Power and the Powers

The Use and Abuse of Power in its Missional Context

. . . .

Andrew Hardy,
Richard Whitehouse, and Dan Yarnell

CASCADE *Books* · Eugene, Oregon

POWER AND THE POWERS
The Use and Abuse of Power in Its Missional Context

Cascade Books
An Imprint of Wipf and Stock Publishers
199 W. 8th Ave., Suite 3
Eugene, OR 97401

www.wipfandstock.com

ISBN 13: 978-1-62564-779-5

Cataloging-in-Publication data:

Hardy, Andrew

Power and the Powers / Andrew Hardy, Richard Whitehouse, and Dan Yarnell

x + 186 p.; 23 cm—Includes bibliographical references and index.

ISBN 13: 978-1-62564-779-5

1. Powers (Christian Theology) 2. Mission (Christian Theology) I. Title II. Whitehouse, Richard. III. Yarnell, Dan.

BS2545.P663 H172 2015

Manufactured in the USA.

Power and the Powers

Contents

Introduction

The Oxford *Complete Word Finder* gives eighteen different definitions of the word "power," the first of which is "the ability to door act" and the last of which is, surprisingly, "a deity, the sixth order of the ninefold celestial hierarchy." The remainder of the definitions range from electrical energy through delegated authority to governmental influence all of which shows what an important and at the same time slippery concept the term "power" can be. Power is something that we all have or use to varying degrees, even if we think of ourselves as relatively powerless. It is, therefore, incumbent upon us to use it responsibly and with reference to the One from whom all power ultimately comes.

Current events, whether we consider conflict in Syria, Iraq, Palestine, Afghanistan, Sudan, or the Ukraine, forcibly remind us of the ideological, political, and military ramifications of the use of power. However, the use and abuse of power is far more subtle than these events imply. Underlying some of these global power plays are issues of power encompassing matters of family, gender, belief, poverty, and wealth as each is institutionalized and formalized into power structures that dominate the lives of players on the larger stage of world affairs. Often, individual players feel as though they are caught between conflicting forces over which they have little or no control.

In the midst of this it is possible to wonder where God figures in the interplay of competing influences and yet, as the Apostle Paul says, "*We know that in all things God works for the good of those who love him, who have been called according to his purpose*" (Rom 8:28; NIV). And it is not just that his purpose was to call us but that he has also called us for a purpose namely to engage in the *missio Dei*—his strategy to bring all the powers in the universe, beneficent and malign, under his rule. Then, and only then, all power and the powers that are behind them will fulfil God's overall purpose of which we are invited to become a part. That is to say that power and the powers are missional concepts that form the background to all the church's missionary activity, which is the primary reason for its existence. This is the reason that we seek to tackle such a topic in this book; it may seem that the church's power has declined in a post-Christendom, postmodern world, but that may become a new opportunity as we begin to realize that the power of Christendom was not always godly and as the church in the West learns to operate from the weakness of the cross on the margins of society in order to challenge its hegemony over the world.

The spiritual landscape in the northern hemisphere has changed dramatically since the last quarter of the twentieth century when, in a burst of triumphalism under the influence of charismatic renewal, the Evangelical, Pentecostal, and Charismatic wings of the church in the West were in the ascendancy and "spiritual warfare" was a fashionable concept. Lately, a note of realism has broken out in face of the realization that mainline churches have steadily, and in some cases dramatically, been losing membership accompanied by an onslaught of almost militant secularism via education and media outlets which has ensured the difficulty of drawing the younger generation into a relationship with Christ. Under these conditions both popular and academic attention to issues of spiritual conflict has waned. It is now time to reassess the theological and practical importance of this issue as we seek to move forward in missional endeavor in the light of new circumstances.

One thing is certain, the urgency of tackling the issue of power in society at large as well as in the church has never been greater. It may be part of Satan's tactics to focus our attention on the church's numerical and spiritual decline so as to identify the social causes without scoping the deeper underlying nature of the spiritual conflict that sits beneath it.

In Terry Hayes's debut bestselling thriller *I Am Pilgrim* the arch-villain "Saracen" wants to destroy his enemy Israel. Realizing the impossibility of this task as an Arab he decides that the way to eliminate his "near enemy," Israel, can best be achieved by targeting the "far enemy," America, that he deems to lie behind it. He plans to do this by starting a smallpox epidemic to wipe out America and thereby render Israel vulnerable. This story carries an insight that has spiritual parallels; behind the near enemy—all of the use and abuse of power in the world and the church that impede mission—lies the power of the "far enemy," Satan, and his manipulation of power structures that broker power in the world. In Hayes's novel the "good guy" an anonymous secret agent who calls himself "Pilgrim" uses every power at his disposal to neutralize Saracen and thwart his plot. However, his use of power is no more moral or humane than that of his opponent since he buys in to the myth of redemptive violence. In our missional calling we have no such luxury; yes, there is redemptive violence, but it took place on the cross where Jesus drew the sting of the principalities and powers that appear to govern this world. He reigns through weakness and calls us to follow in his train.

The way forward from a missional standpoint is to take on the powers in the light of the cross, using the superior force of love. In the pages that follow we explore this theme theologically, historically, and practically in an attempt to reengage the church with *missio Dei*—mission as God intended.

1

A Theological Framework

Richard Whitehouse

The Context of Rapid Global Change

It has frequently been observed that we are living in a global climate of rapid and explosive social and cultural change. This global climate calls into question long held presuppositions about the nature of the world around us and the ways in which people respond to it. To take just one example, the very way in which we view political geography and the terminology we associate with it has shifted dramatically. From a political and economic perspective the world is no longer viewed in terms of the east and the west; the axis has shifted toward a division between the northern and Southern hemispheres of the globe in terms of the distribution of wealth and demography. The average age range of Southern Hemisphere countries is overwhelmingly younger than that of the north. In the main, most of these young people are brought up within a traditional worldview that takes seriously the idea of non-cognitive or suprarational realities. It is at just this time that the center of gravity of the church in the world has shifted to the Sothern Hemisphere.

In this context the church in the northern hemisphere has to reinvent itself in partnership with the South. We live in a post-Christendom—some have argued even a post-Christian—era where a switch to a missional agenda appears to be the only way forward if the church is not to become extinct. We are no longer in a situation where mission can be regarded as a bolt-on activity; rather it is to be seen as the core of the church's nature. The move from "mission" as an abstract noun to the adjectival form "missional" is intentional. Mission can no longer be an activity of the church, it has to be what defines us and a crucial part of this redefinition will be a rediscovery of the fact that we are in the midst of spiritual conflict of epic proportions.

As far back as 1991, David Burnett traced the growth of pagan spirituality in Britain, an issue that Scottish theologian John Drane has also addressed as an evangelistic opportunity. Postmodern questioning of unrestrained post-Enlightenment rationalism suggests a greater openness to the idea of unseen spiritual forces in large sections of contemporary European society. Inward migration from Sothern Hemisphere countries has accelerated this process to some degree by introducing population segments which do not completely share the modernist world view. As part of this mix, African and Asian inner city congregations have forced the issue of spiritual warfare into greater prominence for the largely dying churches in European culture.

In his 1991 introduction to a monograph on the mission implications of the current theological understanding of the nature of spiritual powers in the New Testament, MARC editor Bryant L. Myers wrote:

> In the midst of this climate of rapid change, extreme complexity and almost obsessive pluralism, the Church of Jesus Christ is to be in mission. The good news of Jesus Christ and the claims of his kingdom are needed everywhere . . . Post-Christian Europe needs to rediscover the gospel that was once central to its culture and sense of being.[1]

The existence of unseen spiritual forces is back on the theological agenda; the issue of what has been termed "spiritual warfare" can no longer be relegated to so-called primitive societies, in the twenty-first century it is being taken seriously by theologians as well as missiologists. In this work we will be considering the nature of spiritual conflict in the context of the kingdom of God and the language of "power encounter."

1. Quoted in McAlpine, *Facing the Powers: What Are the Options?*, 1.

Biblical Hermeneutics and the Language of Power

In his 1991 monograph for MARC, the research division of World Vision, Thomas McAlpine surveys a variety of approaches to the classic NT texts dealing with spiritual powers. In it he identifies four theological traditions that handle the texts in very different ways and, as a consequence, come to differing though sometimes overlapping views as to how the church in mission should confront these powers. We will later look at these traditions in more detail noting, as we do so, that new emerging approaches could also be added to McAlpine's four traditions.

For the moment it is important to note that these differing traditions point to the fact that theology is not conducted in a vacuum. We all bring our own theological and hermeneutical assumptions to the biblical text and we first need to scrutinize these before approaching the text in detail. For instance, as far back as 1984 P. T. O'Brien highlighted the inclination of post-World War II European theologians to discount the idea of the powers as personal spiritual beings in favor of a tendency to identify the powers with the structures of society. He notes:

> The problem lies with many contemporary Western theologians and their cultural conditioning; they have allowed the latter to dictate their understanding of the biblical texts with the result that an increasingly fashionable view, viz., that the Pauline powers designate modern socio-political structures, has become the new orthodoxy.[2]

It may be pointed out that O'Brien may not have entirely escaped his own cultural conditioning in his analysis of Paul's use of the same texts. This only serves to indicate the difficult nature of the task of coming to terms with the biblical context before we come to apply such passages to our own situation.

The Hermeneutical Task

Hermeneutics may be described as the science or art of textual interpretation. In the case of the biblical text it enjoys a long history of technical debate and of procedures that forms a study in itself. It is not necessary for us to examine these technicalities here, but we do need to flag up a caution that identifying and isolating a group of key NT texts without reference

2. O'Brien, "Principalities and Powers," 130.

to their literary, historical, and cultural contexts may not be the best way to proceed. This would be the literary equivalent of trying to analyze the events of the 9/11 attack on the twin towers in New York without reference to the culture that produced American foreign policy or at the religious sensitivities of the Islamic groups that produced suicide bombers! It is not possible, or at least, not sensible, to approach the biblical texts with no knowledge of their background (we know it is possible because many groups with a fundamentalist bent do so, but that does not make it a sensible or helpful thing to do).

Two Basic Hermeneutical Principles:

Read the Text in Light of the Wider Biblical Context

The mistake that is often made is to see the biblical texts relating to the powers in isolation from each other and with little regard for the settings that gave rise to them and that they are meant to answer. We need to step back from the classic texts on spiritual warfare in order to consider the general context of spiritual conflict in the Bible. Greg Boyd, after briefly surveying notions of spiritual conflict in a variety of different cultures, concludes that handling such perceived conflict in these cultures is based on a spiritual warfare worldview. He suggests that this worldview is an assumption in biblical literature and he adds:

> The way in which Scripture portrays this warfare world view differs significantly from that of most other cultures. For the biblical worldview is predicated on the assumption that there is only one eternal God whose character is perfect and who is the omnipotent Creator and sustainer of all that is. It is nevertheless clear the biblical authors do espouse a warfare worldview that demonstrates many similarities to the warfare worldviews of other cultures.[3]

We will consider the issue of worldviews later in the context of anthropological and missiological approaches to spiritual conflict and their uses of the language of power. For the present, a worldview may be defined as "a set of basic cultural assumptions that govern individual and societal perceptions about what is real." Boyd contends that such a worldview conditions the way in which the biblical authors approach spiritual realities. Thus, a basic hermeneutical consideration is to take into account the overall

3. Boyd, *God at War: The Bible and Spiritual Conflict*, 18.

thrust of biblical literature as it forms part of the background or stream of thought that moulded the writers of individual texts. This is not only true of the biblical literature itself, but also of the way that this literature has been interpreted throughout the history of the church in the West.

Interpret Passages according to the Light of Their Cultural Milieu, Not Our Own

The second hermeneutical task is not an easy one and it raises a great deal of theological debate. In order to adequately understand the context of particular passages or the thought of a particular thinker, for example, Jesus or Paul, it is necessary to arrive at some determination of the predominant influences on their thought. This is not always straightforward. Both Paul and Jesus lived in cultures that were influenced by Greek, Roman, and Judaic streams of ideas each of which in itself was subject to complex undercurrents, variations, and traditions. The tendency until relatively recently has been to discount the depth of the influence of both the Old Testament literature and intertestamental Judaism on their thinking and thus on the way they chose to express perceived truths.

Only as we attempt to grapple with these issues will we avoid importing our own presuppositions into the text. The tendency of theologians like Bultmann to assume that the language about the powers used by Paul is naïve and mythological, is based on the assumption that it represents an outmoded prescientific worldview that needs to be "demythologized." This is to misunderstand the term "myth"; it does not indicate, as is popularly supposed, a made-up story to explain reality—something that is not true—but, rather, takes the form of a controlling metaphor that explains reality, often in the shape of a story. Opponents of attempts to "demythologize" Paul's terminology have noted:

(a) that "myth" is not to be understood as part of an outmoded primitive worldview, but characterizes humanity in any epoch;

(b) that belief about supernatural interventions in the affairs of human beings is neither mythical, naïve, nor pre-scientific (as the Enlightenment view would imply);

(c) and that belief in demons is not specifically mythical.

O'Brien comments, "Further, it is most important to note that certain third world theologians have often claimed that a biblical, and especially Pauline, perspective on the powers is perfectly intelligible in their own cultural contexts."[4]

The point here is that we cannot avoid bringing our own cultural understandings to the text, but as far as possible we should seek to lay these aside in order to ask, "What was the situation for those who wrote and received the text?" Once we get as close as we reasonably can to their cultural milieu, we will be able to understand what they were saying in their day and then begin to apply their terminology to our own contexts.

Before considering the biblical approach to spiritual conflict and its use of the language of power we will first take a look at some historical approaches to this issue. This will further clarify the way that the church's understandings of the kingdom of God and the language of power have been socially and culturally mediated in the past.

The Early (Post-Apostolic) Church and Spiritual Conflict

Before we attempt an exegesis of any passage in the light of our present circumstances it is necessary to tackle the hermeneutical task of seeking to grapple with the original meaning of the text. Each of the four traditions of interpretation identified by McAlpine in his monograph has, to some extent, avoided this important first step. This is an issue to which we will return later since it is important if we are to ground our practice of spiritual warfare in the Bible. Too many popular approaches to engaging in this important missional task have foundered at this point and have only succeeded in creating misunderstandings and poor practice. What follows is a brief and selective historical survey of ways that the issue of spiritual conflict has been treated since the close of the NT canon of Scripture. The object of this survey is to explore how successive generations of the church have contextualized spiritual warfare.

Each understanding is grounded in a particular historical and cultural context by which it is to some extent conditioned. This simple observation should help us reflect on what is happening when we approach this topic and may help us to avoid importing our own contextual presuppositions into the biblical text when we come to consider it against its own background.

4. O'Brien, "Powers and Principalities," 130.

The Sub-Apostolic Period and the "Church Fathers"

Surviving Christian writings from the period of the so-called "Apostolic Fathers" at the beginning of the second century come from a second generation of church leaders who had either been in contact with some of the original twelve apostles or their immediate disciples. Very little literature from this period has survived, but what we have presents a fairly consistent picture of the church and its teachings. The earliest documents of the second-century church display an acute awareness of the differences between the Christian community and the varied cultural backgrounds of the Roman Empire in which it was set.

Many pagan contemporaries of the emerging Christian movement were obsessed with the influence of a myriad of local and domestic deities who might control business, civic, and family life. Spells, charms, and amulets were resorted to in order to seek to manipulate or harness the power of spirits or minor gods. This was accompanied by a concern about the afterlife and how to enter it unscathed. Clinton Arnold has demonstrated the presence of these attitudes in Ephesus and Colossae in the Apostle Paul's time.[5] Such attitudes may be taken as representative of the cultural milieu of the era. Little had changed as the church entered the second century although a variety of forms of Gnosticism were beginning to emerge from the opening of the century onwards. We will look at the Gnostic heresy later but, for now, it is sufficient to observe that it was an approach to spiritual power based on *secret knowledge* (Gk. *gnosis*) that enabled the devotee to negotiate the passage of the soul through layers of spiritual powers who were regarded as intervening between the worshiper and the ultimate being. To begin with, it was not so much a religion as a spiritual ambience with various teachers, gurus, and spiritual guides. It was a way of thinking much like contemporary new-age philosophy, a sort of pick and mix spirituality that was thought to impart spiritual power.

Against this background the early church writers in the first half of the second century show surprisingly little interest in the principalities and powers referred to by Paul in his writings. They move more in the thought world exemplified by the Johannine writings. Perhaps in reaction to pagan excesses they simply portray Jesus as the conqueror of death; salvation comes through response to proclamation and obedience to a way of life that consists of faithfulness to Christ. A predominant theme is that salvation

5 Arnold, *The Colossian Syncretism, Power and Magic.*

comes through identification with Christ. Pagan religions were often accompanied by traveling thaumaturgists or wonder workers and, possibly in response to this, the earliest church fathers and apologists tend to downplay miracles and exorcism as an approach to dealing with the powers. For these writers the demonic is dealt with through the incarnation of Christ, who came to destroy the works of the devil, and through the indwelling Spirit within the believer; salvation and deliverance come from assimilation with Christ.

In the first half of the second century there appears to be little interest in corporate aspects of demonic activity in society as spiritual conflict is located in the individual and his or her relationship to the church. The concern is to downplay the use of miracles or exorcism as antidotes to demonic activity in favor of proclaiming, receiving, and practicing the message of the gospel. Thus, in contrast to the pagan exorcists who used spells, amulets, magic and ritual in their supposed power encounters with demonic powers, the focus was upon the defeat of the demonic through the incarnation of Christ, his death on the cross, and the believer's obedience to the gospel.

The Second-Century Apologists

The latter half of the second century saw a change in approach to the language of spiritual conflict. At this point we move away from the pastoral concerns of the Apostolic Fathers toward the emergence of Christian apologists whose focus was on mission. They were more concerned to make a case for the effectiveness, as well as the truth, of the Christian message. Many scholars place the longer ending to Mark's Gospel (Mark 16:9–20) in this period; it appears to be a later addition to the original Gospel since it does not appear in the earliest manuscripts. It was probably added as a summary of the church's position in relation to the good news contained in Mark as it connected to mission. It may have been penned in order to round off the rather abrupt shorter ending to the Gospel. Twelftree suggests that this fragment originated in Rome where the original Gospel itself was probably written. He thinks that the resurgence of interest in the language of power in relation to the demonic in the second half of the century was partly due to Roman influence stimulated by the emergence of the longer ending to Mark's Gospel.[6] This is, in part, speculation but the change of emphasis in the writings of the church fathers is clear. We will take three

---

6. Twelftree, *In the Name of Jesus*, 234.

examples from this period: Justin Martyr, Irenaeus of Lyons, and Origen. Justin, who was of Roman descent, was born to pagan parents in Samaria in the town now known as Nablus. As a gentile convert he was concerned to both defend and advance the Christian faith. At Corinth he engaged in a dialogue with Trypho the Jew, who attacked the Christian position. This dialogue was subsequently written down and, together with Justin's *First and Second Apologies*, was to form the cornerstone of his defense of Christianity. Justin's demonology is considerably more developed than that of the Apostolic Fathers. In combating Gnostic views he goes on the offensive. Rather than playing down Christian exorcism he contrasts the effectiveness of the church's approach to that of pagan exorcists. They use incantations, incense, magic, spells, and rituals to achieve their conquest of demons whereas Christians, though they may repeat forms of words, do not rely on them to achieve the desired result. Rather than trust a formula or ritual the Christian exorcists rely entirely on the power of the name of Jesus. Justin describes demons as "strange" and deceitful spirits that enslave people to themselves by devotion to magical writings, which teach people to offer sacrifices and incense, thereby entering into pacts with them that bring about adultery, murder, war, intemperate deeds, and wickedness. They are also responsible for creating heresies and stirring up persecution against the church.

Justin held that demons are also capable of possessing people, but he is not interested in naming particular demons; rather, he sees Satan as the one who heads them up and controls them. However, Jesus has won the victory over both Satan and demons through the cross and "those believing on the one crucified by Pontius Pilate, Jesus our Lord . . . have all demons and evil spirits subject to us."[7]

Ireneaus was bishop of Lyons from about 178 CE where he wrote the apologetic work *Against Heresies.* He evidences miracles taking place in the mainstream church, such as healing the weak, the lame, blind, deaf, and paralyzed and even raising the dead. Over against this he points to Gnostic power-encounters with demons as magical deceptions—just smoke and mirrors—and though he acknowledges they can chase away demons, he claims the best they can do is transfer them from one person to another. Theirs is no permanent victory. Ireneaus contrasts the illusory nature of the exorcisms of false religions and of aberrant forms of Christianity with the genuineness of the church's successful encounters with demons. He also

7. *Dial. Tryph.* 76.6.

points to the difference in motivation for the act of deliverance. Twelftree comments:

> In other words, the exorcisms performed by the church are done in the power of God or in connection with the truth. Also, in contrast to the healings of his opponents, in the healing that takes place in the church, there is "sympathy, and compassion, and steadfastness and truth, for the aid and encouragement of mankind, are not only displayed without fee or reward, but we ourselves lay out for the benefit of others our own means."[8]

Ireneaus appeals to the genuineness of miracles in the church of his time as support for the genuineness of the miracles of Jesus rather than the other way around. At the same time Ireneaus echoes Paul's list of spiritual gifts in 1 Corinthians 12:8—10. His list of charismata includes exorcism, which is absent from Paul's list, focusing as it does on the internal wholeness of the church. Ireneaus suggests that miracles are for the benefit of non-Christians as well. This was accompanied by a concern about the afterlife and how to enter it unscathed. Irenaeus makes a point that the power to perform miracles comes about through Christ's disciples receiving grace from him. It is interesting to note that following this period the act of initiation into the church through baptism was preceded by exorcism; baptismal vows not only consisted of allegiance to Christ but also of renouncing the devil.

Origen was born in Alexandria, Egypt, about 185 CE and died in 254 CE. His father Leonides, a Greek convert to Christianity, was martyred and a youthful Origen, passionate to follow him, was only prevented from going to the arena to meet certain death when his mother hid his trousers! This passion was to mark the whole of his career as he matured. Some authorities assert that he even castrated himself in order to literally fulfil Jesus' injunction to become a eunuch for the kingdom of God's sake. This prevented him from entering the priesthood on the basis of then current rules of the church. Instead he spent his life as an apologist for the Christian faith constantly studying the received Scriptures in order to refute the Gnostics whose beliefs he despised. He engaged in some of the first ever work in Christian literary criticism. In the process he scorned the Gnostic and Marcionite rejection of the Old Testament because he believed in the supernatural origins of both Testaments and their underlying message. He spoke of

8. Twelftree, *In the Name of Jesus: Exorcism Among Early Christians,* 242.

the good things in Jesus Christ shed forth by the Gospel, the Gospel ministered by men and angels, and, I believe, also by authorities and powers, and thrones and dominions, and every name that is named, not only in this world, but also in the world to come, and indeed even by Christ Himself.[9]

Plainly, for Origen, principalities and powers were viewed in Jewish apocalyptic terms as personal beings intervening in human affairs.

As we have seen, Origen was vehemently oppose to the Gnostics, some of whom taught that because the High God was a pure and impassive spirit he could not be tainted by contact with matter, which was considered to be evil. The material world was therefore created by a lesser divinity or "demiurge," gradations below God. Origen, in a daring riposte, characterizes Jesus as the creator-demiurge immediately below God; he plainly does not see him as tainted by matter. Nevertheless he sees Jesus as accomplishing our salvation through his humanity separate from the High God—the Father. It must be remembered that this was at a period when the church was still trying to define the touchstone of his messianic character. In particular Origen focuses on Jesus' high priestly function.

It should be noted here that the church fathers habitually referred to non-Christians as Gentiles and, by implication, saw the church as the continuation of Israel. What is important to notice in this passage is that the enemies seem to be literal while what stands behind them is an opposing power. This interpretation fits in with a later statement from Origen that sees the opposing power, or powers, as structural entities capable of conversion.

At this point, Origen is not clear whether he grants the powers some sort of structural as well as personal status since whole towns are converted along with their tutelary overseeing spirit or whether he sees the powers as redeemable in themselves. Conversion here should probably not be taken in an evangelical sense as much as in a wholesale turning to a Christianized culture. In any case, this should be seen against the background of Origen's tendency to universalism. Nevertheless it points to an understanding of the powers that was conditioned by the philosophical, religious, and spiritual currents of thought of that day.

9. Origen, *Commentary on John's Gospel* (ANF, 1:15).

Third- to Fifth-Century Testimony

Even before the church became a state-promoted religion following the "conversion" of the Emperor Constantine in 312 CE the church had gained influence and membership became more lax. Christainity was no longer a proscribed and derided religion, so it became fashionable to be a Christian and even advisable in order to gain social advancement. In this context standards of faith and of Christian behavior were lowered. In response to this, some who were more serious about their faith and wished to engage more closely with God opted for what was to become a monastic life.

Beginning with St. Anthony, who withdrew to the Egyptian desert around 270 CE in order to engage in solitary prayer and meditation, these proto-monks became the new heroes of the faith in an age when Christians were no longer martyred by the state. The memoirs of these so-called "desert fathers" are filled with accounts of personal struggles with temptation and the devil reminiscent of Jesus' temptations in the wilderness. These personal "power encounters" resulted, they believed, in the overthrow of Satan and the demonic at a personal level through intense spiritual concentration and personal holiness. This came by extreme asceticism, fasting, meditation, and intercessory prayer. The desert fathers were combating the demons that they saw to be the source of evil in the decadent society that they had abandoned; less rigorous Christians often came to them for prayer, healing, and spiritual advice. In the year 314 CE Pachomius set out to live in the desert near Anthony and to imitate his practices. Until this time the desert hermits lived a solitary existence but as their numbers grew they had begun to group into cells. Pachomius felt challenged by God to gather male and female hermits into an informal communal organizational setting led by an abbot or abbess. Subsequently, throughout the Middle Ages, the monastic life continued to be seen not only as one of contemplation and prayer but also in warfare terms as intercession for the world against the inroads of Satan. Later, in 410 CE, when Rome itself was sacked by pagan Germanic tribes from the north, the collapse of the Empire and, with it, Western Christianity, seemed imminent. Against this apocalyptic background Augustine (354–430 CE), bishop of Hippo in North Africa, wrote his famous treatise *The City of God*. In it he traced the fortunes of two cities, the city of God and the city of the world. Augustine comes closer than any other writer in the early church to seeing the principalities and powers in terms of human organizational structures. The book was written to refute the charge leveled by pagans in the Empire that the fall of Rome was due to the Christian religion because of its prohibition of the worship of the traditional gods of Rome. Augustine counters this claim by tracing calamities and misfortunes that afflicted the city before the coming of Christianity when the old gods were worshiped. Indeed he claims that, far from being protected by the pagan gods, the worst excesses of the corruption of manners and the worst vices of the soul can be traced back to the times when these gods were universally worshipped. Augustine goes on to assert that the dilemma for the Christian is that of living under the influence of two conflicting cities at the same time, namely the earthly and the heavenly city. This is somewhat like the conflict between this present age and the age to come present in the New Testament. Alister McGrath comments that. For Augustine: "The complexities of the Christian life, especially its political aspects, are due to the dialectic between these two cities."[10] Augustine traces the progress of the secular earthly city in the Old Testament from the time of Adam's fall onwards and suggests that its origin lies beyond that in the pre-mundane fall of Satan giving rise to the division between fallen and good angels.

Augustine insisted that the flawed nature of Roman society was due to its worship of false gods, a worship he believed to be demonically inspired. Nevertheless, he saw that the organization of civil society was based on concerns common to pagans and Christians alike—he cites family, community, and nation as examples. These concerns are regulated by the secular city by which the Christian, although a member of the heavenly city, is bound. The secular or earthly city however has no right to legislate for matters of religion since its tendency is to demand service (Greek: *latreia*) or worship for itself. In this sense the earthly city is idolatrous.

Due to his insistence that the Christian lives in two cities at once Augustine rejects the idea of the church as a gathered body of saints. The church is exiled in the city of the world and therefore it shares the fallen character of the world—wheat and tares grow together—and it will only be perfected as the city of God at Christ's return. Salvation is inaugurated in the life of the believer but it will only be completed at the end of history. We are perfected in hope but not yet in reality therefore the spiritual battle arises from the tension between the two cities. Present deliverance is thus possible but will only ever be partial. Augustine believed in miracles as an evidence of salvation and gives numerous examples from his own experience in Carthage, but sees them as pointers to the future. For Augustine, the

10. Quoted in McGrath, *Christian Theology*, 468.

tension between demonic and heavenly powers is an eschatological issue that can only be partly resolved in the present. The final power encounter awaits a coming day.

Medieval Approaches to Spiritual Conflict

We do not have space for a detailed historical analysis of the Western church's approach to spiritual conflict. Enough has been said to make the point that the church has dealt with the issues surrounding it and the interpretation of individual biblical texts in the light of the needs of their own times. To this degree, *they brought their own presuppositions to the biblical text* rather than an unclouded attempt to understand these passages in the light of the contexts in which they were originally written. Of course, we all do this to some extent; we cannot approach any text with completely culturally-free minds. However, part of the hermeneutical task is to divest ourselves of as many of these presuppositions as possible. What follows is an abbreviated explanation of what, historically, led up to the way that modern theologians have allowed their own cultural suppositions to influence their reading of the text. It is these cultural readings which have in turn governed most approaches to confronting the powers missionally.

The early medieval period

In the fourth century, Constantine moved the capital of the empire from Rome to Constantinople (modern Istanbul), which was further from incursions by northern Germanic tribes. This Eastern Roman Empire continued to flourish after the fall of Rome to the Goths and Vandals, but during the seventh century the Islamic caliphates invaded North Africa and whole swathes of southern Europe. Later, Constantinople was also to fall to the Islamic Ottoman Empire. Meanwhile, pagan Scandinavian raids into Northern Europe, including Britain, altered the political map as the Vikings drove back the local Christianized populations plundering the monasteries—the main centers of learning—of their treasures, including the libraries. Book learning and scholarship gave way to folklore and camp fire traditional tales many of which focused on Danish and Nordic battle myths. Gradually, the Norse, Saxon, and Danish invaders intermarried with local populations as they settled and began to administer their new territories and the version of Christianity they adopted was battle-focused. What is clear is that

Christianity in Northern Europe was increasingly interpenetrated by pagan ideas. Indeed, earlier conversions to the faith were often cultural conversions beneath which the old pagan customs were buried or even retained with a Christian veneer. Martin of Tours (d. 372 CE), who predates this period, is typical of a missionary strategy adopted in the Early Middle Ages. His biography, written by his friend Sulpicius Severus, contains many apocryphal tales such as one occasion when he is reported, by prayer, to have turned back the flames from a house that caught fire as he was burning down a pagan Roman temple. Spiritual "face-offs" demonstrating the superiority of Christ over demons and pagan practices were practiced by Celtic saints such as Patrick in Ireland, David in Wales, and Aidan in Northumbria. Even where pagans voluntarily embraced Christianity a great deal of superstition still underlay their faith. Although Pauline language was probably not used by these frontier missionaries theirs was, in reality, a battle against principalities and powers. Since these pioneers often chose to advance their cause by seeking to convert pagan rulers and then persuading them to order their subjects to convert, it is clear that they saw the powers in both political/structural and cosmological terms.

The later medieval period.

The High Middle Ages (1000–1300 CE) saw the emergence of small communities ruled by local lords who were granted land rights by the monarch. In turn, the local rulers raised their own militia who could be called upon to fight in the king's battles. Against this background the whole of society in Christianized Europe was underpinned by the notion of "the chain of being" derived from Aristotle's philosophy, rather than from biblical teaching. On this view, the world comprised a series of hierarchical links beginning with God, who as creator stood outside his creation although omniscient, omnipotent, and omnipresent. Below God the angels existed in spirit form—spirit in distinction from flesh was regarded as unchanging and permanent—at the bottom of the chain rock or earth possessed only the attribute of existence, plants possessed life as well as existence, while animals additionally enjoyed the attributes of motion and appetite. Man straddled the divide between spirit, which he shared with those above him in the chain, and mortal flesh, which he shared with those below him. The struggle between flesh and spirit characterized humankind's relationship with God and the spirit world. This way of thinking was the expression of an essentially dualistic view of the world. The way of the spirit brought man closer to God while the desires of the flesh drew him away from God. This "chain of being" is one factor that explained the way in which the medieval church developed. It was a social as much as a religious theory that served the interests of the hierarchical elite. For most of the population, however, life was a struggle and local superstitions and fear of spirit elements that war against the soul dominated existence. Most feudal villages were isolated and learning was centered in monasteries and, later in the period, emerging universities, which were located in cities. For most peasants, and many of their masters, life was dictated by the fight for survival that was thought of as a spiritual battle too. In the main, this battle was not couched in biblical terms; rather, it grew out of the ideological clash stemming from a theology heavily influenced by Platonic/Aristotelian Greek philosophy and repressed pagan superstition.

Bernard of Clairvaux developed the idea of three overlapping spheres of activity—the world, the flesh, and the devil—which warred against the soul. His solution was to work to build up the conscience as a bulwark against sin. This triad, drawn from the NT, became a predominant theme in medieval thought and is still a helpful framework for understanding spiritual conflict. Bernard's influence in the monastic movement and scholastic circles was considerable. Mystics like Julian of Norwich, Marjory Kempe, the anonymous author of *The Cloud of Unknowing*, and Richard Rolle also record battles with the demonic, which would become influential much later. But, as Graham Russell Smith observes, the emphasis on their popular influence

> is often out of all proportion to their actual impact on the religion of ordinary men and women at the time. The "popular" or "traditional" religion of the majority, whilst undoubtedly influenced by paganism and superstition, was nevertheless probably equally influenced by church screens and windows, the enacted Miracle plays as well as orally in rhyming verse treatises and saints' lives. In such traditional religion, we find certain Scriptures regularly used in exorcism or defence against evil.[11]

In the emerging Christendom model of church that came to fruition in the medieval period, church and state were intertwined and the Catholic Church itself began to take on the form of a secular state where the bishops of the church became secular princes as well as rulers of the church.

11. Smith, "The Church Militant."

Thus, the pattern of spiritual warfare changed. As Stuart Murray shrewdly observes, the Christendom church sanctioned "just wars" as part of the underpinning of the State and, as a consequence, increasingly appealed to OT passages for its justification.[12] So, in the medieval period, spiritual warfare was interpreted at two separate levels: that of the struggle within the individual's soul as the believer attempted to resist the snares of Satan and the lure of the flesh in order to achieve union with God, and the political level at which it was permissible to wage physical war on behalf of the church, which was identified with the kingdom of God.

The Reformation Heritage

The Reformation to some extent continued this pattern, but the Roman Church was no longer the arbiter of faith for Protestants. The location of authority transfered to the Bible and its local church interpreters rather than the Pope as the head of the Catholic Church. Some Reformers were protected by local princes who thus became sponsors of the faith while others worked closely with their town council. This meant that although the church was still territorial it was fragmented into what would emerge as nation-states that could go to war on behalf of their theological position. At the same time struggles with temptation and conflict with the devil were regarded as intensely personal experiences

In the later Puritan era a similar pattern prevailed except that the individual's struggle with Satan began as a lead-up to a conversion experience by which a person came into the kingdom. The believer's struggle with sin began at the cross, not at the cradle. *Pilgrim's Progress*, John Bunyan's allegory of the Christian life reflects this trend. This classic tale did much, along with the King James version of the Bible and Shakespeare's works, to form the English language as we have it today. It was also to form the imagination of the British evangelical church regarding spiritual conflict right through to the end of the nineteenth century. It fell to the revivalists of the eighteenth century to rediscover the supernatural. Intense spiritual experiences with sometimes dramatic public manifestations of demonization were not uncommon under the preaching of Whitefield and the Wesley's. John Wesley's class system, which was the bedrock of his Methodist Associations, focused on dealing with sin and the temptations of the devil in everyday life. The touchstone of spiritual experience was the experience of

12. Murray, *Post-Christendom Church*, 120.

new birth, which brought the believer into a spiritual dimension unknown to him before.

By the opening of the nineteenth century, spiritual conflict for evangelicals, on the one hand, was interpreted in terms of social work at home and through encounters with Animism, Hinduism, and Buddhism overseas. As the church entered the era of the modern missionary movement conflict at home began to center on the intellectual battle brought about by scientific naturalism in general and Darwin's evolutionary theory put forward in his book *The Origin of the Species,* published in 1864, in particular. Liberal theologians, on the other hand, took no notice of the Pauline language of spiritual conflict other than to see it as evidence of an outdated mythology abandoned in a more scientific age.

2

More Recent Approaches to Spiritual Conflict

Richard Whitehouse

Further Theological Approaches to Spiritual Conflict: *Christus Victor*

The position that pertained at the end of the nineteenth century is pretty much where things remained until relatively recently. The first signs of change came in the aftermath of World War I when, in 1931, Swedish Lutheran theologian Gustaf Aulen produced *Christus Victor*, a small book that challenged views of the atonement based on the law court in favor of what he saw as the "classic" view of the atonement which he traced in the early church fathers. He argued that the ransom (or *Christus Victor*) theory of the atonement in the church fathers was not based on a legal or business transaction, the payment of a ransom to the devil, but on the rescue of humanity from bondage to sin and death as well as from the power of the devil. On the cross, Jesus defeated the powers and, through his resurrection, potentially restored humanity to its pre-Adamic state. Critics objected that Aulen overstated his case and that a variety of images of the atonement were used by patristic theologians. Nevertheless, the events of World War II also brought about considerable shifts in attitudes toward biblical language about spiritual conflict in general and the Pauline terminology in particular. Dietrich Bonheoffer offered a penetrating analysis of political events in Germany that was biblically grounded. His opposition to Hitler's

Third Reich resulted in direct action, which was to cost him his life. Swiss theologian Karl Barth engaged in a more passive form of protest while working in Germany, but their theology of spiritual conflict was formed by their experience of the evil that confronted them. Meanwhile, shortly after the war, Lesslie Newbigin, then a missionary in India and attempting to grapple with the nature of the missionary task, was soon to comment on these events.

Structural Approaches to Spiritual Conflict

It 1953 Dutch theologian Hendrikus Berkhof produced *Christ and the Powers*, written against the background of the recently experienced horrors of Nazism. In it, he suggested that the powers outlined in Paul's writings were not to be understood in terms of the personal demonic categories portrayed in contemporary and intertestamental apocalyptic literature, but as references to structural aspects of society originally designed by God to serve mankind, which had become ends in themselves and, as such, idols and, therefore, demonic. The way in which to confront these realities in missional terms is to challenge them and to call them back to their original functions. Thus, spiritual warfare becomes social and political action. As justification for this position Berkhof cites Colossians 1:15–20, which says that all things were created by Christ, including principalities and powers, and that God's purpose is that his fullness should dwell in Christ in order to reconcile all things to himself, *"whether things on earth or things in heaven, by making peace through his blood, shed on the cross."* In Berkhof's view, Paul took the current apocalyptic belief in personal spirit powers inhabiting the atmosphere in order to control social and political events and demytholo-gized them by replacing them with the notion of social structures ordained by God but that had abandoned their God given calling. Berkhof's argument, later to be followed by others, was that when Paul referred to *"things in heaven and on earth"* he was talking about two different categories. Much later, Walter Wink, professor of theology at Auburn University in New York, was to develop these ideas further. We will come back to him again, but first we will consider another approach to the Pauline texts that shares some of Berkhof's presuppositions, but suggests a different way of respond-ing to them missionally.

Anabaptist commentators such as John Howard Yoder took up Berk-hof's analysis of principalities and powers in terms of sociocultural entities that are meant to fulfil God's purposes for humankind and to which men are intended to submit. Indeed, Yoder goes as far as to say, "Man's subordination to these Powers is what makes him human, for if they did not exist there would be no history nor society nor humanity. If then, God is going to save man in his humanity, the Power cannot simply be destroyed or set aside or ignored."[1] How, then, are these now subverted and rebellious powers to be brought back to their intended purpose? Yoder's answer from within the Anabaptist ethical tradition is that Jesus proclaims his victory over the powers through the church. Interpreting Paul, Yoder comments:

> What he says is not . . . that the gospel deals only with personal ethics and not with social structures. Nor does he say that the only way to change structures is to change the heart of the individual man . . . the primary social structure through which the gospel works to change other structures is that of the Christian community.[2]

Thus, for Yoder, the church as a gathered body of the saints is a counter-culture that challenges the fallen structures by demonstrating a qualitatively different manner of living from within society. As Yoder sees it, the Christian stance in relation to the powers is one of radical submission exemplified by Jesus who paid the penalty on the cross, so the church is to challenge the powers and draw them back to their intended God ordained function by radical submission; he selects Paul's attitude to slavery and the commands to husbands and wives for discussion, insisting that to submit to them is to draw their sting and challenge their validity. In his view, the powers are already crumbling anyway. Yoder along with others within the Anabaptist tradition points to the kingdom manifesto in Luke 4:16–21, where Jesus read the passage from Isaiah 61 announcing an eschatological jubilee and, after sitting down, proclaimed: *"Today this scripture has been fulfilled in your hearing."* Commentators have disagreed about what exactly Jesus thought he had fulfilled, but Yoder argues for "a visible socio-political, economic restructuring of relations among the people of God, achieved by his intervention in the person of Jesus as the one Anointed and endued with the Spirit."[3] For Yoder, this visible restructuring of relations, therefore, comes through the church. This group of thinkers also appeal to Isaiah 2:2–4, where the nations come to Jerusalem to learn God's law before taking it

1. Yoder, *The Politics of Jesus*, 147.

2. Ibid., 157.

3. Ibid., 30.

back out with them, as justification for their view. Like Berkhof and other expositors within what McAlpine categorizes as "the Reformed tradition," the Anabaptists see the powers as integrally connected to cultures, societies, political parties, and any other human power structures. Insofar as they exceed their divine mandate these powers become a cause of missiological concern, they must be recalled to their intended vocation. In this case, spiritual warfare becomes a matter of confronting the powers with a qualitatively different sort of power that challenges their idolatry through "[t]he formation of a contrast-society (the church!) in the midst of the old structures of domination."[4] McAlpine comments that the actual history and practice of the church weakens this argument considerably. Though, historically, there is a well-documented tendency for actual Anabaptist denominations to see themselves as a gathered body of saints who live differently from the mainstream denominations spawned by the Reformation, it is not one that Yoder would care to make. Gregory Boyd, although not part of the Anabaptist tradition, maintains that it is precisely this failure of the church that makes the point that God's eventual triumph over the powers (whether personal or structural) is purely an act of his grace. Yoder and his associates come to the biblical warfare texts from the standpoint of the ethics of violence, something we will address briefly in the next section as a bridge to our consideration of anthropological approaches to spiritual conflict. Pacifism and nonviolent approaches to politics are deeply embedded in Anabaptist origins and their subsequent history and it is this that has to a large extent conditioned the way they read the Bible in general and the Pauline texts relating to principalities in particular. As we saw earlier, Stuart Murray, who is also an Anabaptist, commented on the Christendom appeal to OT warfare texts as a justification for its statecraft. This is in line with Yoder's analysis of "Constantinianism" as the fundamental sin. Charles Bellinger characterizes Yoder's use of the term "Constantinianism" in this way: "[S]in is the attempt by human beings to control human history, to guide it according to their ends and beliefs, apart from the pathway of suffering obedience revealed in the life of Christ."[5] Pointing to this attempt to take Christ more seriously as part of the equation, Bellinger comments that, for Yoder, "Jesus was, in his divinely mandated prophethood, priesthood, and kingship, the bearer of a new possibility of human, social, and therefore political relationships." Thus, Bellinger says, " . . . We can see Christ clearly

4. McAlpine, *Facing the Powers*, 11, 40.

5. Bellinger, "Yoder's Christ and Girard's Culture," 5.

as the One who is bringing God's new order into a disordered and resistant World."[6]

Yet this account is not fully satisfying. In the Anabaptist view, violence is the very nature of sin, whether in terms of personal envy, domestic abuse, armed robbery, terrorism, or war; violence is at the heart of spiritual conflict. Although himself an Anabaptist, Bellinger suggests that René Girard's anthropological account of the relationship between human culture and violence is a more adequate explanation of sin because it deals with it from an inner psychological standpoint, rather than from a rather disembodied ethical standpoint. In other words, the Anabaptist view tends to deal with the manifestation of sin (violence) but has less to say about what inner forces drive it. This brings us to consider the way missionary anthropology contributes to the discussion.

Missionary Anthropology

Anthropology is the study of variations and differences among different groups of humans; its origins come from an application of evolutionary theory to the contextual development of human group behavior. It therefore focuses on cultural adaptations for survival and an analysis of the somewhat slippery term "culture" is crucial to most anthropologists' interpretation of their observations. This a theme to which we will return in a later section.

René Girard

René Girard (b. 1923) is not strictly speaking a missionary anthropologist, rather, he is a Christian humanist who developed his ideas about the nature of our humanity (a theological anthropology) based on his study of French literature. He was until his retirement in 1995 Professor of French Language, Literature, and Civilization at Stanford University.

From his study of medieval and modern French literature Girard concluded that humans tend to look to successful people as models believing that by imitating them they too will become successful. Basically, we want to have what a role model has because it will make us as important as we see them to be. Girard calls this "mimetic desire." "Mimesis" means "imitative"

---

6. Ibid., 4.

and elsewhere he refers to it as "appropriative mimicry."[7] Initially, we copy the other person's *desire* for an object they possess rather than ownership of the object itself but, since the object is in short supply, it becomes the focus of that desire, thus creating *rivalry*. This rivalry gives rise to violent behavior as we seek to appropriate the object for ourselves. This, according to Girard, is the origin of every manifestation of evil—it is brought about by violence stemming from mimetic desire.

Based on his analysis of primate behavior, Girard theorizes that violence brought about by mimetic desire predates human language and that it was a prehistoric phenomenon that still persists. It can be seen in such diverse area as: the psychology of small children, product brand rivalry among young people, advertising, economics, and intercommunal relationships.

Girard also suggests that when, in prehistory, the level of violence reached intolerable levels the protagonists would look for a victim or scapegoat to blame for the problem and punish him, usually by death. Bellinger comments:

> Killing a scapegoat, or attacking a minority group within society, provides an outlet valve for the build-up of hatreds, resentments, and violent impulses that are generated by mimetic desire. Killing the scapegoat is a cathartic event that creates a new sense of social mimetic desire. Killing the scapegoat is a cathartic event that creates a new sense of social unanimity that did not exist before. Sacrifice becomes salvific for the society, and it becomes the cornerstone of both religion and culture.[8]

According to Girard, the tendency in prehistoric primitive societies to look back at the killing of a scapegoat in one situation was often sufficient to prevent the need for another killing and this led to enshrining the memory of the first event through a ritual action. For him, this typical process is the source of religion, which even gave rise to the genesis of language.

The selection of a scapegoat to divert the destructive energy of violent behavior is based on a shared unconscious lie, since the victim was not the real cause of the original conflict. Girard's mythical account of the mechanism of scapegoating (which can be observed in practice in many current and historical cultural contexts) maintains that ignorance of the lie

---

7. Girard, "Mimesis and Violence: Perspectives in Cultural Criticism," 9–19.

8. Bellinger, "Yoder's Christ and Girard's Culture," 6.

concerning the guilt of the sacrificial victim is essential for the effectiveness of sacrificial violence.

In his book *Things Hidden Since the Foundation of the World* Girard turns his attention to the Bible. He believes that the overall effect of revelation is to expose the sickness of mimetic desire and, thus, to potentially draw its sting. The scapegoating mechanism is clear throughout the OT and the gospel accounts turn it completely around when mimetic desire causes the culture of Christ's day to seize on him as its victim. Here, however, the tables are turned since the Gospels insist that the scapegoat on the cross is innocent. The celebration of God's victory over the mimetic desire that began with the serpent's seduction of Eve in Eden and ends at the cross culminates in the ritual of the Eucharist.

Girard does not defend the Bible or Christianity on the basis of nonviolence; he says that Christianity in its ideal form promises not peace but truth. For him, the subsequent structures of historical Christianity represent a conflict between the deep-seated sacrificial order characteristic of human culture and its rejection of mimetic violence exhibited in the New Testament. On the one hand, the historical churches have partially rejected the insight of the Gospels over almost two millennia; on the other hand, by spreading the gospel across the globe they have undermined archaic sacrificial religions, paving the way for a final tide of revelation that will bring together humanity. In the end, his is a Christian humanitarian eschatological vision of the conquest of evil (for which, read "violence"). As a result, he is scathing about the liberal values of secular humanism, which he sees as a cheap endeavor to intensify cultural freedom liberated from constraining institutions—particularly the church—based on a reckless self-assurance in humankind's capacity to save itself through mimetic desire.

Girard's account has become highly influential in the arena of conflict studies and has even given rise to an academic journal, *Contagion,* which is the official journal of the *Colloquium on Violence and Religion.* The psychological aspects of his theory are endorsed by a number of clinical psychologists and have even been adopted by some as a therapeutic tool. The anthropological aspect of his work is, however, highly speculative and lacks grounded validation as an account of the source of evil and the rise of religion. Moreover, his theory fails to provide, on the basis of mimetic desire, a satisfactory account of how and why human beings frequently choose to cooperate to achieve beneficial ends. His biblical exegesis avoids treating Satan as a real entity, much less the Pauline passages on the principalities and powers that one assumes he would see as personifications of mimetic desire or as structural embodiments of it since he sees the biblical defeat of mimetic desire as a demystifying of the peace of this world.

In the end, his is a flawed theory, even from an anthropological standpoint. We have chosen to give so much space to his thought because of its contemporary importance and its practical impact on much modern thinking. From a biblical perspective he does not address the classical spiritual warfare texts, although he takes the overall conflict setting of Scripture seriously as he applies his theory. The treatment of conflict as an overarching theme in Scripture is something to which we will return in the next chapter, but it must be said that in Girard's case a theory is brought to the text rather than being read out of that text. This perfectly illustrates our thesis, that is, that the hermeneutical process is too often distorted by our own contextual presuppositions. Girard's assumptions are derived principally from his analysis of medieval and modern French literature, both of which carry their own cultural assumptions; it is a kind of literary cultural "double whammy"! It is this emphasis on the notion of "culture" that will drive the rest of our excursion into missionary anthropology.

Charles Kraft

Kraft has been professor of anthropology and intercultural communications at Fuller Theological Seminary in Pasadena, California since 1969. Prior to that, he was for thirteen years a Brethren missionary in northern Nigeria. During this period he developed some of the skills and the viewpoint of an anthropologist. Unlike most academic anthropologists, however, he did not become sufficiently disengaged from his subject matter to adopt or even to affect neutrality in the matter of the views of spiritual conflict that he encountered in his research, which grew out of his missionary experience.

To begin with, Kraft adopted a neutral viewpoint on the phenomena under investigation, but after his return to America and some years adopting the normal academic stance he was exposed to the viewpoint of a number of students from Pentecostal and charismatic backgrounds. This caused him to reflect on the exponential growth of Pentecostalism worldwide and its greater ability to deal with the spiritual worldview of people in "undeveloped" cultures. It was at this time that he came under the influence of John Wimber whose experience of healing ministry drew on Methodist missionary Alan Tippett's language of power encounter. Kraft traces his personal development in the first chapter of his book *Christianity with Power* written for a popular audience. In it, he claims to work from a position of critical realism and in the process he examines at a popular level the notion of a worldview, a category frequently used by anthropologists. He notes that our worldview teaches us to interpret reality in culturally approved ways. It teaches us to treat the evidence around us selectively and causes us to accept things that confirm what we have already been taught through the lens or filter of our cultural assumptions. He draws a helpful diagram to illustrate this:

FIGURE 1

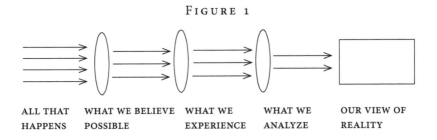

| ALL THAT HAPPENS | WHAT WE BELIEVE POSSIBLE | WHAT WE EXPERIENCE | WHAT WE ANALYZE | OUR VIEW OF REALITY |

In discussing what constitutes a worldview he says we constantly make cultural assumptions:

> These assumptions and the channels or guidelines we form based on them make up what we call worldview. We will here define worldview as *the culturally structured assumptions, values, and commitments underlying a people's perception of reality.*[9]

In a July 1991 article Kraft distils Alan Tippett's earlier investigations into "power encounter" in the context of the Polynesian worldview. He notes Tippett's observation that "most of the world's people are power oriented and respond to Christ more readily through power demonstrations." Kraft insists his missionary experience endorses Tippett's thesis that "Gospel messages about faith, love, forgiveness, and the other facts of Christianity are not likely to have nearly the impact on such people as the demonstrations of spiritual power."[10] This is because the worldview of such people encompasses conflict in unseen spiritual realms that controls, or at least affects, most of their daily experience. Kraft goes on to suggest that, for missionaries, power encounter on its own will not be sufficient to alter

9. Kraft, *Christianity with Power*, 20.
10. Kraft, "What Kind of Encounters Do We Need in Our Christian Witness?," 258.

the worldview of such peoples. It needs to be complemented by two other encounters, namely a truth encounter and a commitment encounter. Of this he says:

> The three encounters—power, commitment, and truth—are not the same, but they are intended to initiate a process crucial to the Christian experience aimed at a specific goal.
>
> The concern of the truth encounter is understanding. The vehicle of the encounter is teaching.
>
> The concern of the commitment encounter is relationship. The vehicle of the encounter is witness.
>
> The concern of the power encounter is freedom. Its vehicle is spiritual warfare.
>
> Truth and understanding have a lot to do with the mind; commitment and relationship rest primarily in the will; and freedom is largely experienced emotionally.[11]

Clearly, at this point Kraft is moving beyond a neutral anthropological stance as he applies categories learned from this discipline as an evangelistic tool in a missionary context. He sees this as part of spiritual warfare. In this article he observes that missionaries need to use these three types of encounter together rather than separately.

Kraft objects that in missionary situations challenges to commitment to Christ are usually couched in abstract terms. Western missionaries have focused solely on truth encounter when what is needed is a demonstration of those truths at work in the spirit realm. He laments, "We have encountered Satan's counterfeit 'truths' with the exciting truths of Christianity, but often in such an abstract way that our hearers have seen little verification of that truth in our lives." Earlier he comments:

> We encounter commitment to other gods and spirits with challenges to commitment to Jesus Christ. But when the people need healing, or seek fertility, or when there isn't enough rain, or there are floods, too often our answer is the hospital, the school and modern agriculture. We provide secular answers to what to them (and the Bible) are basically spiritual issues.[12]

Kraft observes that, in the missionary situation, converts and even some national pastors display a dual allegiance because missionaries have countered allegiance to other gods and spirits without taking seriously the

11. Ibid., 260.
12. Ibid.

spiritual realm they inhabit. He is so convinced of the applicability of this analysis that in recent years he has spent a considerable portion of his time beyond the classroom engaging in a counselling, deliverance, and healing prayer ministry

In his work, Kraft rightly appeals to the ministry of Jesus as well as the Acts of the Apostles and refers to the first chapter of Colossians as well as the classic warfare passage in Ephesians 6:1–16 as a foundation for his views on spiritual conflict. However, coming, as he originally did, from a conservative evangelical position he applies these texts almost exclusively to individual battles with unseen forces. His move to a less traditional view of the reality and potency of such forces at the individual level comes as a result of allowing personal experience of individual power encounters to help him reinterpret the biblical text. It is curious that his starting point as a missionary anthropologist *does not seem to provide a structural perspective* on the nature of these powers to any great degree.

Paul Hiebert[13]

Hiebert was a more academic missionary anthropologist who was born on the mission field in India. It was from personal experience and his field studies in India that he formulated his understanding of the nature of spiritual conflict that governed his approach to the relevant biblical texts.

Hiebert's main concern was to enable missiologists and missionaries to effectively communicate the gospel cross-culturally. While not denying the need for power encounter, he naturally tended to focus on *the importance of truth encounter* as a means of effectively conveying the good news, although he did not self-consciously use these category labels in his discussion. He insisted that cross-cultural misunderstandings, which occur at the cognitive level, and ethnocentrism, at the affective level, are the two main barriers to effective missionary work. For him, anthropology was a tool to strip away these hindrances to communicating the gospel; it was a means of evaluating cultures in order to get inside them. However, he saw relativism

13. Born on November 13, 1932, in Shamshabad (a suburb of Hyderabad), Paul represented the third generation of a Mennonite Brethren missionary family, in 1977 he became a missionary anthropologist at Fuller Theological Seminary until 1990 when he moved to Trinity Evangelical Divinity School (Deerfield, IL; 1990–2007) where he spent his last seventeen years, first as professor of mission anthropology and South Asian studies and later as Professor of Anthropology and Mission, as well as chair of the Department of Mission and Evangelism, and Associate Dean of Academic Doctorates.

as one of the dangers of an anthropological approach to understanding cultures. In an article for *Perspectives on the World Christian Movement* he says that while maintaining respect for the integrity of other cultures missionary anthropologists end up espousing a relativism that obscures truth.

Hiebert goes on to affirm that we must progress beyond relativism, "As Christians we claim another basis for evaluation, namely, biblical norms."[14] The process of arriving at these biblical norms is not as simple as it sounds since missionaries do not come to the Bible free from their own cultural presuppositions. Hiebert was not the first to observe that to thoroughly contextualize the gospel there has to be a three way process of evaluation; David Hesselgrave—among others—makes a similar point.[15]

Different cultures arise from or produce differing worldviews—Hiebert compares a worldview with spectacles through which people groups within particular cultures view reality and shrewdly observes: "Often we become aware of our own worldview only when we live deeply in another culture, and then return to view our own culture through outside eyes, with a different belief and value system."[16] People within a given culture would probably be unable to relate what their worldview is since it constitutes the "givenness" through which they make sense of the reality around them. Hiebert uses the analogy of an iceberg to explain the relationship between culture and the worldview that embeds it. "Behaviour and beliefs," he suggests, "are what we see above the surface of the ocean. The worldview is the large hidden mass beneath the surface that holds the whole iceberg up. If we convert only beliefs and behaviour, in time the worldview will take the Christian beliefs captive."[17]

What is needed for the Scriptures to be more fully understood is a mutual process of worldview transformation. Hiebert comments: "The process of doing theology in a particular setting must be that of critical contextualization in which the culture is studied, then Scripture, and finally Biblical truth and morality are used to judge and correct the culture and its worldview. This is the key to worldview transformation."[18]All of this carries implications for the way we do theology; as we seek to engage in what he calls "philosophical theology" (i.e., systematic theology), which seeks

14. Hiebert, "Culture and Cross-Cultural Differences", C-17.

15. Hesselgrave, *Communicating Christ Cross-Culturally.*

16. Hiebert, *Conversion and Worldview Transformation*, 85.

17. Ibid., 84.

18. Ibid.

to synthesize biblical themes, or biblical theology, which takes a more narrative approach. He suggests we should be open to what he proposes as "missional theology," by which he means an attempt to interpret the Bible contextually in terms of the culture being addressed.[19] In his 1997 article he comments: "The process of doing theology in a particular setting must be that of critical contextualization in which the culture is studied, then Scripture, and finally Biblical truth and morality are used to judge and correct the culture and its worldview."[20]

The church plays a decisive role in this process as it is meant to be a hermeneutical community of scholars, exegetes, practitioners, and social commentators, which facilitates the process of engaging cross-culturally with Scripture and the task of making it relevant to other cultures. This observation will later bring us back to Hiebert's reflections on the relationship between evangelism, the church, and the kingdom of God, which he sees to be crucial to the issue of addressing issues of mission in a cross-cultural context. He begins by contrasting Hindu, Western, and biblical worldviews in order to alert us to the issue of contrasting cultural understandings of the relationship between the spiritual and material realms.

In his earlier article on culture and cross-cultural differences Hiebert illustrates the case of attempting to translate the gospel for a Telegu Indian in the Hindu context. He begins by showing the difficulty of substituting the word "sin" in one language for that in another since the terms in either context are already freighted with culturally embedded meanings.

Moreover, in Telegu there are at least three options for translating the Hebrew word for God. Hiebert comments: "The problem is that each of these carries the Hindu connotation that gods have exactly the same kind of life as human beings, only more of it. They are not categorically different from people."[21] The same problem occurs in trying to convey the notion of incarnation because in Hindu thought gods are thought of as constantly moving up and down in different levels of the same category as humans. There is no way within that language of portraying an infinite God crossing the gulf between one category of being and another. In any case, in this way of thinking, the infinite is not personal. In the Western way of thinking there are only two tiers of existence, the material and the spiritual, whereas in the worldview of many other cultures there is a third, intermediate level

19. Tiénou and Hiebert, "Missional Theology.".

20. Hiebert, *Conversion and Worldview Transformation*, 84.

21. Hiebert, "Culture and Cross-cultural Differences," C-19.

of activity. There are similarities between the Indian concept of life and the medieval view of the "great chain of being" with which we dealt in the previous chapter. This is because, while the Hindu framework may predate Plato's thought on which the medieval view depends, both are drawn from the same circle of ideas. Post-Enlightenment thought has moved away from a so-called "three decker" view of the universe for one excluding the middle semi-supernatural realm that features in many animistic cultures and in Hinduism. This is what Hiebert categorises as "the flaw of the excluded middle." Other cultures share a less rigid view of the difference between the sacred and the secular. In some senses, for them, all of life has a sacred dimension. The division between private faith and public truth just does not exist.

Toward the end of his life Hiebert wrote an important, if brief, article on spiritual warfare that brought his anthropological studies into sharp focus.[22] In it, he notes that the current focus on the issue on the part of Western missionaries is a step forward, because it

> comes as an important corrective to the earlier emphasis in many western churches on the Gospel as merely truth, and on evil as primarily human weakness. Both truth and power are central themes in the Gospel and should be in the lives of God's people.[23]

However, he notes that this new emphasis has been forced on practitioners as a result of their encounters with demon possession, magic, and witchcraft. This has caused many to base their views on experience and then to look for Bible texts to justify their stance. For Hiebert this signals a failure to think biblically and theologically about the issues. He comments: "They fail to examine the worldviews they use to interpret both Scripture and experience. These are hard to see because they are what we think with, not what we think about."[24] In the ensuing analysis he suggests that there are varying worldviews on spiritual warfare, each of which will affect the approach taken to the biblical texts.

To begin with, he identifies the modern Western worldview growing out of the Post-Enlightenment Cartesian dualism with its separation of reality into two realms; the supernatural realm inhabited by God, angels, and demons and the natural physical realm, which includes man, animals,

22. Hiebert, "Spiritual Warfare and Worldviews."

23. Ibid., 1.

24. Ibid.

plants, and inanimate matter. This then results in the denial of the possibility of spiritual warfare on the part of secular humanists who only admit to the existence of the material realm; the rest is mere folklore and superstition; thus they demythologize Scripture. The other version of the modern worldview takes spiritual warfare seriously from a purely cosmological standpoint: "God, angels and demons are involved in a cosmic battle in the heavens, but the everyday events on earth are best explained and controlled by science and technology." This is the stance of many modern missionaries, who

> affirm the cosmic battle between good and evil, but deny the realities of witchcraft, spirit possession, evil eye and magic in the cultures where they serve. Consequently they fail to provide biblical answers to the people's fears of earthly spirits and powers, and to deal with the reality of Satan's work on earth.[25]

Hiebert's second category is what he calls "the tribal worldview" where demons, ghosts, the spirits of ancestors, and gods are all considered to be real. Most of these are not considered to be wholly good or bad. Rather, spiritual warfare is a matter of ongoing conflict between shifting alliances of supernatural beings who affect life. These allegiances are often an issue of territory based on ethnicity—the battle is not so much between good and evil as between "us" and "them." When a tribe, village, or group is conquered by a more powerful group they experience conversion to their more powerful gods through a sort of power encounter. Thus the territoriality of gods and spirits is an important part of tribal spiritual warfare. Hiebert considers that this view has influenced the ideas of some Christians as they seek to understand conflict between Satan and "territorial spirits"—a view for which he finds little evidence in Scripture.

Hiebert labels his third warfare category "the Indo-European worldview." This worldview arises from Zoroastrianism, Manicheism, and Hindu cultures; it is based on a cosmic dualism between good and evil—the Buddhist ying-yang motif on the Korean national flag is a symbol of this. He says that, "In it mighty gods battle for control of the universe: one seeking to establish a kingdom of righteousness and order, and the other an evil empire." The consequence is that "Humans are innocent victims caught in the cosmic struggle. The outcome is uncertain for both sides are equally strong." Good in this context is not thought of in terms of absolute rightness (or

25. Ibid.

righteousness). The gods sometimes sin—they are good not because they never do wrong but because they are on our side. Victory is never complete or fully assured since good and evil are equally powerful. Hiebert maintains that morality in the Indo-European worldview is not based on truth or righteousness but on equal opportunity to win—the protagonists are thought of as being more or less equal in power.[26] This means that, where it occurs, victory is brought about through *the myth of redemptive violence.*[27] He goes on to suggest that, though the Indo-European worldview has little religious significance in the West, it still acquires moral resonance through Hollywood drama and the rules of the sports field.

Hiebert's final spiritual warfare category is that of the biblical worldview. He concedes that the OT is full of warfare imagery that may be both spiritual and politico-physical in character, but by the time we get to the NT the focus of the battle is a more spiritual one. Demonization is present, Jewish exorcists sought to control it through techniques, whereas Jesus simply relied on the authority of his spoken word. He concludes: "If the cosmic struggle between God and Satan is not one of power, what is it about? It is the establishment of God's reign on earth as it is in heaven."[28]

Hiebert insists that the cross is central to a true biblical understanding of the nature of spiritual warfare. He appeals to Colossians 2:15 and Hebrews 2:14 for his justification and maintains that at the crucifixion Satan sought to provoke Christ to use his divine powers inappropriately whereas Jesus, as Messiah, refused his tormentors' challenge to come down from the cross and wage physical warfare. Instead the cross is "the demonstration of victory through weakness. At the cross Satan, not Jesus, stands judged because he put Christ, God incarnate as perfect human, to death."[29]For Hiebert the cross is not an end in itself:

> Rather it removes the obstacles to God's purpose of creating people fit for His Kingdom . . . a biblical view of spiritual warfare points to the final establishment of the Kingdom of God throughout the whole universe. When we focus too much on the current battle, we lose sight of the cosmic picture in which the real story is not the battle, but the eternal reign of Christ.[30]

26. Ibid., 3.
27. The idea that in the end it is revenge that will establish justice.
28. Ibid., 4.
29. Ibid.
30. Ibid.,.5.

In personal interviews recorded on video, Hiebert traces his pilgrimage from a missionary to a missionary anthropologist. In it, he says he began as a missionary evangelist seeking to establish the church and bring in the kingdom, but latterly he came to see that the kingdom of God is what gives rise to both church and evangelism; to understand this rightly is the key to a biblical hermeneutic and to understanding spiritual conflict.[31]

In closing, we have majored on Paul Hiebert's thought, allowing him to speak in his own words as far as possible because he neatly brings us full circle to the hermeneutical issue with which we started this section. As we move on to the next chapter to consider some of the biblical conflict texts in some detail it is important to bear in mind the debate in which we have so far engaged. As we come to consider the Bible on its own terms in relation to spiritual conflict it is vital, as far as we can, to allow it to speak for itself. In order to do this we need to shed as many of our own cultural and literary presuppositions as possible. We also need to work hard to see the biblical worldview from within its own context(s).

31. www.globalmissiology.org/cms/index.php?option=com (accessed June 2011).

3

The Bible and the Powers

Richard Whitehouse

Introduction

Any approach to individual texts on spiritual conflict in the Bible needs to be seen in the context of the whole canon of scripture. The Bible was gathered into its present form by the Christian church in the conviction that it reveals what God has to say to his people. Clearly, the canon of Scripture records a development both of human thought and of divine revelation. This means that the particular detail of any given subject needs to be set within the context of the whole. We will, therefore, make a selection of relevant passages on spiritual conflict, taken in a roughly chronological order, that contribute to a biblical understanding of the topic.

Creation and Combat Motifs in the Old Testament

In his comprehensive work on conflict theology[1] Greg Boyd begins his task by examining the biblical worldview, which he sets in the wider context of the cosmic warfare worldview of the Near East in Old Testament times. It is important to do this because, as he convincingly maintains, the Old Testament writers particularly in the Psalms, the restoration prophets, and the book of Job draw on ancient Near Eastern cosmic warfare imagery in order

1. Boyd, *God at War*, chapter 3.

to explain the relationship between God and the existence of evil within his creation. This does not mean that the biblical authors uncritically adopted Canaanite cosmology, they merely "baptized" some of its terms into their radically different account of creation and the nature of evil. There are, however, sufficient commonalities between the two sets of accounts to make the use of this imagery appropriate as an apologetic device having explanatory power for the first readers of the biblical narrative.

This imagery had "bite" for their readers because the cosmologies from which it was borrowed were current throughout the OT period. Warfare imagery formed part of the cultural ambience of Egyptian, Canaanite, and Babylonian religion against which the faith of Israel was constantly pitted. It was, therefore, useful to appropriate it, thus subverting it to serve the more adequate cosmology of the biblical revelation. This use of pagan mythological themes as an apologetic device is itself a form of cultural spiritual conflict evidenced by the fact that the cosmology lying behind the outlandish creation stories contained in most ancient Near Eastern texts is based on a dualism that is absent from the biblical account. These accounts of the creation feature jealous and warring gods from whose quarrels the world was formed, not created, since matter was already presumed to exist. The main concern of these mythologies is to contain the chaos that always threatened a world produced by competing deities. In these accounts the hostile sea was viewed as a cypher for raging chaos. In their limited worldview, the sea always threatened to break out of its bounds and produce disaster. As Boyd points out, the Israelites shared the conviction with all ancient Near Eastern peoples that the earth rested upon waters:

> When the author of Genesis 1 begins his creation account by referring, without explanation, to "the surface of the deep" (*'hôm*) and "the waters" (1:2), no ancient Near Eastern person would have had trouble understanding what he was speaking about. This was "the deep" or "the waters" on which everyone believed the earth had been founded (Ps 24:1–2)."[2]

The Genesis creation account demythologizes the pagan versions that saw the personified waters as hostile to creation, a viewpoint that is to some extent reflected in later OT references, which appear to take on some of the pagan mythological version of hostility and warfare having been built into creation from the beginning. Boyd observes that the pagan accounts are erroneous but still resonate with the Hebrew view of reality where creation

2. Ibid., 84.

is based on a cosmic covenant of peace, which is somehow disturbed by hostile forces.

In Israelite thought, the raging sea is often used as a picture of the nations who were in conflict with God. This imagery is prominent in Psalms and the book of Isaiah, for example. In the biblical account the sea is constrained and confined; whether the sea refers to the created order or to the nations, Yahweh has the potential conflict under control. The biblical writers also borrow the imagery of Leviathan, the ancient twisting serpent, the monster of the deep who is the possible origin of NT serpent/dragon imagery used in connection with Satan. In the ancient Near Eastern worldview Leviathan represented disorder and conflict with the gods whose personal battles produced the world in the first place. The whole point of the culmination of the book of Job, which grapples with the issue of unexplained evil in the life of a righteous man, is that "Yahweh can do what Job could never do: stand up to and subjugate Leviathan, as he did at the time of creation."[3] The prologue to the book of Job presents this Leviathan figure, under the guise of Satan, as Job's accuser and the attempted provoker of conflict in the court of heaven.

In the hands of Isaiah, Leviathan, and thus the deep that is his habitat, will be defeated through the future reign of God. *"The Lord with his cruel and great and strong sword will punish Leviathan the fleeing serpent, Leviathan the twisting serpent, and he will kill the dragon that is in the sea."* (Isaiah 27:1; NIV). This is an exact parallel with the Ugaritic mythological combat text, which is turned on its head since there is no hint here of ontological dualism;[4] the conflict is real, the power of the enemy is great but the outcome is never in doubt.[5]

God's OT Conflict with Supernatural Beings

In view of the attitude of the culture surrounding its formation, the OT, especially in its earlier stages, is remarkably reticent about the existence and the nature of the demonic. The Hebrews exhibited a radically different attitude toward the spirit world than that of their pagan neighbors who were preoccupied, even obsessed with either manipulating or appeasing evil spirits who were thought to be in intimate control of their daily lives. Boyd

---

3. Ibid., 94.

4. That is, we are not dealing with a battle between equals.

5. Longman and Reid, *God Is a Warrior*, 78.

comments: "Indeed, given its cultural context, it is remarkable how little the Old Testament says about evil spirits. Even when it does refer to evil spirits, it makes little of them."[6] Wherever they are referred to it is clear that Yahweh is in control and that they present no long-term threat to his rule. Indeed, at points they are used for his purposes even when they attempt to subvert his rule. What is clear is that they are not pawns used to achieve his sovereign will; rather, they have an independent will of their own even though they end up serving his purposes in the long run. This observation helps to clear up some of the more puzzling OT references to evil spirits sent from God to achieve his purpose. What they do on the errands on which God sends them is of their own volition—there is no meticulous divine supervision here. Nevertheless, the errand itself is itself an act of judgment for sin or rebellion on the part of those who are thus afflicted.

Although the OT does not major on the spirit realm in term of demons and other evil spirits it does highlight the existence of other gods besides Yahweh. Psalms even speaks of a heavenly council of these so-called gods (82:1–6), as do Job, Jeremiah, and Isaiah (Job 15:8; Jer 23:18; Isa 6:2–8). A body of scholarship interprets these and several OT passages as based on Ugaritic, Canaanite, and Babylonian texts that portray a divine council existing to preside over the cosmos.[7] The main difference between the other Near Eastern texts and that of the OT is that the biblical text is deliberately vague about the composition of the heavenly council and nowhere, with the exception of the figure of Satan in the prologue to Job, identifies specific personalities or deities.[8] The OT takes for granted the existence of other gods—witness the commandment "You shall have no other gods before me"[9]—which is set precisely against the background of liberation from the gods of Egypt and the magic arts of their priests.

It is clear that these gods were conceived of as real entities over against the God of Israel and it is he that gave them existence but how does this relate to biblical monotheism?[10] Parts of the OT tradition seems to suggest that these "gods" were thought of as originally being angelic or spiritual

---

6. Ibid., 8.

7. E.g., Miller, "The Divine Council"; Mullen, *The Divine Council*; Heiser, "Divine Council."

8. Cf. Seinfeld, *New Interpreter's Dictionary of the Bible*, 145.

9. Exod 20:3.

10. For a discussion of how this relates to radical monotheism, see Boyd, *God at War*, chapter 4.

beings who were given responsibility for nations or territories and who violated their trust and exceeded their mandate in rebellion against Yahweh. *If this is the case it would at least pave the way to a degree for a structural understanding of the nature of the jurisdiction of the powers in later apocalyptic and Pauline thought.* While some OT passages grant these gods ontological status Jeremiah, Isaiah, and certain passages in Psalms mock them as "no gods" and the idols that represent them as powerless. Part of their divine status is what is attributed to them by their worshipers, but the Bible, throughout, treats them as real and as God's opponents whom he will demolish in due course.

Warfare and the Supernatural

In their book *God Is A Warrior* Longman and Reid, leaning heavily on von Rad's earlier work, trace the connection between the concept of holy warfare and conflict with the false gods of Israel's enemies. Yahweh even physically intervenes in some of Israel's battles, as with the drowning of the Egyptians at the Red Sea and Deborah and Barak's victory over Sisera in the book of Judges. The point is that God is seen as employing the forces of his creation as weapons in his battle. In other places it is made clear to the Israelites that there is a heavenly host of God's angelic beings who also fight on their behalf. The heavenly host is on occasions identified as God's army standing with Israel when they are obedient to his will. We see this in 2 Kings 6:17 when God reveals his heavenly army to Elisha's servant when they were trapped in Dothan by the Aramean army.

Not all of Israel's later battles were regarded as acts of Holy War; in the time of the kings much of the warfare is apparently purely political. Warfare is only holy when sanctioned by God. In the Holy Warfare Tradition[11] recorded, certainly up to the time of David, this is signaled by the ritual preparation of the soldiers before battle to rid themselves of uncleanness and the fact that the plunder was regarded as belonging to God. This is because Israel's battles on these occasions were seen as war not only against physical but also against unseen enemies. The fact that Israel was on God's side does not mean that he was their tool in warfare; Longman and Reid comment:

---

11. For an early definitive work on this theme, cf. Rad, *Holy War in Ancient Israel.*

He would not provide the victory for them in any and every situation. They had to obey the covenant; otherwise, they were liable to God's judgement. At such times God turned against Israel as an enemy. This reversal of Holy War came about particularly when the King trusted his weapons more than the Lord.[12]

It is quite clear that whenever Israel was unfaithful, God abandoned them in battle or is said not to have gone out with them. In the later period, when Israel's apostasy became so great that they were worshiping false gods and practicing sexual immorality even within the temple precincts, God said he would abandon not only them but also the temple in which they trusted as the symbol of his presence. They thought that as long as the temple was in Jerusalem they could not be defeated. However, it was God, not the temple, who was their defense and Jeremiah warned that they would be carried into captivity as a punishment. Ezekiel, who was himself forced into exile, also pronounced that Israel's plight was due to God's abandonment of the temple as a punishment for turning to false gods. It was still a Holy War but Israel was now the enemy and Yahweh was even prepared to use his own spiritual enemies to chastize them. This underlines the fact that God was in control of the nations and may even relate to the idea of a heavenly council of supernatural beings over whom he is, in the end, in control.

The Day of the Lord: The Future Warrior

During the period of the Judges and then of the divided kingdom under the monarchy, the nation experienced cycles of ascendancy followed by moral failure leading to complete apostasy. These times of apostasy were brought about by following the gods of other nations or when Israel was conquered by these same nations. These times of defeat led to an expectation that "the Day of the Lord" would arrive when Yahweh would defeat his and their enemies in a final judgement that would place Israel in charge of the nations. This would be the culmination of God's cosmological battle ushering in a time of prosperity and empire. However many false prophets inspired by lying spirits might come along to predict victory for Israel, prophets who were faithful to God's covenant consistently proclaimed, firstly, that on the day of the Lord Israel would be equally judged and punished along with the other nations and, secondly, that this would eventually be followed by restoration based on justice springing from true worship of God. By

12. Longman and Reid, *God is a Warrior*, 60.

implication this involved the rejection of demonically-inspired foreign gods. God's enemies would be used to chastise the nation even though their demonic idols were no-gods, but it would be Yahweh who would prove himself by ushering in a justice-based kingdom. To some extent cosmological warfare was being expressed in terms of ethics.

If we accept the commonly received view among Bible scholars that the final form of the book of Job dates from the Exile, this process can be seen at work at a personal level. The effects of the secret attacks of the accuser were not to be explained by the theological sophistry of Job's friends but by the creator God who in his extensive wisdom and creative power is able to tame the cosmological monsters of the Babylonian combat myths. The lesson was meant to be applied to the nation as a whole; Yahweh is both Lord of the conflict and the restorer of fortunes for those who are faithful even through extreme adversity.

The restoration of a faithful Israelite remnant under Ezra and Nehemiah proved to be a bitter disappointment. Haggai records that even while they were meant to be building a new temple the people fell away from their high ideals by paying more attention to establishing their own wealth than to a building project that was meant to put God at the center. During the rebuilding of Jerusalem Nehemiah ruthlessly attempted to prevent intermarriage with neighboring tribes, which might eventually lead to a hybrid faith. By the end of the OT canon Malachi complains that the nation had returned to its old ways, desecrating temple worship so badly that he calls for its doors to be closed. Meanwhile, he foresaw acceptable sacrificial worship fires rising to Yahweh from the very nations who were currently given to false gods.

It is against this background that Israel entered a four-hundred-year prophetic silence that gave rise to lurid apocalyptic literature that reappropriated cosmological language. During the intertestamental period the religion of Israel took some unexpected turns. Historically it was a period of social and political conflict that saw Jewish returnees to their land under considerable pressure as they were successively ruled over by the Persians, the Greeks, and then the Romans. There was a roughly 100 year break when they asserted quasi-independence under the Hasmonean dynasty after the Maccabean revolt. N. T. Wright convincingly demonstrates that the bulk of Jews in the land regarded themselves as still being in exile even though living in their own land.[13] The experience of subjugation and oppression

13. Wright, *The New Testament and the People of God*, chapter 10, esp. 301.

under other rulers gave rise to a variety of expectations—Wright points out that it is misleading to label Jewish religion at this time as "Judaism," as there were several different "Judaisms" or brands of the Jewish faith. There were clear longings on the parts of some for a warrior Messiah to come and liberate Israel from foreign domination. For many this was accompanied by a burning hatred for their foreign overlords and the idols that they worshipped, which were thought of as being demonically infested. These feelings were intensified when Antiochus Epiphanes IV marched into the temple and burnt swine's flesh on the altar as a calculated insult to the Jews (this is probably the "abomination of desolation" predicted in Daniel and referred to by Jesus in the context of his expected second advent).

It was during this period that the kind of apocalyptic literature appearing in the OT in Daniel chapter 7 came to full flower. This literature consists of symbolic imagery accompanied by lurid visions and hyperbolic imagery. Many of these apocalyptic tracts spoke of a messianic invasion heralded by the imminent collapse of the natural realm with stars falling from the sky, earthquakes, and other natural phenomena working the purpose of Yahweh in overcoming the powers in heaven and on the earth. There were sometimes astrological references; the world was conceived of as being surrounded by layers of heavens stretching from the atmosphere surrounding the earth through to a seventh heaven where God dwelt. The Jewish concept of God became more remote and both the earth and the heavens were thought of as being populated with evil spirits, the inspirers of the foreign gods. A divine incursion was often promised, widely thought of as a second exodus, a full return to the Promised Land sometimes conceived of as a renewed Eden. There was, of course, a wide variety of expectations painting different scenarios but most of them culminated with the same results. The cosmological imagery, often borrowed from Persia or Babylonia was used to tell a different story of the defeat of the hostile powers bringing about a return to the earth's pristine state with Israel at the head of the nations. Some apocalyptic versions of the future predicted more than one Messiah—usually featuring a priestly messianic figure accompanied by a warrior Messiah-King. The term Messiah (Hebrew: *mashiac*) means "anointed" and both priests and kings in the OT were "anointed ones" who fought God's battles, one in the spiritual and one in the physical realm.

One group, the Essenes, formed a brotherhood the bulk of whom withdrew to form a monastic society on the shores of the Dead Sea in expectation of the coming battle. Their *War Scroll* outlines vivid expectations of a future divine conquest to which they had to contribute nothing except to be spiritually prepared through holy communal living, which featured frequent baptisms for personal sin and devout prayer interceding for the expected battle to come.

The origin of the pharisaic movement is somewhat obscure but they emerged out of a group of wise men and scribes of Torah who traced their origins back to Ezra the scribe. The name comes from the Hebrew פְּרוּשִׂים (pĕrûšîm), which means "set apart." This name was probably adopted as a protest against the tendency of some Jews to adopt Hellenistic values. Their movement was partly a political party and partly a social movement in Judaism. They maintained that observation of the Torah in daily life was more important than the Temple ritual. Unlike the Sadducees who controlled temple life they accepted a wider canon of Scripture embracing the prophets, the historical books, and the Wisdom literature as well as the Pentateuch. They awaited a general resurrection of the righteous from the dead whereas the priestly party who only regarded the Pentateuch as Scripture did not believe in an afterlife. The Pharisees were concerned to apply ritual and moral purity in daily living believing that Messiah would come if the whole of Israel kept the Law perfectly for one day. For them, spiritual conflict was an ethical matter—they followed in the ethicizing tradition.

It is more difficult to find reliable information about the Zealots since most of what we know comes from the Jewish first-century historian Josephus whose description of them is based on pro-Roman political propaganda. He tends to use the term to cover any rebel faction prior to the destruction of the Second Temple in 70 CE. This does not seem to have been a cohesive movement. However, there appears to have been fanatical groups whose approach to the coming of a Messiah was political and various groups acclaimed their own leader to be the Messiah in hope of raising a popular following against the Romans. We have no inside knowledge of the thought forms of Zealot groups since they have left no literature by which we can judge. They are only known to us from external accounts of their activities, most of which are prejudiced. However, they do have a historical context that suggests a thoroughly Jewish background, which probably drew upon some of the extant circle of apocalyptic thought. The very fact that they used messianic language confirms this. In the end, their protest against foreign domination included the rejection of foreign gods but it was as much a social protest; for them, the kingdom of God was meant to come by force of arms.

Each of these sample responses to Israel's historical situation leading up to the opening of the NT engaged in spiritual conflict at different levels. It is clear, however, that they tended to see Israel as a nation still in exile, even though in their own land, and that their hopes centerd on a restored Israel sometimes couched in terms of a fresh Red Sea type deliverance. They looked for a future theocracy in which God's Messiah would reverse their fortunes. Apocalyptic thought and the practices that grew out of it were essentially eschatological. This was expressed in terms of reestablishing God's rule over a rebellious creation currently presided over, or at least dominated by, opposing spiritual forces.

Conflict Motifs in the New Testament

Mark's Gospel, widely regarded as the earliest of the Synoptic Gospels, avoids any account of the birth and boyhood of Jesus; instead, Mark begins with the title-like announcement: *"The beginning of the gospel about Jesus Christ, the Son of God."*[14] As far as Mark is concerned Jesus *is* the good news and this statement is firmly attached to the perception that he is "the Son of God." Although this opening statement came to be seen by the church as an assertion of Christ's divinity it is also a term that was used of the Messiah in intertestamental literature and should probably be initially taken in that sense.[15] This fits with the announcement of John the Baptist appearing in the desert in fulfilment of Isaiah's prophecy: John prepared the way for the Lord by proclaiming a baptism of repentance for the forgiveness of sins—a scandalous demand for the Jews to undergo the same kind of ritual cleansing required of converts to Judaism—the significance would not have been lost on his hearers. John's announcement of the coming of the Messiah who would baptize not with water but with the Holy Spirit is a clear eschatological statement that would probably have been regarded by his hearers in apocalyptic terms. Both Matthew's and Mark's accounts record John's assertion that repentance and baptism were necessary because "the Kingdom of God is at hand." This is a theme that Jesus takes up after his baptism and the contest with Satan in the wilderness. Bosch makes the point that "kingdom" is a warfare term. He says of Jesus' kingdom ministry:

---

14. Mark 1:1; NIV.

15. See Psalm 2 and other places where this title is applied to kings and spirit beings.

[I]t launches an all-out attack on evil in all its manifestations. God's reign arrives wherever Jesus overcomes the power of evil. Then, as it does now, evil took many forms: pain, sickness, death, demon-possession, personal sin and immorality, the loveless self-righteousness of those who claim to know God, the maintaining of special class privileges, the brokenness of human relationships. Jesus is, however, saying: If human distress takes many forms, the power of God does likewise.[16]

Bosch speaks about "the assault of God's reign on evil" but this comes about not through violence but through a new kingdom manifesto, which is laid out in Jesus' sermon in Matthew 5–7, which envisages a different set of values from those of the imagined apocalyptic kingdom featured in Jewish speculation. In Luke's account the kingdom manifesto is set out in Jesus' sermon in the Nazareth synagogue in chapter 4.

Mark omits the details of the temptations merely commenting that Jesus was tested by Satan in the desert for forty days. The scene is set for a conflict account of Jesus' ministry. He is the warrior at odds with a fallen spirit-world as it impacts God's people and the rest of creation. The remainder of Mark's Gospel focuses on miracle and exorcism as much as it does on Jesus' teaching. The structure of the Gospel reflects a Galilean ministry where growing conflict with the authorities is followed by the transition to Jerusalem and the final showdown with both the religious establishment and the Roman administration, which led to his death. In Mark, exorcism of an evil spirit in the synagogue at Capernaum follows the call of the first four disciples. This is probably meant to signal that God's warfare is not only with foreign powers or disembodied spirits but also with spiritual strongholds even within Israel's religious establishment. Longman and Reid comment on the Capernaum synagogue exorcism: "The question of the demon in verse 24—which may just as well be read as an exclamation ('You have come to destroy us!')—accentuates the warlike mission of Jesus against the demonic world."[17] They provide details of the alleged divine warrior motif elsewhere in Mark, although, in places, they seem to stretch the evidence to breaking point.

The clash with the Pharisees over casting out demons recorded in each of the Synoptic Gospels is central to the understanding of spiritual

---

16. Bosch, *Transforming Mission*, 32.

17. Longman and Reid., *God Is a Warrior*, 98.

conflict.[18] Mark places this event early in his Gospel after the choice of the twelve apostles, in itself an implied eschatological statement. At this point the religious leaders accuse Jesus of demon possession, *"He is possessed by Beelzebub! By the Prince of demons he is driving out demons"* (Mark 3: 22; NIV). Mark makes the point that Jesus replied in parables; nevertheless he clearly states that Satan has a kingdom, which, by implication, is parallel to his own. Thus, if Satan were to drive out Satan his end truly would have come! (Longman and Reid read this as an eschatological irony.) Jesus' reply, "But if I drive out demons by the Spirit of God, then the kingdom of God has come upon you" is paralleled in Matthew and Luke (Matt 12:28; NIV—cf. Luke 11:20, which has "finger of God," i.e., his executive power, instead of "Spirit of God"). Clearly, Jesus is signaling a clash of kingdoms; the casting out of a demon is not merely a case of psychological or spiritual healing it is a declaration of war on Satan, whose domain will eventually be plundered. Jesus contrasts his own ministry of exorcism with that of Jewish exorcists who also cast out demons. Jesus goes on to say, "In fact, no one can enter a strong man's house and carry off his possessions unless he first ties up the strong man. Then he can rob his house" (Mark 3:27–28; NIV). Here Jesus is serving a warning on his demonic opposition; he will bind the strong man and, in good time, plunder his goods.

Spiritual conflict is a theme in all four Gospels and it is significant that both Matthew and Luke begin with a cycle of birth stories embedded in a context of conflict. Matthew's birth account clearly states that Joseph was to give him the name Jesus (the Greek form of Joshua, which means "the Lord saves") linking this with the Isaianic prophecy of a virgin who would give birth to a son called Emmanuel ("God with us"). Mary's song, when she visits Elizabeth, is cast in thoroughly apocalyptic, yet this-worldly terms (Luke 2:46–55). The scene is set for God's invasion of the earth and the implied restoration from exile. Scarce wonder that, after the visit of the Magi, Herod seeks to kill the child who escapes with his parents to Egypt.

Luke presents the ministry of Jesus in terms of a new exodus. At the transfiguration Jesus speaks with Moses and Elijah about his "departure" which he was about to accomplish in Jerusalem—the Greek word is *exodon*, which translates literally as "exodus." At the Last Supper on the eve of his death Jesus celebrated the Passover in terms of a new covenant in his blood. Clearly, Luke sees Jesus as the Passover Lamb and interprets his death in

18. Mark 3: 22–27; Matthew 12: 24–29; Luke 11: 15–22.

terms of redemption not from bondage in Egypt but from bondage to sin and by implication from the powers that bind men.

In John's Gospel we leave Jesus' Galilean ministry and the focus turns to Jerusalem. At first sight the Gospel appears to carry few references to spiritual conflict themes (it does not feature exorcisms and the healing miracles in John seem to have more to do with purely physical cures). Each of John's recorded miracles is taken as an opportunity to deal with wider theological concerns as John reflects on the actions of Jesus. On closer inspection, John's approach to spiritual conflict is, in fact, even more thoroughgoing than that of the Synoptics. In spite of the lack of individual exorcisms, it may be argued that John views the ministry of Jesus as one great exorcism as he seeks to deal with Satan's domination over the world. This exorcism finds its completion in the death and resurrection of Jesus. In order to unravel this, we need to examine some of the major themes of the Gospel. John deals with a number of polarities such as light and darkness, above and below, God and the devil, and flesh and spirit. We do not have space to deal with all of these in detail, but we note that these central themes that illustrate the point of Jesus' battle with the powers.

Paul's Conflict Terminology

Preliminary Concerns

We do not have space to examine every one of the Pauline passages on spiritual warfare, but it must be observed that they are far more extensive than is often supposed. Both Boyd and Longman and Reid point out that several cosmological warfare motifs underlie more than the handful of classical Pauline references to the principalities and powers. However, the two main approaches to Paul's thought are divided between interpreters who arrive at a structural approach to the identity of the powers and those who see the powers as personal entities.

The main advocates of the structural approach include Berkhof, Yoder, and Wink each of whom tends to "demythologize" the powers; indeed, they contend that Paul himself already went down this route compared with beliefs about the powers that were current in first-century society. There is some merit in this argument as we shall see, but for the most part the proponents of this view, apart from Wink, do not engage in a sufficiently serious cultural or literary exegesis in coming to their conclusions, their approach to the texts is governed by a concern for social ethics.

Advocates of a personalised view of Pauline thought including O'Brien, Arnold, and N. T. Wright (who takes a somewhat mediating position) tend to engage in a more thorough exegesis of the passages, which they set against the general first-century background and of the specific situational context of each passage.

Cultural Background

Paul's cultural background was that of a first-century diaspora Jew born in the cosmopolitan city of Tarsus in Cilicia (now southern Turkey) and trained in Jerusalem by Gamaliel, one of the most famous Pharisaic scholars of his day. Saul, as he then was, persecuted the fledgling Christian church until his famous conversion experience on the road to Damascus. His encounter with the risen Jesus and the call that accompanied it was to define the rest of his career. Insufficient notice has been taken of Paul's account of his commission from the risen Christ, nor of the fact that his view of Christ and the church was conditioned by this encounter. Paul testified before King Agrippa that Jesus commissioned him with the words:

> I have appeared to you to appoint you as a servant and as a witness of what you have seen of me and what I will show you. I will rescue you from your own people and from the Gentiles. I am sending you to them to open their eyes and to turn them from darkness to light, and from the power of Satan to God, so that they may receive forgiveness of sins and a place among those who are sanctified by faith in me. (Acts 26:16–18; NIV).

Luke wrote this after Paul had written most of his letters. Nevertheless it may be taken as coming from the mouth of Paul underlining the fact that it defined Paul's attitude to Satan, the powers of darkness, and his own mission. It is likely that Paul's call was at the back of his mind whenever he addressed the issue of spiritual powers even if his exposure to Greek thought had developed his thinking on other matters. Paul was clearly conversant with Greek literature, but his early training under Gamaliel and his strict religious pedigree (cf. Philippians 3) would ensure that the OT and first-century Judaism, informed as it was by intertestamental currents of thought, played a significant part in moulding his ideas.

The Language of Power

The Bible in general is replete with power language, which is particularly rich and diverse in the NT. Here the same or similar terms are applied indiscriminately to both human and supernatural holders of power.[19] Let us see how Paul uses this language in a series of key passages:

Romans 8

The whole chapter is an eschatological statement; Paul is looking not only to present life in the Spirit, but also life after the resurrection of the dead, which is, in some sense, already realized through life in the Spirit. He links this to the coming restoration of the whole of creation. The thrust of the passage is based on hope. The situation of the believers in Rome might seem to deny this hope so Paul asks the question in verse 35, *"Who shall separate us from the love of Christ?"* and from verses 37 on he produces a list of entities that cannot part the believer from the love of God in Christ. This apparently random list seems to throw together physical and spiritual realities. Thus it is likely that Paul is deliberately mixing up categories since he is convinced that God's sovereign purpose is fulfilled in Christ, whom he has freely given in the incarnation and crucifixion. This is the language of power encounter.

Colossians 1 & 2

Paul's letter to Colossae was occasioned by an emerging heresy that related to angel worship, ascetic practices, ceremonies that appear to have involved dietary prohibitions, religious festivals with an astrological flavor, and angel worship. Clinton Arnold's groundbreaking research into inscriptions and amulets from this era excavated in the region around Colossae shows that magic practices involving the veneration of angels were common, both in pagan and Jewish cults. Arnold convincingly argues that what Paul was dealing with in this letter was a form of Christian syncretism that attempted

19. Wink, *Naming the Powers*, 11.

to import some of these features into the church with a consequent down-playing of the importance and centrality of Christ. Therefore he affirms Christ's Lordship over creation and develops the metaphor of Christ, who is the fullness, as the head of the body, which is the church.

In chapter 1, Paul's hymn to Christ as the image of the invisible God who is the creator of all things exalts him as the firstborn of all creation since he was the first to rise from the dead with a resurrection body. This makes clear that all the powers, both heavenly and earthly, are subservient to him since he created them. It seems clear that Paul is speaking about structures and the different designations of power seem to be mirrored in heaven and earth. This notion fits more closely with a common idea in Jewish apocalyptic literature, seen in also in the OT (e.g., Isa 24:21–23), than with Platonic philosophy.

Paul's statement about the reconciliation of all things, earthly and heavenly, has been a cause of contention. Wink sees it as grounds for believing that hostile social structures and the spiritual influences that lie behind them will all one day be redeemed. He believes that the powers are "the necessary social structures of human life and it is not a matter of indifference to God that they exist. God *made them*."[20] They are cultural and political entities meant to further God's purposes for order in human society but they have fallen away from their intended functions and have taken on an idolatrous life of their own. According to him, they are not angelic or demonic powers but human institutions with an interior spirituality that need to be reconciled to God by being called back to their original purpose.

Arnold counters that there are good reasons for rejecting this reading. He says, "It is certainly true that this passage is unique in extending reconciliation to 'things/beings in heaven,' but it is nowhere explicitly stated that the heavenly beings are redeemed."[21] He notes that in 1:21–23 reconciliation terminology is applied to believers, but not to hostile powers. Indeed, earlier in the chapter believers are spoken of as being rescued from the dominion of darkness and being brought into "the kingdom of the Son he loves." That is, their reconciliation is couched in Exodus-type terms—which some scholars believe Paul has in mind here—and we know that the forces of Egypt were overthrown. Arnold also makes the point that: "The notion of the redemption of the hostile powers is also difficult to maintain in light of the Jewish apocalyptic framework that informs Paul's thought.

20. Wink, *Engaging the Powers*, 66; emphasis original.
21. Arnold, *The Colossian Syncretism*, 267.

This world view looked forward to a time of final battle in which there would be a losing side. God would intervene and triumph over his enemies."[22]

Arnold devotes a whole chapter in his work on Colossians to the issue of the meaning of the term *stoicheia*. Arnold's extensive discussion of the use of the term in magic and astrology as well as the demonology and angelology of Jewish folk belief at the time, convincingly establishes that in the Colossian context the *stoicheia* are to be understood as evil spirit powers to be equated with the principalities and powers—or rulers and authorities—referred to in Col 1:16 and 2:10 and 15. He says that "the *stoicheia* were an integral part of the present evil age. They function as masters and overlords working through various means—including the Jewish law and pagan religions—to hold their subjects in bondage."[23]

In the Colossian passage (2:1–15) Christ is pitted against these elemental spirits but this is no dualistic contest between equals since the fullness of deity dwells in him in bodily form. What is more, the Colossians themselves share in his fullness and so have all the weapons at their disposal to overcome astral spirits and false worship based on hollow deceptive philosophies and human tradition (he may have surrounding pagan traditions in mind, here). There is no need for ascetic practices to subdue the flesh since their baptism into Christ is like a circumcision that put off the flesh. It is at this point that Paul insists that they have been made alive in Christ since they were buried in baptism and have been raised with him. Thus, the resurrection is the guarantee of what Christ accomplished on the cross, which Paul portrays in terms of a Roman general's triumphal procession, where the enemy is stripped of his powers and paraded before a watching world as a defeated foe.

Longman and Reid see this as a reintroduction of the OT warrior motif baptized into Paul's current context within the Roman Empire. Here it is applied to Christ's victory over the powers, which strips them of their legitimacy.[24] The consequence for the Colossian Christians is that neither demonic powers nor human structures should be allowed to hold them in bondage.

Paul's answer to domination by these powers is not to engage in public protest, nor to cast out the demons but to remember that Christians are seated in the place of victory with Christ at the right hand of God. The

22. Ibid., 268.

23. Ibid., 194.

24. Longman and Reid, *God Is A Warrior*, 151.

contrast between earthly and heavenly is not between the material and the non-material, but between the temporal and the eternal. As with the closing of the parallel letter to the Ephesians to which we will now turn, spiritual warfare, for Paul, always ends in prayer for his missionary ministry, which is conceived of as part of God's cosmic battle. This fits with the whole of Paul's orientation with regard to the powers: his and the church's battle with them is part of the missional thrust to reconcile and redeem the nations.

Ephesians 6:10–20

Paul's Ephesian letter should be seen in the context of his founding of the church in Acts 19:1–41[25] where he spent at least two years in the city in a ministry of teaching and proclaiming the gospel, which involved exorcisms. As a result of this ministry a number who had responded to Christ who formerly practiced sorcery brought their scrolls together and burnt them publicly—an estimated 50,000 drachmas worth (a drachma amounted to a day's wages for a laborer). This account fits with what we know of an Ephesian society that was dominated by occult activity centered on the Temple of Aphrodite, one of the Seven Wonders of the ancient world. The worship of Aphrodite or Artemis, who was a fertility goddess, was based on cultic sexual practices. The cult also identified Aphrodite with the Egyptian deities Hekate and Osiris, who were gatekeepers to the underworld. An enormous amount of inscriptions and pottery fragments featuring magic spells, amulets, and charms, together with household idols and figurines based on the worship of Aphrodite and other Gods, have been uncovered.[26]

The letter to the Ephesians should be read against this background; Paul was addressing a real spiritual battle for the soul of the city. Part of the key to understanding the letter is his fivefold use of the Greek word *epouranos*, which is used in several other places in the NT, but nowhere else in ancient Greek literature and, therefore, must be interpreted in light of its context. It is an intensive form of the normal word for heaven (*ouranos*) and appears to be used by Paul in the sense of "the spiritual dimension." In the light of chapter 2:1–3 it may refer to the atmosphere in which angelic forces, both good and bad, were thought to operate. This is the dimension in which the warfare which Paul describes is to be conducted. Paul says,

25. We take the letter as being genuinely authored by Paul.

26. For details of these and the regional influence of the Temple of Aphrodite, cf. Arnold, *Power and Magic*.

"[O]ur struggle is not against flesh and blood but against the authorities, against the powers of this dark world, against the spiritual forces of evil in the heavenly realms" (6:12; NIV). The Greek text piles up the categories and connects them with the repetitive use of "*pros*" (against). Fee says:

> This description of the "powers" collects into one place a variety of terms and language from throughout the epistle that ensures (1) that we have been dealing throughout with malevolent "spirit" beings, (2) that they inhabit what Paul has referred to frequently as "the heavenlies," and (3) that this is a major concern of the letter.[27]

It is clear that while Paul may also have structural elements in mind, he sees the devil as the ultimate driving force behind the spiritual opposition in Ephesus. He is the one whose schemes are to be resisted and against whom the Ephesians are to make their stand by wearing the whole armor of God. The protective or defensive pieces of the armor are aspects of Christian character (truth, righteousness, readiness, faith), to which is added the offensive weapon of *the sword of the Spirit, which is the word of God.* Fee suggests on linguistic grounds that when speaking of the "sword of the Spirit" Paul is referring to Spirit-inspired proclamation of the gospel about Christ rather identifying it with a book not yet written. It is a word that comes from God.

In the context of Ephesians 6, the Christian is called to a constant battle against the dark powers warring over their world, manifested through spirit beings and the social and political structures of the city. As he penned these words, Paul may well have thought back to the founding of this church. At that juncture, spiritual conflict touched personal lives, demons, the religious establishment, the economic infrastructure, and the political order. Paul is probably not using the various terms randomly in order to demythologize the powers as some have alleged. Rather his terminology is layered. Perhaps we should read between the lines here, for when he says, *"Our struggle is not against flesh and blood,"* he probably means something like "Our struggle is *not so much* against flesh and blood as against the rulers against the authorities, against the powers of this dark world." Paul was certainly aware that he was dealing with flesh and blood realities in his encounters on his first missionary journey, for instance, when he confronted Elymas the sorcerer who influenced the Roman proconsul in Cyprus. Thus, personal entities form the first layer of conflict, but Paul was calling the

---

27. Fee, *The Empowering Presence*, 725.

Ephesians to see that behind them lay the embedded roles given to them, that is, as rulers, authorities, and powers—as Berkhof, Yoder, Newbigin, and Wink cogently argue.

However, Boyd, Arnold, and Longman suggest that the term "*kosmokratoras*" can also apply to spirit forces. (Boyd translates "*kosmokratoras tou skotous*" as "the cosmic powers of this present darkness.")[28] What is clear is that Paul identifies a third pervasive layer: "the spiritual forces of evil" who operate in the "heavenly realms." Thus, each layer is influenced, if not controlled, by the one above—though the spatial metaphor should not be taken literally, it indicates a mode of operation. This final layer should be ultimately equated with the activity of the "ruler of the kingdom of the air" in Ephesians 2:2 (the Greek rendered "kingdom," here, is *exousias*, which denotes "the power of authority"). The "air" probably refers to the apocalyptic notion of the first heaven surrounding the earth and hence is often thought of as "the atmosphere." At any rate it means much the same as "the god of this age" who in 2 Corinthians 4:4 is said to blind the minds of unbelievers.

For Paul, the locus of the battle for the liberation of the world lies in the church as it defies the rule of the pretender, Satan, and his false kingdom in its manifold varieties. Bosch elsewhere speaks of Paul's churches as "the vanguard of the new creation."[29] We, along with them, are called to take up the challenge to bring the future into the present as we challenge Satan's rule wherever it confronts us in this world.

28. Boyd, *God at War*, 281.
29. Bosch, *Transforming Mission*, 172.

4

Cultural Analysis of Western Spiritual Power Encounters

Andrew R. Hardy

The Scope of Modern Culture's Effect on Spiritual Influence and Power Theology

The terms "spiritual warfare," "power encounter," or "demolishing strongholds" seem to be used interchangeably within popular Christian literature.[1] The rise of Pentecostalism as a worldwide phenomenon has led to a mass resurgence in the two-thirds world populations of the practice of exorcism (the topic of a later chapter).[2] It has also entered the West through Pentecostal Christian migrant diasporas that now live in the West. Modernism's Enlightenment heritage did much to challenge Western views that there is an unseen world of angels and demons[3] (this is known technically as demythologization—the German liberal school of theology, led by scholars like Rudolf Bultmann conceived the need to rid theology of what they considered ancient myths and folk tales). The Jesus of modernism needed to be reshaped without his first-century cultural mythological trappings to communicate the gospel to modern people; theologians like Bultmann

---

1. White, *Spiritual Warfare*, chapter 1.
2. Kim, *Joining in with the Spirit*, 130.
3. Hansberger and van Gilder, *Church Between Gospel & Culture*, chapter 8.

feared Christ would have no power to influence modern persons. Jesus the exorcist and miracle worker was not considered credible to modern German theologians (of the nineteenth and first half of the twentieth centuries), or the society they wanted to influence with their modernized version of Christianity minus its premodern folk stories.[4] They did not consider these stories to be acceptable to a world of reason and critical rationalism, which only believed in what could be verified through the five senses (that is, empirical research).[5]

This liberalized program of reinterpretation of the Christian story meant that the worldview of modernism had to be addressed via a language that pictured Jesus as an ethical teacher, who sought to bring about a better society based on service, love, justice, God's mercy, and forgiveness as principles to live by. Following philosophers like Kant,[6] Descartes,[7] Hume,[8] and Hegel,[9] this school of thought was happy to believe that God did not intervene in the world in supernatural ways; rather, it embraced the notion that God had in some way initiated the beginning of the universe but had then left it to its own devices (this view is known as deism—although an existentialist, Bultmann was not deist).[10] From this perspective a supernatural interventionist God who sought to free human beings from the devil and demons was considered impossible for Western modern people to embrace. Such a world was not compatible with their conscious or unconscious worldview. What they *could* embrace was a faith in Jesus Christ that would lead to a better society and a sense that service and love would be a superior means for people to coexist together ("existentialism"[11] is the most useful philosophical term to describe this phenomenon).

However, the rapid growth of Pentecostalism particularly in the Sothern Hemisphere, and the influence of Charismatic views on some of the mainstream evangelical churches in the north, most notably the Catholic Church in places like South America,[12] has challenged the functional

4. Bultmann, *Theology*, 268, 269, 295, 298.

5. Mimi, *Biblical Interpreters*, 261–67.

6. Brown, *Philosophy*, 21, 27, 90–106.

7. Davies, *Philosophy of Religion*, 694–95.

8. Ibid., 230–32, 233–38, 281, 290.

9. Ibid., 8.

10. Clayton and Simpson, *Religion and Science*, 346.

11. Mimi, *Biblical Interpreters*, 262.

12. Kärkkäinen, *Ecclesiology*, 74.

deism of many Christian people in the West. This Charismatic interest in the unseen world of the spiritual, including a fascination with evil spirits, has been embraced by some Christian groups, such as Salt and Light (in Oxfordshire)[13] and the charismatic evangelical Alpha movement (with its base at Holy Trinity Brompton),[14] and with Vineyard churches (based on the ministry of John Wimber). Although it may be argued that many, if not most, of the mainstream traditional churches in Britain do not actively practice so-called spiritual warfare ministry, or power encounter ministry against demons, there is a small constituency among the indigenous white churches that does. The US church scene is broadly divided between non-charismatic and charismatic churches. In this context mainstream denominations or networks choose their view of charismata based on the views of the churches they ally themselves with.

What this discussion indicates is that although Western theology may seek to contextually filter out the supernatural and unseen it is still embraced by a significant minority. My initial theological training embraced literary and historical critical methods with its avowed demythologizing agenda with regard to deliverance or healing ministry. However, my view on spiritual powers has changed significantly over the past twenty-five years. It may be argued that the practice of deliverance itself takes the focus of the Gospels seriously concerning Jesus as deliverer/healer, not to mention the practice of deliverance in the early church's baptismal services.[15] Authenticated instances of healing and apparent deliverance from disease create an empirically verifiable chain of evidence that also deserves consideration. The emergent postmodern world is once more asking questions about the unseen world.[16] Included in this trend is the validation of university religion departments that offer courses at undergraduate and graduate levels, exploring the phenomenology of spirituality,[17] and, by extension, the unseen spiritual dimension.

Moreover, as Robinson rightly points out, a resurgence of interest in "spiritual Warfare" has been brought with ethnic Christian groups coming from the poorer South to the richer West to re-evangelize Europe.[18] The

---

13. Salt & Light, 2010, saltlight.org (accessed April 3, 2015).

14. Holy Trinity Brompton, htb.org (accessed April 3, 2015).

15. Kraft, *Christianity with Power*, chapter 1.

16. Fee, *People of God*, 1.

17. Holder, *Christian Spirituality*, chapter 1.

18. Robinson, *Winning Hearts*, chapter 1.

multicultural texture of European and North American culture has also led to pluralism of beliefs,[19] which means differing cultural worldviews are embraced by diverse ethnic groups in the West.[20] Charles Kraft classically gave particular significance to emergent worldviews that led him to a new cultural analysis concerning the issue of power encounter and types of ministry based on power. Postmodernism and secularism dominate the Western worldview and have jointly changed the outlook of people thus influencing former European spiritual worldviews. This is important as perceptions are culturally determined through upbringing, socialization, and acculturation.[21] Kraft comments:

> We see then that perception influences all of our interpretations and responses. But how did it happen that we interpret in the way we do, rather than in some other way? Our elders taught it to us, to put it simply. Through the process of being taught our culture, and especially the worldview of our culture, we are trained to see as the other members of our society see. We are strongly indoctrinated long before we seek to make any of our own choices in perceiving reality. [22]

It is important to apply Kraft's insight to an appreciation of a broader cultural analysis taking as its starting point the observation that each ethnic and culturally divergent group in Britain has been shaped by differing views of reality that often are significantly dissimilar to the Western European understandings. Part of the cultural analysis of the terrain of "power encounter" theology needs to take into consideration that multicultural ethnic churches have come with their own package of theological and cultural heritages. These include a strong belief in the world as a battle ground inhabited by a personalized devil and demons who are involved in cosmic conflict with God.[23]

Moreover, other cultural groups including Hindus, Buddhists, Muslims, and Shamanistic traditions coming from Asia, Africa, and South America have brought other theologies of spiritual powers with them.[24]

---

19. Ibid., 156.

20. Kraft, *Christianity with Power,* 24, 51, 53, 54.

21. Barnard and Spencer, *Cultural Anthropology,* 513. Friedl, *Cultural Anthropology,* 375–84.

22. Kraft, *Christianity with Power,* 18.

23. Kim, *Joining in with the Spirit,* 128–32.

24. O' Donnell, *World Religions.*

The emergent multicultural West is also multi-faith and pluralistic so that people in society see reality in different ways subject to the differing world-views they bring with them. Even a brief consideration of this emerging ethnic and cultural tapestry raises important phenomenological issues regarding spiritual practices and it does not stop there.

There are new movements that have particularly found a foothold within the West that have grown out of far older theological trends, which may be traced back to the dawn of the emergence of modern man.[25] These include the reemergence of Gnosticism,[26] renascent Paganism, the Occult, and the ill-defined "New Age mysticism." Exploration of these movements, for movements they are, in a culturally diverse environment will be further pursued later in this chapter. In terms of a Christian theology of "power encounter" these are forces to be reckoned with as each may arguably be said to have its own character and spirit. The term "spirit" is used here in the sense of traits that seem to define these various movements. The use of the word "spirit" is permitted in anthropological terms due to its contextual relevance to the present field of contextual analysis.

Secularism, pluralism, science, humanism, individualism, consumer-ism, and materialism may also be said to have their own faiths. All of the above may be considered important for cultural analysis in a missiological venture such as this. We will examine the forces of secularism later. The landscape of some of the renascent forms of power theology will be mapped out as a set of cultural vignettes in what follows. It will not be possible to delve too deeply into everything that has been mentioned so far. What will be attempted is a critical analysis of how to go about local contextual examination of the terrain these so called "powers" inhabit. Before entering the discussion it is important to remind ourselves of a definition concern-ing what the term "powers" might mean from a biblical and theological perspective. Six New Testament texts iterate concerns about the "powers."[27] Much work has already been done in earlier chapters to delve into the bibli-cal language of power. All we need at this juncture is to remind ourselves of some basic concepts that will help us to engage in relevant discussion for this chapter. For instance, Ephesians 6:12 comments: *"For our struggle is not against flesh and blood, but against the rulers, against the authorities,*

---

25. Gnosticism, Paganism, and the Druid faith are a few examples.

26. Pannenberg, *Systematic Theology*, 19, 211, 248, 276, 435.

27. Rom 8:38; Eph 6:12; Col 1:16, 2:15; Heb 6:5; 1 Pet 3:22.

against the powers of this dark world and against the spiritual forces of evil in the heavenly realms."[28]

The Greek term used for power in this verse is *kosmokratoras.* It may be translated as "powers of the world," or "monarch of the world," or as "a power paramount in the world of the unbelieving and ungodly."[29] The conjunction of these "powers of this dark world and against the spiritual forces of evil in the heavenly realms" distinguishes a link with what was probably a proto-Gnostic idea. Gnosticism came over from Hellenism and was part of a syncretization movement that came to full flower during the second century AD. Gnosticism often pictured the whole of the world including the ground, the air that was breathed, and the sky as the habitations of gods or demonic forces, that sought to subject humankind to them.[30] Both Ephesians and Colossians were probably written to liberate early Christian communities from the notion that they were any longer subject to these powers that sought to block the path to the divine.[31] These evil "spiritual forces" that inhabited the pagan views of the *epouranios* (Greek word meaning heavenlies) depicted a kind of demonic blockade to stop a spiritual seeker making positive contact with the ultimate reality (God) of the cosmos. Paul's message to the Ephesians was that this evil spirit of the heavenly realms was defeated by Christ, so that its power might no longer keep them from the power of Christ's saving actions in their lives.[32] For *"by grace you have been saved,"*[33] and this was salvation from *"the ruler of the kingdom of the air, the spirit who is now at work in those who are disobedient."*[34]

This *archontatesexousiastou aeros*—(ET: "ruling authority of the air")—according to Paul only had authority over those who did not belong to Christ, but not over those who belonged to the Lord. Hence "rulers," "authorities" and "powers" (both earthly and heavenly) were joined in the Pauline worldview in a conjunction of interrelationships. Rome was the prime claimant to being a purveyor of these evil powers for Paul and the Revelator. This gave rise to the theology of the victorious Christ or *Christus*

28. NIV.

29. Moulton, *Analytical Greek Lexicon,* 238.

30 Wink, *Powers That Be,* 15.

31. Guthrie, *New Testament Introduction,* 545–51.

32. Eph 2:1–10.

33. Eph 2:8; NIV.

34. Eph 2:2; NIV.

Victor[35] in the second and third centuries, which designated Jesus as a higher power than the Roman emperors and any evil forces that were thought to dominate those who were not Christians. It was these same evil powers that inspired rulers to persecute and martyr Christians for not paying homage to Roman emperors as gods.

Theologically, it may be argued that the basis to all missiology, beginning with that of the Apostle Paul, had to do with some real appreciation of power encounter. The theologian Walter Wink did much to texture this view as we have already noted earlier, recognizing that in the modern era earthly governing powers acting as domination systems,[36] are as much part of the territory for power encounter, as was the case for first-century Christians confronted by Rome. In terms of a cultural reading of the modern/postmodern "powers," it is important to recognize that in order to be able to successfully influence people for Christ, it is essential to appreciate their contexts and what forces or "spirits" define their psychological, cultural, and sociological experiences. The theology and missiology of this section is driven by such a reading.

Reading the Postmodern "Power Encounter" Landscape

What ensues under this heading is a discussion of the landscape of ideas that a potential postmodern reading of power encounter might offer to help understand them better. It will be informative to begin with a brief analysis of the driving forces of multiculturalism and pluralism that influence Western beliefs.

The inevitable result of multiculturalism is cultural diversity and eventual positive discrimination[37] that second-generation immigrants have fought for so robustly in the West. This has been hard won but mostly welcomed in the West, partly on economic and politically expedient grounds as it provides new work forces that help the economy. Positive discrimination rightly sought to adjust an imbalance that is justly considered to have been anti-humanitarian. Martin Luther King Jr. is a classic North American hero of black civil rights who signalled that positive discrimination was won by ethnic groups who brought a justice seeking Christian liberation theology with them. Partly due to their efforts, this liberation theology in

35. Aulén, *Christus Victor.*

36. Wink, *Powers That Be,* chapter 2.

37. Haralambos and Holborn, *Sociology,* 386–87.

practice sought to win justice and equal rights for ethnic groups in society, work, and politics. Hence the discriminating forces or powers that tried to limit ethnic minority group participation in society have broadly speaking been undermined and at least theoretically silenced in the USA. These so-called powers of discrimination may be thought of as representative of one form of power encounter that met with significant success in a more tolerant multicultural Britain in the shape of social justice or a social gospel.[38] In North America similar racial integration policies have redressed power imbalances between whites and blacks. Power encounter is contextualized in these cases by a kind of liberation theology. A European version of liberation theology[39] has for a number of reasons, including what has been felt by ethnic Christians who are part of the old colonial mission project of the nineteenth century, developed into a fight to reconnect with their ethnic roots. The aim is to help ethnic groups who are seeking their racial and cultural roots achieve an expression of Christianity that is contextually relevant and true to their ethnic and cultural heritages.

Kim comments that colonialism tended to reject any worldview but its own while the new postcolonial context has turned the tables:

> Nowadays Western Christians often expect that the expression of Christian faith should vary according to culture; and when visiting another part of the world, they are inclined to be disappointed if the Christianity there appears "very Western."[40]

Kim points out that the people of the Western church today expect diverse cultural expressions of faith from different ethnic groups—especially when encountering them on holiday or travel. Part of the reason for this must be because multiculturalism and religious pluralism have forced Western people to accept the reality of divergent[41] expressions of worldview. Postmodernity is a reaction to modernism, which is probably trying to work out what diversity of beliefs mean when it is less than certain if any one belief system can be accepted as the right one.[42]

---

38. McManners, *History of Christianity,* 411, 414, 443.

39. Bosch, *Paradigm Shifts in Theology,* 432–47.

40. Kim, *Joining in with the Spirit,* 42–43.

41. Barker, *Cultural Studies,* 126, 275, 456.

42. Greene and Robinson, *Metavista,* 5. Hunsberger and van Gelder, *Church between Gospel & Culture,* 113–72.

Renascent Paganism

In keeping with this, the reemergence of paganism in Europe is another part of the postmodern landscape that is trying to touch base with some of its earlier tribal roots before the Christianization of the eleven tribes of Europe took place.[43] This finds expression in the current interest in Celtic roots, druidic religion, and other ancient practices.[44] This is very much a nature religion—connection with the rhythms of nature is part of its life-blood.[45] In terms of power encounter this form of renascent paganism seeks to celebrate everything on a more earthy level. [46] Morality has far more to do with seeing a person as part of the greater cycle of nature. Connection with what is natural is the important issue. Sexuality, and its expression in various ways, is natural to the extent that it is a drive that needs expression—often outside of long-term relationships. Connecting with the spirit of nature and the world is grounded in a form of pantheism[47] that sees god as being in everything, and everything essentially as being god. The powers that hold pagans[48] captive may be considered, in Christian terms, to be based on a religion based on the book of nature and its cycles. In biblical terms a comparison may be made with ancient religions like Baal worship, which celebrated cultic rites that were derived from fertility myths of a rising and dying god.

The scriptures of paganism are the natural world and its processes. The idea of a special revelation of a transcendent and immanent God does not readily resonate with pagan belief, which holds that such a theology does not exist. There is an animistic view, which sees everything as possessing spirit or spirits. Because animism is considered to be a less enlightened form of religious belief by most theologians, who consider monotheism to be more open to proper theological reflection, there is a basic inability to dialogue with proponents of this naturalistic spirit-infused world on a more robust theological level. If theologians influenced by postmodernity are to take a step toward engaging in mission with pagans, then it is important to

43. McManners, *History of Christianity*, 85.

44. Pagan Theology: A Personal Enquiry into the Nature of the Gods and Goddesses, 2006, pagantheology.com (accessed April 3, 2015).

45. Merton, *Contemplation*, 357.

46. Meyer, *Four Old Irish Songs*, 8–9.

47. Wink, *Powers That Be*, 20.

48. McManners, *History of Christianity*, 40–41, 61, 65, 66, 74, 75, 76, 85, 89, 97, 108–9, 224, 310.

make a decision about effective means of engaging the powers that dominate their worldview. One such step may be to seriously consider how to combat the spiritual forces that are hidden behind this religion.

The website www.pagantheology.com discusses the earthy rites of neo-paganism. The following rather long quotation is very informative about pagan ritual as it relates to its avowed theology:

> While I won't go into a survey of the extensive theory of ritual, we do want to understand why our rather detailed set of ritual practices relates to our experience of the Gods and Goddesses, and our experience of Pagan religion.
>
> We can start with the circle. One time my circle was holding discussions on various aspects of ritual and belief. Sort of working our way through the ritual process, trying to learn more about the elements of ritual. I had both the cheekiness and misfortune to volunteer to start the series with the ritual element of casting the circle. So I merrily went off looking for the theory, history, and background of circle casting. I expected to find a lot of discussion. Not so much.
>
> Why do we cast the circle? Circle forms have a long association with magic and Pagan religious practices. The Greeks saw a circle as important for sacrificial rites to the Gods. Classical and ritual magicians incorporate the magic circle as a protection from, and container for, spirits and other entities. In modern neo-Paganism the circle casting is seen as less a protection than a two-fold mechanism for containing energy raised, and for creating a sacred space for the performance of ritual.
>
> If the Gods and Goddesses are immanent in the world, as we have discussed in previous columns, then the world is in some ways itself sacred. Because the Gods and Goddesses are not practically or conceptually "other" but they are with us and the world in the same way we are with each other in the world, then the world itself and our gatherings take on an element of the special character of the Gods and Goddesses. They are sacred, they are deity, and thus through our encounters with them we engage in a mystery that creates a special attribute in the world.[49]

This rather fulsome description of what it means to "create the sacred" by drawing the energy circle of the earth's "God's and Goddesses" indicates the pagan belief that participants themselves are endued with the "energy" that is part of what the "circle" demarcates. Hence, modern pagans consider

---

49. pagantheology.com.

that they possess, and interact, with real life energies that come from earth spirits. This pagan expression of the search for meaningful connection with the spiritual dimension seems to indicate the potential for a missionally significant charismatic definition of encounter with these powers.

Renascent Gnosticism

At this point, some consideration needs to be given to modern-day Gnosticism as another power or spirit of the age. Gnosticism comprises an assortment of devout movements customarily considered by adherents to be Christian. Greek thought dominated the culture of ancient society around the Mediterranean basin[50] but there is no definitive evidence that can locate its origins. This emerging way of thought flourished from roughly the era of the institution of Christianity to the suppression of the Gnostic movement in the fourth century AD. For many centuries the main sources of our knowledge of it were found among the church fathers who opposed Gnosticism, although, more recently, original Gnostic gospels and writings have been unearthed.

The latter part of the nineteenth century witnessed a number of popular monographs utilizing newly discovered primary-source materials to forward study of this religion, which was really a pluralism of faiths. It was also during the nineteenth century that a newly founded Gnostic movement emerged in France. Later in the twentieth century the discovery of the Nag Hammadi library in Egypt (1945)[51] made it much easier to pick out from its fragments what early Gnostic sects believed. The subsequent translation of this library into English led to a widely available literature that furthered the dissemination of the renascence of the movement.

Today there are a number of Gnostic sects that focus on some of its theological facets and ancient practices. Gnostic sexual groups base their views concerning spirituality related to sexuality on Gnostic sources. The early church accused Gnostic groups of practicing group orgiastic sex rites as part of their religious practices.[52] This accusation has been challenged by some modern scholars. However, that modern Gnostic sexual magic groups practice sexual rites as part of their journey is undisputed by today's

50. Trigg, *Origen*, 15, 16, 20, 257, 270.

51. http://gnosis.org/naghamm/nhl.html (accessed 1 June 2015).

52. The Book of Revelation mentions the Nicolaitan Gnostics in these terms, Rev 2:15.

devotees. Part of the ancient Gnostic belief system emphasized that the body was evil, as it was made of evil matter—only the immaterial spirit was considered to be incorruptible. Some Gnostics appear to have taught that indulgence in as much sex as possible was a way to liberate the adherent from bondage to the material body. Hence, sex in excess led to coming to disdain it, thus liberating the adherents into a heightened awareness of the spirit, which now no longer desired its fleshy dwelling or its pleasurable benefits.

Modern Gnostic sexual magic began with Paschal Beverly Randolph.[53] The nature of power encounter here may be said to relate to an ethical and moral arena. Lust may be its specific area of potential bondage, which requires deliverance. Moreover, more broadly, any modern Gnostic theology can lead to disdain for materiality because of its heightened sense of otherworldliness, which may be lead to a denial of the pursuit of justice and of the environmental and social gospel. The net result is often a denial of engagement with positive social change for the good of humanity. Put in other terms, it backs out of responsibility for aiding others who are in physical need because of its material origin. This antimaterial view of reality could give too much license to exploitation of the environment and indifference to injustice. Thus, the powers of industrialization together with consequent political and economic abuse of the poor of the world could be left to the domination systems to exploit at will.[54]

Other consequences may arise from the central Gnostic thesis that the material world is less important than the unseen immaterial spiritual world. These may be mirrored in Charismatic and Pentecostal theologies whenever esoteric ecstatic experiences, focusing on the immaterial world of the spirit, are treasured above tangible social action. Worship services can become events where individual encounter with God in an "out of the world" experience is thought to be more valuable than what happens in the physical world. A net consequence can be that Christian spirituality is disengaged from the material world. The Semitic Judeo-Christian worldview knew nothing of this duality in its earliest expressions since it called on believers to holy engagement equally in body and spirit.[55] Indeed the

53. Catherine Yronwode, Luky Mojo, 1994–2014, luckymojo.com (accessed April 3, 2015).

54. Wink, *Powers That Be,* chapter 2.

55. A classic biblical verse often quoted to demonstrate the holistic nature of the Semitic Hebrew view of spirit and body comprising the human soul is to be found in Genesis 2:7, 8.

material world and much of the spiritual world were bed fellows.[56] It could be argued that Western Charismatic Christianity has become too focused on getting a spiritual fix, as the avowed highest good, with an unwillingness to engage in social gospel activism in the material world, which is part and parcel of a biblical, sacramental view of spirituality that includes both material and spiritual aspects as one entity affecting every niche of life.

However, it must be noted that Pentecostal Christians in places like South America are powerfully engaged in liberation theology, sometimes seeking alliances with Marxist liberation ideology to improve the lot of a downtrodden poor. This may be seen as a power encounter against the mega-economic and political domination systems of international commerce and national affluent totalitarianism. Kim comments:

> Both liberation theology and the Pentecostal-charismatic movement in Latin America are concerned with the problem of poverty but they offer two very different solutions to it. Liberation theology locates the problem in unjust structures in society such as hierarchy and capitalism. Pentecostals and Charismatics tend to identify supernatural forces of evil—Satan and evil spirits—as the cause of poverty and suffering . . . [transformation is the aim for both] . . . the net result may be similar in both cases. The base communities' struggle to change social structures also results in personal transformation and spiritual growth.[57]

What Kim's analysis details is the possibility for two dissimilar movements to achieve similar results and even to find some level of contextual ground for working together. It is possible for similarity to be a fulcrum for dialogue and change of unjust structures in society. If this can happen in Latin America then it can happen elsewhere.

Reverting to neo-paganism, it might be argued that some useful contextual dialogue could start with a discussion about the unseen world of the powers/energies and how this motivates an eco-missiology. Pagans are often very much interested in the balance of the environment. In turn, this could lead to an encounter with the Christ of power that a charismatic and Pentecostal missiology might seek to employ in this dialogue.

---

56. Psalm 19 is another wonderful example of the joined-up nature of the physical world and the landscape of the spirit as of equal wonder to the Hebrew mind.

57. Kim, *Joining in with the Spirit*, 129.

In his book *God at War: The Bible and Spiritual Conflict* Gregory Boyd helpfully summarizes the issue as some Christian power encounter theologians see it:

> The truth [is] that God's good creation has in fact been seized by hostile, evil cosmic forces that are seeking to destroy God's beneficent plan for the cosmos. God wages war against those forces, however, and through the person of Jesus Christ has now secured the overthrow of this evil cosmic army. The church as the body of Christ has been called to be a decisive means by which this final overthrow is to be carried out.[58]

It may be argued that if a Pentecostal/Charismatic power encounter is to be effective with groups like neo-pagans, or Gnostics, then some level playing-field for interaction needs to be identified. Hence a little historical divergence at this point will seek to raise some important insights that might aid a dialogical missiology toward such groups.

Writers coming from outside the Christian worldview see how the church has approached the so called powers historically in rather different terms. Their views may be helpful in order to gain some insight into a non-Christian viewpoint of what previous non-Christian generations have encountered when being missionally engaged by the Christian church. Kevin Hearne in his article, "The Demonization of Pan," discusses how the early church developed a policy that led to identifying all the so-called pagan gods with the devil or demons. From Hearne's perspective this was the wrong approach, probably committing what for some anthropologists is the ultimate sin, that of damaging a different culture with a more dominant worldview. Hopefully this might help us understand what is driving Hearne's critique of historical Christian missions. It may also help to obtain a non-Christian perspective on what is considered an aggressive Christian mission agenda.

In relationship to power encounters with renascent paganism it might be said that Hearne's concerns reflect the outlook of pagans subject to a clumsy insensitive approach seeking to condemn or subvert their worldview. What this journal article articulates well is a non-Christian perspective on what the demonization of the god's of paganism meant to them in the earlier church period. You may wish to read the following with the question in mind, "How might this strategy be effective for modern mission with pagans of today?" In terms of a cultural reading it makes for

58. Ibid., 19.

important critical evaluation of the results of the early church's missional strategy faced with a so-called pagan society.

> Believing in only one God and forsaking all others, Christians had a tendency to equate all pagan deities with demons. Eusebius, writing in the early fourth century, was the first to take aim specifically at Pan. In responding to Plutarch's account of Pan's "death" during the reign of Tiberius (who reigned during the time of Jesus' crucifixion), Eusebius interpreted the story as evidence that God had rid humankind of its biggest demon. "As the pagan deities were demons, in the Christian view, Eusebius' equating Pan with the demon, seems natural and unforced." By the time of Eusebius, it might well have been natural to make such an equation; but according to A History of the Devil, such slander would have been impossible without the emergence of the Septuagint and the concept of a devil.
>
> The concept of the Devil was also aided by the development of the concept of evil demons. At first, demons are morally ambivalent like the gods. Then two groups of demons are distinguished, one good and the other evil. Finally, a shift in vocabulary occurs. In the Septuagint, the good spirits are called angels and the evil spirits demons wholly evil spiritual beings. These are now easily amalgamated with the Devil, either lending their traits to him, or being spirits subordinate to him.
>
> It is not difficult to see here how Pan's rampant sexuality so sinful to Christians made him an ideal candidate for demonization. This defamation of a once pastoral god was part of a vast campaign of religious propaganda designed to put the fear of the devil (where the fear of God didn't seem to work) in the people's hearts for Christianity had several pantheons of old gods to conquer, and a personification of evil was efficacious in helping the process along. Thanks to Christianity, Pan literally became the world's biggest scapegoat.[59]

The Christian "diabolization of pagan forms" was no accident. The question is if such a strategy would work again with such movements as neo-paganism? It would seem fraught with difficulties compared to the way the nature of society in the time of the conversion of the tribes of Western Europe took place. For instance, it would not now be possible for a

59 Hearne, "Demonization of Pan."

totalitarian potentate to order conversion or death as the king of the Norse tribes did in the eleventh century. In any case, the Christian faith is built on mutual respect; moreover, the cultural mores of postmodernism favor permiting differing and even contradictory belief systems to go hand in hand. Hence to directly confront neo-pagans with a power-encounter approach by a Pentecostal demonization of pagan "gods" and "goddesses" would result in a wall of resistance. Any type of success may be better sought by dialogue and sharing of worldviews. Building relationships with pagans may be a way to begin this process. It is suggested that present day power encounter in the West requires a softer approach that grows from trust together with an affirmation of the value of others to God, which is forged in longer-term relationships. A power encounter with God's love might be the most important thing for seekers to experience through long-term friendships with Christian communities who model tolerance and patient grace. This might be the most powerful tool to engage in postmodern power encounter.

From this perspective, a theology of power encounter brought by ethnic Pentecostal migrants to the West may not be effective as a primary missional tool to engage neo-pagans. This is an important conclusion to draw from this cultural analysis though there may still be times when it is warranted to engage the powers head-on.

The Occult and Power Encounter

It would be less than thorough to avoid dealing with the occult in a section focused on a cultural analysis of the powers. It has been noted that there are probably more practicing witches in Britain than ministers of religion. The term "witch" can be very misleading given that many who own this designation do not actively associate themselves with dark forces, or Satanism. Wicca, for instance, is more fixated on what is often termed "white magic" rather than "black magic."[60] It would seem that Wicca finds a ready ally with neo-paganism to the extent that it is concerned with health and balance in life. It is important to recognize that what may be considered to be the inbuilt power of Wicca is mostly not considered evil, or malicious, by its adherents.

However, it is important to note that more formal members of the occult may consider themselves involved with dark forces. One definition of witchcraft, along these lines, is that the witch seeks to manipulate things

60. Witchway, 1999–2013, witchway.net (accessed April 6, 2015).

and people for personal ends. There is a realm of power encounter here with darker or negative forces in the minds of practitioners.

It is important to note that not all of those who term themselves witches consider their so-called magic to be based on active malice toward others. Rather the uppermost desire is to live in harmony with themselves, nature and others. Forces are considered to inhabit an unseen realm and these can be manipulated through spells and magical objects that are considered to contain power to work magic in the unseen dimension. Hence it is argued that those who consider themselves occultist devotees, or adherents of Wiccan, do believe they can manipulate unseen forces or powers to meet their own ends. Hence supernatural power encounter may be part of the language for an analysis of these practices.

Given that many TV programs have some sort of occult or magical theme it may be claimed that interest in these areas is popular. Programs like *Medium*, *Psychic Sally*, *Most Haunted*, *Supernatural*, *Buffy the Vampire Slayer*, *The X Files*, *Paranormal*, to name a few, constitute a genre of popular entertainment that suggests significant interest in this topic. The success of the *Harry Potter* novels and films as well as *Lord of the Rings* must not be neglected, or more recently *Game of Thrones*.

How might the missional leader engage in dialogue with people in the light of these interests? It could be that it will come about more by building relationships with neighbors, friends, and work colleagues so that useful dialogues might begin. It is important to remember that interest in TV programs like these does not mean viewers are more than interested in exploring the possibility of different potential supernatural powers, or realities without becoming devotees of the powers they portray. This postmodern interest indicates a useful bridge for engaging in missional dialogue. It may be worth seeking a strategy to engage the powers that attempt entry into postmodern people's lives through the popular media. However, it is not easy to identify a ready answer to stemming the current trend of interest except to become a player in the spiritual market place, seeking to be an alternative voice that provides a Christian view on the powers.

Conclusions

What this chapter has sought to achieve is a cultural analysis of some of the aspects of power encounter in the Western world. It aimed to identify some of the religious or spiritual sources whilst seeking to promote debate about the need, firstly, to identify what the spiritual powers are considered to be; secondly, to identify some of their characteristics and how these may lead to meaningful dialogues, which are crucial in the light of Christianity's main characteristic as a faith based on a relationship with a relational deity. Thirdly, it is important to recognize the views of differing spiritual movements, like renascent-paganism, as to what their interpretation of the powers they relate to means for them. If this cannot be determined, then it will not be possible to dialogue effectively with those we seek to engage in missional power encounters. Fourthly, any direct challenge mounted against the powers that indwell the more avowedly supernatural movements discussed in this chapter, will need to be approached with sensitivity and prayer. A direct frontal attack, without any relational integrity expressing the love of God to any community we have discussed in this chapter must surely be ill-advised if not downright bad practice. Fifthly, there will inevitably be a time in missional dialogue with other faiths that the powers that inhere the Christian faith and other's faith, will come face to face. However, as Clark Pinnock suggests, it may well be that the Holy Spirit has already won hearts from varied faith backgrounds to himself without them even knowing they have met the third person of the Godhead simply because they have opened their hearts to the Holy Spirit without knowing it.[61] Hence extreme caution is needed when seeking to work in this area of mission especially in terms of the cultural analytical task required to construct an approach.

We have not discussed the New Age movement, or other religions such as Buddhism, Sikhism, Taoism, Rastafarianism, Zoroastrianism, Shintoism, Shamanism, Hinduism, the Jewish faith, and Islam. Each of these faiths may entail their own kinds of power encounter. Hans Küng[62] did much to consider mission among the world religions. Meantime, philosopher and theologian John Hick,[63] in his later life, embraced a misguided, more universalistic theology that portrayed all major world religions as essentially different paths to God. Universalism represents yet another set of views about the powers personified in the world's faiths. More formalized evangelical and mainstream Christian theologies tend to consider universalism to be a loophole that gives ground to the powers that be. Recently, the popular devotional commentator and writer Rob Bell seemed to em-

---

61. Pinnock, *Flame of Love*, 199.
62. Küng, *World Religions*.
63. Hick, *God Has Many Names*.

brace a degree of universalism in his book *Love Wins*,[64] as Brian McLaren appears to do in his more recent publications.[65] Bell is not as such arguing for universalism, where anyone can be deemed part of God's coming kingdom despite which world religion they belong to. However, his contributions have caused him to be criticized by many denominations, as he has not made his position clear regarding the particular salvation that is said to only come through saving faith in Jesus, compared to classical universalist theology where saving faith in Christ is not the primary requirement for becoming part of the divine and future life.

Moreover, power encounter also has to do with dealing with powerful ideas. It has been noted that it is important to approach other faith-orientations, be they neo-paganism or Wicca, with respect. It takes time to adjust to their worldview since it takes time to get to know people and their beliefs. It also takes time to build relationships. An approach like this focuses on the need to approach missional dialogue with due care by taking the time to win the right to be heard.

Military planners often speak of a warfare strategy that can cause us to win a battle and lose the war. In the same way it is possible to win a tactical battle when encountering the powers but to lose the war in the more important strategy of achieving a person's obedience to Christ. Cultural analysis of the powers is the first step to personally researching a particular group or individual's worldview in this regard. Next, it is important to build friendships that will, it is hoped, win the right to engage in dialogue so that, eventually, meaningful spiritual engagement may ensue. I would argue that the most important power encounter is to face someone with the love of God in Christ Jesus through the presence of the Holy Spirit rather than directly to confront people as part of an activist agenda. Christ loves all people and gives all the right to choose whom they serve. We too must base our contextual missiology on an attitude of grace and collaborative friendship on areas we can all agree with.

64. Bell, *Love Wins*.

65. McLaren, *A New Kind of Christianity*.

5

Ethnography and Understanding Power Encounters

Andrew R. Hardy

The previous chapter focused for the most part on the so-called supernatural domain in terms of power encounter as an anthropological and cultural reality. In this chapter we will analyze postmodern secular society. Cultural anthropologists seek to see the world from the inside out in order to understand a particular cultural group. This is often achieved by what is known as participant observation or ethnography[1] as a research technique. It involves the enculturation of the anthropologist as an accepted member of a cultural group.[2] Hence it develops an intra-group participant insider's view of the world; allowing the researcher to become one of the cultural participants offering insights into how a given group sees the world, talks about it, thinks about it, and interacts with it.[3] This insider's view is considered to be an important contribution to research and it is often reported in narrative terms by researchers who seek to explain a given culture under study.[4] Stories of what the researcher has taken part in are narrated as the primary data of the shared research.[5] Sometimes research may be based on iterating a narrative in this fashion without critical observation or analysis being

1. Haralambos et al., *Sociology*, 831–35.
2. Monaghan and Just, *Social and Cultural Anthropology*, 13.
3. Ibid., 13.
4. Bryman, *Social Research Methods*, 410.
5. Ibid., 560.

included—others do this on the basis of a research narrative. Of course the researcher may incorporate analytical and methodological considerations as well.

It is clearly very difficult to untangle ourselves from the present Western postmodern culture we live in, or to be fully aware of just how much power the forces of secularism exercise over us. It is fair to say we need to identify means to help ourselves gain some insights into what forces dominate the church and the life of its people.[6] In this chapter we will consider how cultural studies, which use some of the insights offered through ethnography, can help us to understand the challenges of sharing the gospel with postmodern secular Westerners.

The Need to Understand Culturally Different Groups

Western European or North American indigenous people will naturally have many blind areas that need pointing out by those who come from outside the West. This is where outsiders who are now coming to live here may be invaluable in helping Westerners obtain such insights. For instance, Christian black Africans entering the West will see obvious differences in the way they understand their faith compared to native Westerners.[7] For instance, many black Pentecostal Christians consider it to be un-Christian to drink alcohol where Western Christians often will. Kim comments on this in the following terms:

> Until we are challenged, we humans are "ethno-centric." We tend to regard our own homeland as the center and standard of the world and others as eccentric or "remote." The name Mediterranean literally means "the center of the earth" and for the Romans the British Isles were a far-flung outpost . . . North American maps often have the USA in the dominant position and split the Eurasian landmass in two. As author Bill Bryson has shown us, looking at Britain from the USA, it is just a "small island" off the edge of a continent.[8]

Ethnocentric power is a force to be reckoned with in the minds of the culture that dominates, as it creates blind spots that make it hard for any given culture's indigenous indwellers to see beyond. It would be invaluable

6. Kraft, *Christianity with Power*, 53, 54, 182, 192.

7. Kim, *Joining in with the Spirit*, 1–6.

8. Ibid., 6.

to create opportunities, perhaps through mentoring relationships, with people who come to Europe from outside its emergent postmodern world-view to obtain alternative ways of viewing the West. It is important to note that one of the powers that may be acting as a domination system over the Western church is its own ethnocentric location in secular society. How might missional leaders raised in the West obtain new alternative lenses to view their own culture? This is where the encounter of a Christian culture from outside the West, that has not planted churches in the West, can provide the Western church with the ability to see things in new ways through different lenses. Cross-fertilization can happen through cross-cultural missional collaboration to bring the gospel back to the center of the West.[9] Friendships between different cultures like black Africans with Westerners can be very useful to help Westerners to unpick some of their cultural assumptions. The power of secularism has become so pronounced in the Western church that it may be difficult to differentiate between many of the normative behaviors of Christians and their non-Christian neighbors. Peoples from outside the West could help us to obtain new views of how to relate to the secularization of the church.

The power of mass-media in the West has arguably done much to desensitize its people about issues like sex before marriage, alternative views on heterosexual and homosexual relationships, violence and greed, and so on. The subconscious message that sex as a recreational pastime between consenting adults is normal, must surely create a subconscious expectation that it will be part of everyday life among loosely acquainted couples, or groups (group sex is a powerful phenomenon of postmodern hedonism).[10] Christians who are joining us from outside the West often look on what people watch on their televisions with shock. The writer has recognized the differences in outlook on what it is permissible to watch on TV between native white students and black students in his classes. Hence, just considering the potential impact of TV as a normalization agent may be said to be one of the powers that need to be encountered probably beginning within the Christian community. Censorship laws exist[11] but in a liberalized democracy they only have as much power to enforce things as society will allow;[12]

9. Ibid., 6.

10. There are programs on TV like, "Sexetera" that emulate the value of group sexual encounters as healthy fun that won't hurt any consenting adult.

11. Rainie and Wellman, *Networked The New Social Operating System*, 288, 289

12. Haralambos and Holborn, *Sociology*, 338, 341–42.

democratic government is possessed by the domination agency of the majority who often profess secular antipathy toward Christian morality.[13] The Western secular demon (I use the word metaphorically) has enforced its dominion in almost every home through the agency of the forces of the media. Of course the East is also becoming increasingly influenced by these forces, as much of the other Two-Thirds World probably will be as well.

Moreover, the relativity of secular morality generally allows even hard forms of pornography with minimal censoring on cable and satellite TV.[14] The sexual revolution of the 1960s, as a cultural phenomenon, was once a powerfully contested countercultural uprising itself, which has now led to new norms of sexual relationships on many levels. The intention is not to condemn an amoral society; this has never worked as a means of subverting the powers that be. It is rather to highlight the all-encompassing topography of the sovereignty of TV, media, internet, and so on, in a globalized world.[15] It is a hugely powerful force and a gigantic player in promoting the worldview of secularism and postmodernity.[16] It must not be forgotten that the phenomenon of globalization through internet communication, TV media, satellite, and so on, has led to the spread of Western ideas to the emergent Sothern Hemisphere's cultures.[17] It may be argued that just as Alexander the Great sought to promote Greek culture and learning through his conquests changing that era significantly, so TV and the global web are forming a secular way of seeing the world, bringing with it the much vaunted power (demon) of relativity and secular ideology, which may be termed "the domain of confusion."

This "domain of confusion" designates what postmodernism has brought with it. It is a powerful force that delineates the present *zeitgeist* of the West. Postmodernity may be well described:

> Postmodernism: (a) Cultural style marked by intertextuality, irony, pastiche, genre blurring and bricolage; (b) philosophical movement which rejects "grand narratives" (i.e. universal

13. One cannot speak about the sexual revolution of the 60s without discussing sex, gender, and feminism as forces to be reckoned with. Barker, *Cultural Studies,* 238–45.

14. Haralambos and Holborn, *Sociology,* 735.

15. The power of the media is of huge importance to cultural studies as well as missiology. It is therefore vital to consider it power and influences over people in society. Barker, *Cultural Studies,* 35, 160, 266, 426–27.

16. Haralambos and Holborn, *Sociology,* 717.

17. Or globalization, a huge missiological subject and force to be considered. Barker, *Cultural Studies,* 155–67, 254, 334–38.

explanations of human history and activity) in favor of irony and local knowledges.[18]

This needs unpacking a little: essentially postmodernity is what some believe to be a between-times state of affairs, awaiting what comes next. It does not accept any one given narrative explaining the way the world is or might be.[19] Postmodern ideology is based on a confused spirit, which in many ways disempowers people from assuming any kind of meta-story. The need for certainty and purposive directionality is something that people often seek to determine for themselves so that they can structure their lives around a harmonizing narrative to live by and to make sense of life. Hence when the postmodern ethos permeates the minds of people there is a sense of confusion accompanied by an attendant search for meaningful experiences to help escape this dissonant spirit of the age.[20] This is where an encounter with the existential living Christ through the Spirit is vital in terms of Christian missiology. The church in the West has to learn to speak a new language to help non-Christians, from generation Y particularly, to understand why it is important to meet him.[21]

This new language is based on the insight that people have long been alienated by the church's didactic preaching and teaching. What is needed in its place is the power of personal narratives.[22] The story of what God is doing in a person's life may help postmodern people to connect with the living Christ through narrative reality. The historical Christian faith can offer plausible narratives to help postcritical people escape the anti-metanarrative Western secular world. The best way for Christians to approach the use of narrative may be by building stronger alliances with non-Christian groups in their local communities, as well as developing deeper more meaningful relationships with them. In this way people can read the narratives of the living Christ as it is acted out in the behaviors of God's people who act as "living human documents," showing to those who observe the way they face life's challenges as Christians what difference knowing Christ makes to the way they behave. It is in this sense that non-Christians can come to understand what differences believing in Christ

18. Ibid., 485.

19. Kimball, *Emerging Church*, chapter 16.

20. One example of the need to find identity and security is to be noted in the work of UK Tribes, www.uktribes.com (accessed April 6, 2015).

21. Greene and Robinson, *Metavista*, 233.

22. Ibid., 188–89.

make to changing the way Christians are motivated to behave by following Christ their example.[23] Deep friendships of this kind may help the confused seekers of postmodernity to consider seeking an experience with the Christ of the Spirit.

Having noted the confusion of postmodern people, it must be recognized that God's people may be equally confused, or in bondage, locked away, in their church domains. This locked-in feeling often gives rise to a sense of frustration that it is hard to talk to people in society about faith matters.[24] Secularization has affected the church in the West in more subtle ways than it is at first recognized. The church itself has become secularized in a rather strange turn of circumstances. It has become subject its own "genre blurring." This took place because the church has anchored itself in a previous modernity and is still trying to maintain the supposed certainties of a bygone modernistic age.[25] It has allowed itself to be allocated its special location in the sacred private sphere where it is ensconced behind church walls and limited to sharing its beliefs only in church services and private meetings. As long as it remains neatly categorized this privatized zone can be left to its own devices. However, if it tries to interfere with secularism's dominant zones of education, economics, politics, medicine, science, and the arts, it finds itself conflicted. From this perspective the domination agencies of the powers inhering secularism have effectively shut the church away to its sacred space.[26] The Western church too often concurs with its particular exile in its own secular space; consider Kaiser's comment:

> Normally, secularization is viewed as a characteristic of the state or of other strictly secular areas of life. But the sacred, too, can be secularized . . . in the sense of being made peripheral or restricted to the private domain. Even God can be secularized in this sense. That is, the action of God can be relegated to personal experience and stories about ancient biblical times and completely eliminated from the stories and processes that govern public life.[27]

Challenging the powers that may be termed "the secularized domination system" will involve what Robinson and Smith[28] call the reclamation of

23. Gerkin, *Human Document*, 25.

24. Greene and Robinson, *Metavista*, 213–16.

25. Kimbal, *Emerging Church*, chapter 5.

26. Hunsberger and Van Gelder, *Church between Gospel & Culture*, 91.

27. Ibid., 91.

28. Robinson and Smith, *Invading Secular Space*, chapter 11.

secular space. That is, numerous areas of society will need to be reclaimed for the kingdom of God.[29] This may be termed a cosmic reclamation of domains such as politics, education, science, medicine, research, economics, media, sports, art, theater, film, literature, and fashion to the reign of God. It is not to argue that it will be feasible, at first, to make a significant impact in terms of numbers engaging in bringing a Christian voice into these spheres, but it is to argue that the Lord's prayer calls Christians to pray, *"Thy kingdom come, thy will be done on earth as it is in heaven."*[30] It indicates that Christ taught his disciples to actively pursue the transformation of society at every level inviting it into the kingdom of God. This implies an activist approach to engaging in kingdom power encounters with Western domination systems. The parable of the mustard seed is both realistic and encouraging in this context.[31] It is practical as it asserts that the kingdom starts small,[32] and realistic in that as the seed is actively planted it exhibits natural and encouraging signs of growth.[33] It becomes a large enough entity in the end to offer shade and habitation to other creatures. In terms of the agrarian world of the ancient Middle East the animals and birds would have indicated that the kingdom mustard plant would attract many other kinds of partners as it grew in its position of dominance in the world.[34] This may have also reflected that other kingdoms would come to join the kingdom of God in the semiotics of first-century culture. This view fits well with Second Temple Judaism's expectation for the final restoration of its fortunes,[35] including the Isaianic panoramic vision of other nations coming to pay homage at Mount Zion—joining in with its messianic kingdom dominion system through which Yahweh would rule the nations with justice and mercy.[36]

What were the kingdoms and principalities (powers) of the first century world if not the many small geographical regions ruled by monarchs, often petty monarchs, acting as titular representatives for Rome? Today they might be compared to the secular domains of postmodern society, with its

29. Ibid., 202.
30. Matt 6:10.
31. Matt 13:31, 32.
32. Sider, *Interpreting Parables*, 223.
33. Ibid.
34. Ibid.
35. Wright, *Victory of God*, chapters 6–8.
36. Isa 2:1–4.

smaller divisibility, branded by sociologists as tribalism, or as niche market groups that have been identified by marketing agencies.[37] These tribes, like earlier titular kingdoms, need to be reclaimed and restored to a relationship with God. Newbigin, following Karl Hartenstein,[38] considered that *missio Dei* (Latin: God's mission)[39] was to be cosmic in its compass, reclaiming every tribe and every space for the kingdom of God.[40] This theology was based on Paul's comments to the church at Ephesus:

> And he made known to us the mystery of his will according to his good pleasure, which he purposed in Christ, to be put into effect when the times will have reached their fulfillment—to bring all things in heaven and on earth together under one head, even Christ.[41]

This bringing "together under one head" in "Christ" is the central locus of Newbigin's cosmic missional theology.[42] What concentration on the cosmic dimension of this kingdom mission indicates is that the coming of the kingdom of God in power[43] means that the prevailing powers will be confronted, and with time, toppled from their positions of dominance, or, following Wink, restored to their intended purpose.[44] How this looks in biblical terms is illustrated by the way that Paul's mission in Ephesus, of two years, led to the silversmiths and shrine-builders of the local household gods being seriously economically compromised leading them to riot.[45] The sign and foretaste of the coming kingdom in Ephesus was the disenfranchisement of the other spiritual powers in that ancient city.

In other words, the kingdom of God came in power as people burned their magic books and pagan paraphernalia in the streets, thus dispensing with the silversmith's services.[46] Power encounter happened simply by the communication of the gospel and the superiority of Christ in the

---

37. UK Tribes..
38. Engelsviken, "Missio Dei."
39. Newbigin, *Open Secret*, 18.
40 Ibid., 18.
41. Eph 1:9, 10; NIV.
42 Newbigin, *Open Secret*, chapter 4.
43. Acts 19:20.
44. Wink, *The Powers That Be*, chapter 4.
45. Acts 19:24–27.
46 Acts 19:24–27.

new believer's lives forming a serious counter-cultural movement[47]—over against the powers that animated the Artemis cultus (the sexuality and fertility goddess of that region).[48]

It might be claimed that a gospel message that does not transform a culture will be a short-lived phenomenon as Schreiter indicates.[49] A gospel missiology that creates a significant counterculture will probably lead to significant change in postmodern communities, which, like the ancient Ephesians, will destroy the equivalent of the modern-day magic books and symbols of their paganism leading to radical missional change. This subverted the associated artisan domination system, which provided for the local economy of Ephesus and its society. The artisanal guild-based trade system was similar to those that existed in Rome and other provincial centers at the time. When the dominant spiritual and economic powers are challenged it is important for other forms of spiritual and economic forces for good to be put into place in order for a community to sustain itself after the old powers have left. Otherwise the power of the gospel to bring about spiritual transformation could too easily get lost in the ensuing suffering of people who have not been equipped through the exercise of the practical social gospel to support and care for their society in their new-found faith situation.

Constructing Local Theologies (Schreiter)

In his book *Constructing Local Theologies* Schreiter sets out some important principles to help us "read" a community. Robinson declares his conviction that even atheists have a belief/faith. Moreover, as Schreiter[50] sees it, they also have a theology even if it is "a-theology" (my term). Indeed the atheist biologist Richard Dawkins, in his book *The God Delusion*,[51] engages with theology, be it "a-theology." An "a-theology"—where the initial "a" indicates the negative, not to believe in God—has to start with the question at some point that if there might be a God then why is it not really proper to believe in one. Dawkins even finds himself reasoning along similar lines, which has him pose certain ideas about his version of God in order to contend

47. Greene and Robinson, *Metavista*, 193–94, 233.

48 Acts 19:24–27.

49. Schreiter, *Local Theology*, chapter 1.

50. Schreiter, *Local Theology*, 124–42.

51. Dawkins, *God Delusion*.

against belief in him. Hence he comments: "Arguments for the existence of God have been codified for centuries by theologians, and supplemented by others, including purveyors of misconceived 'common sense.'"[52]

The popular books produced by Dawkins are almost fundamentalist in their passion to decry belief in God. In essence, Dawkins has tried to become the champion of a new a-theological fundamentalism that harks back to the Enlightenment for its vision of a future without God. Dawkins could be called the bishop of the atheist community.

Schreiter has carefully identified the ways differing communities construct their own worldviews, which will have a theological or "a-theological" construct as part of their conscious or unconscious cognitions, which has been socialized into their mimetic programing. What I term a "mimetic program" here is based on the conviction that differing cultures and subcultures tend to have shared values, norms, mores, customs, beliefs, and philosophies/theologies that are intrinsic as well as extrinsic to the way they morphologize members of their communities to obtain cultural identities.[53] The word "program" is of course not to indicate a formalized systematic checklist of data, but an informal shared set of cultural memes (a meme, or meme memory, is a term used to describe an evolutionary advantage that is passed on as a mental behavior that aids adaptation and survival, it is particularly through memes that cultural intelligence develops).[54] Hence a local cultural group will construct its own beliefs and theology—be it the subculture of a church group or a support group.

However, this raises a rather troubling aspect concerning middle-class communities particularly. There is a tendency for people not to engage even with neighbors who live next door except for an odd nod or hello. Rampant consumerism and the niche market-driven economy that seeks to meet numerous individual needs has led to the consumer cult of the individual, living apart for some of their time in private dwellings.[55] This might be termed the individualistic consumer cult of power. It has its own "a-theology"—if I am allowed some latitude to blur the term—in the sense that the secular world has removed God to the domain of the sacred with some Christians hiding their faith in their private lives in church buildings. Hence secularism has confined this important competitor in what might be

52. Ibid., 100–101.

53. Haralambos and Holborn, *Sociology*, 436–37, 446.

54. Forster and Marston, *Science and Faith*, 108–13.

55 Haralambos and Holborn, *Sociology*, 237–42, 422, 439–40, 459, 594.

termed its own limited sphere; such a theology capitulates to the ethos of the cult of material consumption and the worship service of shopping. The god of the shopping mall can take many forms of brand and niche market products that create identities for the new worshippers at the altar of consumerism. Consumer trophies may be designated as the sacred objects of the consumer cultus that are brought home and used to extend a new kind of secular worship behavior, watching TV, creating beautiful homes, and keeping up with the neighbors—and it is a power to reckon with.

With community life giving way to investing in making homes places to retreat from the world and to relax in, with specific needs and wants having been met, it is possible for people not to build relationships with others on a communal level. The TV, internet, Facebook, Twitter, blogging, and social media seem to meet the ultimate need of the cult of the individual. One does not need to venture out to meet others as it can all be done at home when not working or shopping. What the consumer cult reinforces is the possibility to have the means to live unto ourselves. Hence community contact is subverted and the possibility of making contact with people who feel satisfied and entertained in their own richly endowed domains in order to share the gospel is severely restricted. This is where the missional church needs to think in creative ways to bring Christ even more fully into the internet cyber world in order to reach people with the gospel. The power that holds much of middle-class society in check numbs the possibility of any felt need that leads to the will to action or to engage with the other outside this self-contained home domain.

Having noted a few of the major powers of consumerism, individualism, home entertainment, affluence, and the diversity of the niche market driven economy in society we live in, as well as recognizing people do have theologies or a-theologies, we will now turn to some important insights from Schreiter that may help us to unpick some of the problems we face confronted by the forces of secularism; that seems to castrate Western society of its ardor for communal conjunction.

To begin with, Schreiter challenges the church to consider what the real struggles are that originate with forces they are encountering.[56] He rightly starts with the church, and emerging church, as the focus of change if we are to have any chance of transforming secular communities that are held subservient to the powers that constitute postmodernity with its lack

56. Schreiter, *Local Theologies*, 1.

of passion to embrace a courageous faith rather than to sit on the proverbial fence musing lukewarmly about which faith to follow!

The earlier part of this chapter charted a potted history of power encounter by an ancient church that historically was sure about which powers it faced. Things are far different faced by discontinuous change in postmodernity.[57] The confused homage of competing faiths that is postmodernity is bewildering—the equation leads to confusion even for the church faced by this discontinuity and lack of narrative cohesion or metanarrative. The age of relativity is probably about to consume the heart and soul of the Western mind. Might burnout await our confused and exhausted Western society? Moreover, anything within reason seems to be permissible but when anything goes it can just as easily imply that *everything* might go—hence the impending fears of imminent global environmental apocalypse.[58]

Faced with ecological disaster[59] here is something that might arouse passion for an ecologically relevant gospel in the face of the powers of rampant industrialism[60] and over-consumerism that have led to the rape of natural resources.[61] The writer's fear is that the passion might be to protect personal interests, selfishly, not to selflessly protect the future for future generations. However, theological reflection is merited here; might it not be argued that the God and Father of Jesus has the cosmos in his hand? There was a time in the history of Christian mysticism in which Mother Julian of Norwich[62] was faced with a vision of a nut in the palm of a hand. When she asked what it meant the answer was that it represented all that had ever been made. Might not *Elshaddai* (Hebrew for God Almighty), the father of all reality,[63] end up saying with Julian, "All that is well will be well."[64] The perspective we take here will largely determine whether we join with the eco-ethicists in calling for the preservation of our world's eco-environment. Maybe this will be so—however, the postmodern condition challenges the

---

57. Roxburgh and Romanuk, *Missional Leader,* 7, 8.

58. Meilander and Werpehowski, *Theological Ethics,* chapter 1.

59. Ibid..

60. Haralambos and Holborn, *Sociology,* 108–9, 291, 437, 473–82, 754.

61. Meilander and Werpehowski, *Theological Ethics*, chapter 1.

62. *Showing of Love* 13.41 (trans. Julia Bolton Holloway, "The Westminster Cathedral/Abbey Manuscript of Julian of Norwich's *Showing of Love*," http://www.umilta.net/westmins.html [accessed 26 May 2015]).

63. Eph 4:6; NIV.

64. *Showing of Love* 13.41.

church to be honest about the faith it avows, so that it might actively live it in order that some may be tempted to climb off their uncertain, confused postmodern fence. Faced with new appealing choices Schreiter comments: "Without the presence of outside experience, a local church runs the risk of turning in on itself, becoming self-satisfied with its own achievements."[65]

Schreiter's cultural analysis at this point recognizes that self-satisfaction may circumnavigate a "local" church's ability to engage with the community in a real way, or to engage the broader issues of ecology, whether they be local *or* global. It is possible to live for the reinforcement of the community's own ends to such a degree that the powers that dominate the local secular community are not considered to be worth a second thought. There is not even the chance of effective power encounter happening if the local Christian community adulates its members for being just what the church wants them to be. Rather subtly, the power that motivates this kind of perspective has nothing to do with the mission of God to reclaim secular space. The powers that be may sit securely within their secular domains when the church reneges on its true missional nature in this kind of way.

Schreiter challenges us further by pointing out three significant factors that have made the church even less than certain about how to engage the phenomenon of postmodern culture. The first of his three factors to consider focuses on how new questions demand new answers, he comments:

> Specifically, three recurring concerns threaded their way through all the different theologies that were emerging in the Southern Hemispheres and among marginated peoples of Europe and North America . . . First, new questions were being asked, questions which there were no ready traditional answers. Indeed, so many new questions were emerging that the credibility of existing forms of theology was weakened.[66]

Schreiter also urges us to consider what, if any, application accepted answers used by one culture for a particular period of time have in terms of relevance to a new context:

> Second, old answers were being urged upon cultures and regions with new questions. People outside the North Atlantic communities felt that the older churches were not taking their questions seriously, or were trying to foist their own agenda upon them.[67]

65. Schreiter, *Constructing Local Theologies,* 19.

66 Ibid., 2.

67 Ibid., 3.

Schreiter also challenges the missional church to engage in critical theological reflection on how new contextual situations that people face need new ways of addressing them:

> Third, the realities of new questions and old answers pointed to a concern that recurred in churches around the world: a new kind of Christian identity was emerging apart from much of the traditional theological reflection of historical Christianity. The theology emerging out of this new identity had particular sensitivity to three areas: context, procedure, and history.[68]

What Schreiter demonstrates clearly is that the Western church faced with the rapid growth in the Southern Hemisphere could not address many of the complex issues that preaching the gospel in new cultures requires. By extension this is also true of the church in the Northern Hemisphere (the West) faced with the new postmodern culture. What Schreiter suggests as key to action is to allow people who might come from postmodernity to affirm the Christian faith, to form a "new identity," into which present church structures do not seem to be making any inroads. What is exciting here is that those who discover the present power of Christ to reach them in their postmodern condition can be given much latitude to form new identities suited to reach other postmodern people the church cannot reach due to their present images. This is where a new wave in terms of the postmodern spirituality movement is exciting. Some have termed it the "New Fourth Wave"[69] after the Third Wave of Wimber's charismatic revival.[70] This new wave may be termed New Monasticism.

It is probable that within the next twenty years many small Western churches will close as members die and no new converts are won from the predominant postmodern society unless new people start coming to faith. This might be considered a bleak forecast suggesting the spirit of the age has won a major battle. However, this is where I am tempted to suggest that New Monasticism will play a part. During the so-called Dark Ages as the pagan tribes of Europe were Christianized, the mainstay of the Christian faith, its Scriptures and its learning were to be found in the monasteries. The Celtic monks played a significant role in taking mission to the tribes of

---

68 Ibid.

69. Lyons, "The Fourth Wave," 169–80.

70. Wagner, "A Third Wave?," 1–5. Wagner, "Third Wave," 843–44. A full development of this can be found in Wagner, *The Third Wave of the Holy Spirit*.

Europe.[71] In like manner it may be suggested that missional leaders from amongst the whole body of Christ need to be equipped to take mission into new communities where God is already at work ahead of them, to develop lasting alliances with community movements that can be transformed by small new monastic movements who live among them. In order to do this it will be more important to create a sense of community as New Monasticism is seeking to do, where people support their missional efforts along with the rhythms of some kind of communal life lived in private homes that are in the midst of communities to be reached with the gospel. Silf discusses one means to achieve this in terms of creating retreat opportunities on a do-it-yourself level.[72]

What is important to recognize here is that the missional leader (the ordinary member working with leaders who equip them to discover God's imagination, leading to small missional experiments)[73] will need to be spiritually fed and shaped, as they encounter the powers including the associated temptations to lose the zeal for local *missio Dei*. Indeed this is where the spiritual disciplines will need to firmly weld the missional leader's spirit to God's Spirit in intimate terms—so that the power of the Spirit of Christ might continue to enable the possibility to take authority over the prevailing powers in any given local community. What is vital to grasp is that in order to engage in God's mission, it is vital to follow the undomesticated Spirit of God[74] into the community where he is at work already, speaking to secular hearts and minds, despite what the church may like to consider as its job. To achieve this requires divine detectives who have spiritual sensitivity and the means to discover what the Spirit is doing in a community as he encounters the prevailing powers that be. Hence it is vital to join in with the Spirit of re-creation[75] as he recreates the kingdom of God in the midst of secular spaces. Missional leaders may join in with what they identify as the Spirit's work in these realms, as they encounter the demon of secularism as co-creators (sharers) in the recreation of "new identities," as the Spirit shapes new ways of being church in the midst of those who will hopefully be liberated from the evil powers.[76]

---

71. Robinson, *Winning Hearts*, 22.

72. Silf, *Soul Space*, part 1.

73. Roxburgh and Romanuk, *Missional Leader*, 151.

74. Newbigin, *Open Secret*, 56.

75. Ibid., chapter 6.

76. Eph 2:1–3.

To further the discussion it is important to consider what many of those coming from Pentecostal backgrounds, from the Southern to the Northern Hemisphere might be bringing with them that will help to refocus missional power encounter approaches that can be used to effectively engage evil powers. As long as the encounter is built on the solid foundation of winning a right to be heard, based on true friendships that have taken some time to really evidence that people are ready and willing to listen, then a theology of practical power in action will be useful. Schreiter comments:

> If ethnographic models look to issues of identity and continuity, liberation models concentrate on social change and discontinuity. Put theologically, liberation models are keenly concerned with salvation. Liberation models analyse the lived experience of a people to uncover the forces of oppression, struggle, violence, and power. They concentrate on the conflictual elements oppressing a community or tearing it apart . . . Christians move from social analysis to finding echoes in the biblical witness in order to understand the struggle in which they are engaged or to find direction for the future. Liberation models concentrate on the need for change. [77]

Where ethnography as a cultural analysis tool has often fallen short is that it has only gone so far in identifying what is happening without actively engaging in necessary cultural change in order to really reach a new local people in a language they can relate to. If the gospel does not change culture, then it will only end up with short-term success. It is vital to transform cultures. This can only be done if missional leaders give new converts the continual opportunity to reimagine what the church of the twenty-first century in the West should look like. Hence it will be vital to help them spiritually connect in meaningful mentoring relationships that empower them to imagine a new future and to discover God's imagination for themselves, by the Spirit, so that new ways forward may be discovered. What this means is that a new type of leader is needed, one that "listens out of people" the Spirit-inspired imaginations that have been given to them, along with all of the gifts of the Spirit at work in them. Surely this implies the church will need to march to new drum beats that will often look very different from the traditions and behaviors that have circumscribed a secularized church ensconced in its sacred domain in the West. This would seem also to imply that we need to learn the language of being *the guide at the side,*

77. Schreiter, *Constructing Local Theologies,* 15.

rather than *the expert with all the answers*, as leaders who know how to equip others to employ their gifts and skills for mission. As spiritual guides, like ancient abbots and abbesses, we will need to "listen out" new visions and imaginations inspired by the Spirit in those we seek to equip.[78] However, we need to be careful not to attach the morals of our society as part of the new focus on purity of living that new monasticism brings in its wake.

There is a danger of making Christian morality an agent for engagement with the powers rather than the gospel. And it is vital to remember that the gospel is not so much an idea as the living empowering Spirit of Christ. As the Orthodox theologian Zizioulas rightly says, Christ is dead to the church if there is no room for the Holy Spirit.[79] The power that enlivens the church's ability to engage the powers is the Spirit of Christ—his living person that "blows wherever it wishes".[80] Ellul makes this point in his own inimitable fashion:

> In the minds of most of our contemporaries, Christianity primarily means morality. The spiritual aspect is forgotten except among a few, and the other aspect that calls for notice has to do with the Christian festivals. It is typical that the questioning of Christian truth arises mostly at the level of the conduct of Christians, and the judgment that is passed is moral in character . . . First, the Hebrew Bible the Torah is not a book of morality, whether as constructed by a moralist or as lived out by a group. The Torah, as God's Word, is God's revelation about himself. It lays down what separates life from death and symbolizes the total sovereignty of God. Similarly, what Jesus says in the Gospels is not morality. It has existential character and rests on a radical change of being. [81]

What Ellul nuances for us is that as soon as we make Christianity a missional morality it becomes the morals of a given constituency. The only proper mission is the presence of the living Christ. As Paul iterates the fruit of the Spirit are qualities not quantities.[82] Morality quantifies things, the Spirit makes them qualities. In other words qualities based on the power of the inner Christ empower the whole person to discover the "mind of

---

78. Roxburgh, *The Sky is Falling,* chapter 12.

79. Kärkkäinen, *Pneumatology,* 67–72.

80. John 3:8.

81. Ellul, *Subversion of Christianity,* 69, 70.

82. Gal 5:22–26.

Christ" on a deeper spiritual, dialogical level.[83] The power of Christ is incarnated in the missional community as grace, forgiveness, unconditional positive regard, and welcome.[84] God's reconciling love works through the actions of his grace, which forgive all completely in Christ Jesus. All sins past, present, and future have been atoned for.[85]

Conclusion

This chapter has discussed some very powerful forces that challenge the church in the West. Secularism, consumerism, the niche market economy, hyper-individualism, and radical withdrawal from community engagement are some of the forces that have been identified. Postmodernity has enthroned the disempowering force of confusion robbing people of certainty and purposive direction. The church has arguably largely become secularized by accepting its place in the niche market's societal boundaries. Its voice is not heard if its people do not mobilize to discover the power of God's imagination, to become divine detectives, seeking movements of the undomesticated Spirit amongst lost communities; in order to join with them and encourage them to take on the shape of the reign of God. Meaningful friendships will mean that love has to win the right to enact its omnipotent potential to transform hearts and minds; once secular people give evidence that missional friends have won the right for the gospel to be given a hearing from Christians who really genuinely and deeply care for people. This hearing may include sensitively aiding people to be liberated from "the powers that be" by the power of the living Christ.

83. 1 Cor 2:16.
84. 2 Cor 5:16–22.
85. Rom 6:1–10.

6

Deliverance & Exorcism

Dan Yarnell

Introduction

Of all the many challenges and issues that face a missional understanding, awareness and practical engagement of the powers, nothing has seemingly caused as much help as well as controversy and misunderstanding as that of the practice of the ministry of deliverance and exorcism. From popular and academic literature, radio, and TV programs,[1] film,[2] and stories of those affected by this approach to the powers, it is apparent that some coherent theological reflection and good working practice is needed. Having been personally involved in this over many years, and having recently seen some of the apparent abuses when praxis is not carried out well, it is a matter of

---

1. Various TV and radio programs have sought to bring under investigation the practices and issues that this type of ministry entails, usually noting the excesses. Some examples include: *Satanic Panic—BBC Conspiracies* (2001); *Britain's Witch Children*, Channel Four Dispatches (2010); a live exorcism took place on channel four in Feb. 2005; a new reality television show is entitled *The Real Exorcist* with American Rev. Bob Larson; the Vatican is teaming up with the Discovery Channel to host a new TV series focusing on past possessions entitled *The Exorcist Files*; there is also a DVD series on Islamic Exorcism in the UK (2009); and Radio 4 produced a recent program entitled *So You Want to be an Exorcist* (5th August 2011).

2. The classic film is *the Exorcist* (1973). More recently such films as, *Stigmata* (1999), *Devil's Advocate(1997)*, *Bless the Child* (2000) and *The Exorcism of Emily Rose* (2005).

concern that we explore this important issue as part of our understanding of engaging with the powers.

Many of those from the developing world will have working practices of this type of ministry and might wonder what all the fuss is about. Conversely, in Western nations, there will be quite a mixture of ways of considering this topic and any subsequent expression of ministry from cultural relativism (which would normally distance itself) to daily practical experience of ministry.

Biblical Reflections

The practice of exorcism and deliverance from evil spirits is found in many ancient cultures.[3] The biblical materials indicate that, as with many of the powers references, there is little clear support in the Old Testament for the practice of deliverance. However, there are occasional regulations found in the Torah on dissuading active engagement with spirits (Lev 19:31, 20:6, 27; Deut 18:14). These seem to relate primarily to seeking and understanding the future will of God or the gods, particularly in times of battle. Leviticus 20:27 clearly states that anyone found within the community involved in the practice of being a medium or spiritist is to be put to death. This is in keeping with the strong Levitical holiness framework, which seeks to set the community apart for God's purposes.

One could infer that King Saul was subject to a demonic spirit that could only be subdued by the music of David's lyre and song (1 Sam 16:14). The wording in the text says he suffered from an evil spirit sent from the Lord. This story seems to be broadly about healing of the troubled spirit of a leader who has lost the Spirit of Yahweh, which has now passed on to his successor. There is no indication that the use of music and song is a strategy for use against deliverance of spirits.

Saul's encounter with the witch or medium of Endor (1 Sam 28:7ff.), indicates at least that there were other malevolent spiritual forces at work during his reign of which he was aware. This occurs after he tried to communicate with Yahweh, but found he was unresponsive to his requests. Perhaps out of a sense of desperation Saul sought the counsel of the medium to provide direction and comfort and reconnect to spirituality of some sort through necromancy. After all, he had already banished mediums and

---

3. This includes the Sumerians, Shamanistic cultures, and various Greek and Roman religions. See Yamauchi, "Magic in the Biblical World," 169–200.

spiritists from his kingdom thereby demonstrating his obedience to the laws on such matters.

Even during the time of the Exile, Isaiah notes that there was a continuing temptation to consult spirits (Isa 8:19). He clearly notes that the response to the judgment on Egypt will result in consulting idols, spirits of the dead, mediums, and spiritists, which will eventually lead to nothing (19:3). As with Saul, a sense of desperation seems to lead to this practice.

Beyond this, we are in the realm of the speculative and often fanciful. Certainly within the intertestamental period, we find a more fully developing theology of angels, devils, and demons.[4] This may be related to the encounter with Iranian-Chaldean syncretism during the Babylonian exile creating a dualistic framework of good vs. bad, angels representing the good and demons the bad. This is especially posited in various theological reflections on Genesis 6:1–4. Whatever the details this provides a ready framework for the world of the New Testament and the ministry of Jesus.

Jesus is just one of a number of his contemporaries who was involved in the work of exorcism and more broadly that of magic.[5] There are various texts from both ancient Greek and Roman religions, through to the influence of Judaism and Qumran[6] that offer support to the existence of such an approach to healing and the understanding of the work of evil spirits.

Böcher highlights a typical approach to this ethos and the practices associated with it in this type of literature:

> Because the unclean spirits were localized in the elements, exorcism and a defense against them were accomplished magically and homeopathically with fire and smoke, liquid (water, blood, wine, oil, saliva), air, and many solid substances (earth, gems, ashes, salt, etc.) as well as with the powerful word of a physician and exorcist.[7]

---

4. See further the helpful discussion in Böcher, "δαμων, ονος, ὁ δεμον," 271–74. Also Bietenhard, "Demon."

5. The Jewish historian Josephus attributes the ability of Solomon to practice exorcism to God himself (*Antiquities* viii.42, 45). In the book of Acts, there is an account of some Jewish exorcists who were struggling to exorcize a demonic presence (Acts 19:13–16).

6. From the postbiblical Judaistic writings, see *1 Enoch* 6–11; *Jubilees* 5:1–10; *Testament of Reuben* 5:5–7. Rabbinic Judaism also engaged in this speculative reflective thinking. For one such example, see *Gen Rab* 20 [14a]. The community at Qumran were also involved (1QS3:24–25; 1QH 3:18; 1QM 7:6).

7. Böcher, *Exegetical Dictionary of the New Testament.* 271–74.

It is beyond our scope to explore these in detail and we will take this context as read and turn to the contribution of Jesus.

A Brief Look at the Encounters of Jesus

The author of 1 John claims that Jesus came into the world to destroy the works of the evil one (1 John 3:8). This can be evidenced in various ways, but in the present context, we will primarily consider his work as an exorcist.[8] There is not scope to explore all the various references; instead we shall concentrate on two groupings: first, the four longer exorcism accounts in Mark[9] are perhaps the most obvious beginning point to see how Jesus dealt with the challenges of evil spirits in his ministry. This is not an exegesis of the texts[10] so much as a consideration of Jesus' approach to exorcism.

The Demoniac in the Synagogue
(Mark 1:21–28 / Luke 4:31–37)

The first thing to notice is that this direct encounter with an evil spirit comes right at the beginning of the Galilean ministry. This is consistent with the encounter during the desert temptation, whereby Jesus' identity is challenged. It is perhaps surprising that this takes place within an acceptable Jewish spirituality setting (synagogue)[11]. The connection made between his ministry and his authority, both in his teaching and in the exorcism performed, is also noteworthy. We can also note the unusual statements, partly in the plural ("*What do you want with* us?") and partly singular ("I *know who you are*").

---

8. Twelftree's works on this aspect of the ministry of Jesus is vital reading. Three of his works in particular deserve mention: his published PhD thesis, *Jesus the Exorcist*, the subsequent work, *Christ Triumphant: Exorcism Then and Now,* and finally, *In the Name of Jesus: Exorcism among Early Christians*, where he amends some of his earlier views.

9 I am assuming, along with the majority of New Testament scholarship that Mark's Gospel is the earliest and was used as a source by the authors of Matthew and Luke.

10. On these exorcism texts, see further the discussions in the commentaries of France, *Gospel of Mark*; Guelich, *Mark 1–8*; Evans, *Mark 8:27—16:20*; Hooker, *Gospel according to St. Mark*; Lane, *Gospel of Mark*.

11. This is as shocking as if it took place in a local church today. I have known this to happen in my own experience and in the experiences of various other colleagues.

The Gadarene Demoniac
(Mark 5:1–20 / Matt 8:28–34 / Luke 8:26–39)

We now find Jesus moving outside the comfort and "safety" of the Jewish setting and crossing over the lake, into a Gentile area. This departs from Jesus' normal practice of focusing his ministry on the Jewish community.[12] The Gadarene demoniac is very clearly an outsider, having been removed from family and community because of aggressive behavior attributed to the demonic presence, which now finds him living on his own. His spiritual state of separation is now mimicked by his natural surroundings. We note once again the change in speech between plural and singular. Here Jesus asks for his name, which is not a repeated practice

The Daughter of the Syrophoenician Woman
(Mark 7:24–30 / Matt 15:21–28)

This unusual account finds Jesus once again ministering outside the normal Jewish boundary. The mother requests Jesus' help but, surprisingly, Jesus never sees the girl nor confronts the demon, rather the exorcism is done through faith via the request of the mother.

The Epileptic Boy
(Mark 9:14–29 / Matt 7:14–21 / Luke 9:37–43a)

This is a troubling account where Jesus brings his own authority into the situation because the disciples were unable to bring about the requested restoration and release. Upon seeing Jesus, the spirit reacts, as in other accounts, but no human speech is forthcoming. Presumably this is because the lad is dumb and cannot speak due to the influence of the spirit's presence. In this account, Jesus names the spirit and commands it to come out.

None of these four are identical, except that an evil or unclean spirit or demon is affecting someone and Jesus is able to cast it out. Jesus does not seem to use one distinctive approach rather he works in each situation as it demands.

It is also worth mentioning the commissioning and sending out of the Twelve (Mark 6:6b–13 / Matt 10:1, 7–11, 14; Luke 9:1–6) and the Seventy

---

12. "I was sent only to the lost sheep of Israel" (Matt 15:24).

(Luke 10:1–20), since part of their ministry experience relates to the expulsion of evil spirits. What is unique in these synoptic stories is that Jesus is willing to entrust this ministry to his emerging leadership of apostles and disciples. It seems from the reading of the Gospels that they have had limited training, and yet Jesus encourages and then sends them out. This then becomes one expression of the coming of the kingdom, as Jesus answers the query of John the Baptist from prison.[13]

Review of Jesus' Approach

There are some important considerations to note: Twelftree[14] provides a useful summary of the salient aspects of the four main exorcism accounts in Mark's Gospel as a way of understanding how Jesus pursued his ministry. Firstly, there was a dramatic confrontation between Jesus and the central figure in the story, which is mainly the demonic presence. This is then generally followed by the words from the demons, often in a defensive posture. The exorcist then pronounces clear, straightforward words of challenge or rebuke. Fourthly, the demon might offer a plea to Jesus in response. Finally, the cure or healing culminates with the expulsion of the demonic presence.

This summary helpfully illustrates that Jesus was not limited by the normative practices found in other magical literature and practice, but finds a simple and powerful direct approach to these challenges.[15] The ministry of exorcism is part of the much wider work of healing and restoration. The *shalom* of God was, in effect, the intended outcome. This should not be overlooked. Focusing on one aspect (exorcism) can skew the way in which we consider the overall missional practice of Jesus. Surprisingly, Jesus offers no specific training or direction with regards to exorcism. If this is such an important aspect of missional engagement, one would have thought there might be some teaching about it. In addition, Jesus does not follow a set formula but engages various approaches depending on the context and need.

13. Matt 11:2–6 / Luke 7:13–20. Unusually, Jesus does not specifically mention exorcism in his list of outcomes of the coming of the kingdom to John.

14. Cf. *Christ Triumphant*, 59–71, where these five points are more fully developed.

15. It has been often noted that there are some similarities between the approach taken by Jesus and the workings of Apollonius of Tyana. Cf. Barrett, *New Testament Background*, 83–84. While one should not press this too hard, the similarities are nonetheless noteworthy.

Finally, in a broader sphere in John's Gospel,[16] Jesus' teaching was considered to be from a demonic source when he worked his signs and wonders, which indicates that the ministry of exorcism itself, while beneficial to the recipient, was a threat to other forms of spiritual leadership and power. It seems the powers were at work within the accusers as well as the demonized individuals.

Historical Developments

How much should we consider that the ministry of Jesus is a model to emulate? Do we follow the "What would Jesus do?" approach or are there subtle and important differences to discern in aiding us in our own involvement? This leads to some specific explorations as to how followers of Jesus have engaged in this type of ministry at differing times. What follows is a very brief set of highlights, noting some of the various expressions of exorcism throughout the past 2,000-year history of Christianity.

Early church practices

One of the most challenging issues is to discern how the earliest Christians understood the role of exorcism as a part of its mission. Outside of the synoptic stories, the earliest documents are from the apostle Paul, yet in his own writings he has surprisingly little to say specifically about exorcism. However, the author of Acts does indicate that Paul himself was involved with exorcisms as were others in the early church. The key story is the girl with the python spirit whom Paul subsequently exorcizes (chapter 16). There are some important similarities with Jesus. We can note both the confrontational approach of the demonic spirit and the straightforward approach to deliverance. Other New Testament authors mention the ministry of exorcism more subtly.

There is clear evidence that the practice of deliverance and exorcism continued into the sub-apostolic period.[17] Various authors of the second and third centuries make mention of the practice,[18] and yet there is a varied

16. John 7:20; 8:52.

17. Leeper, "The Role of Exorcism in Early Christianity," 60–61; Brown, *New International Dictionary of the New Testament*, 119–46.

18. Including Justin Martyr, Hermas, Tatian, Tertullian, Origen, Cyprian, and Eusebius. Some catechetical instruction including the renunciation of evil spirits prior to

approach to the topic and to its interpretation. Clinton Arnold's[19] commentary on this period is positive whereas Twelftree is much more cautious and critical.[20] He devotes two full chapters of his book to discovering that there was a varied understanding and approach to this topic, from the earliest writers showing no interest at all, to an understanding that it is all covered in the ultimate defeat of the evil one, to a renewed interest in Rome from the mid-second century. He also notes that the early critics of Christianity hardly mention the practice of exorcism as something for which the Christians were noted. Whichever way the evidence is to be read, in time a framework was needed to assist these new struggling churches that would assist the ongoing practice.

Liturgical Frameworks for Exorcism

Jesus apparently gave no overt training to the disciples nor did the apostles seem to instruct the early Christians, but the need for some orthodox guidance for those involved in this type of ministry became increasingly apparent and perhaps inevitable. This is especially so as the early church developed a discipling process that followed a catechetical framework. All of the three main expressions of Christianity have historical and current frameworks enabling the practice of this type of ministry.

- The Catholic Church traces its practices back to at least the writings of the *Apostolic Constitutions*, possibly even prior to this. The key elements to note include: the exorcism is only done by a priest, making use of various elements (holy water, crucifix, relics of the saints, and vestments), and goes through quite an extensive exploration. The rite of exorcism was updated in 1999 from the original of 1614.[21] There does seem to be a renewed interest in this type of ministry and training, which is offered by the *Althaneum Pontificium Regina Apostolorum* in Rome.[22]

---

baptism can be found in the *Apostolic Traditions*. This becomes important in the development of liturgical practices.

19. Arnold, *Crucial Questions*, chapter 2, "Can a Christian Be Demon-Possessed?," esp. 107–12. See also Skarsuane, "Possession and Exorcism."

20. Twelftree, *In the Name of Jesus.*

21. Online here: http://www.catholicdoors.com/prayers/english/p01975b.htm.

22. See Samuel, "How to Become an Exorcist."

- The Orthodox Church, like the Catholic Church, traces it experiences to the earliest church fathers. Like them, the priest is the key in the expulsion of demons. Here is a helpful summary of understanding and practice:

> The demonic possession of individuals and even of objects has been accepted by the Orthodox Church today in the Sacrament of Baptism, in exorcising satanic powers in the case of the evil eye (vaskania), and in exorcising the devil in the case of a possessed person. In the early Church exorcisms were performed by a person especially trained and appointed to pray to drive out evil from those about to be baptized. Since the fourth century the place of the exorcist, as well as other functions and ministries, have been taken over by the priest. The exorcisms are prayers that invoke God to expel evil spirits. The priest prays to expel all evil, the spirit of error, of idolatry, of covetousness, of lying and every impure act that arises from the teachings of the devil. The renunciation of the devil in baptism is used in every baptism that is performed in the Orthodox Church.[23]

- The Anglican Communion, as a main Protestant church, also follows much of the previously mentioned practices of both the Catholic and Orthodox Church, where the role of the priest is central and some set liturgical frameworks are used as a structured guide. An important document entitled *Exorcism*[24] was produced in 1972 from the findings of a commission convened by the bishop of Exeter. This came from the combination of the growing concern of bad media publicity during the 1970s as well as many requests from parishioners in need.

Twelftree[25] documents some of the history, which initially focused on pastoral practices which went wrong in Barnsley in 1975. The ensuing backlash in the media created the backdrop for both the Anglicans and Methodists to begin to question the clergy involved. This lead to a series of letters in the *Times* ultimately leading to an open letter by sixty-five theologians who raised a number of theological issues, framed within a modernist construct. The evangelical theologian Michael Green was invited to add his

---

23. Rev. George C. Papademetriou, "Exorcism in the Orthodox Church," www.goarch.org/ourfaith/ourfaith7079.

24. Petitpierre, ed., *Exorcism*, for a good summary and updated appraisal. Cf. Malia, "A Fresh Look," 65–88.

25. Twelftree, *Christ Triumphant*, 11–19.

signature to the letter, but declined.[26] Clearly for those within a modernist framework, the idea of exorcism seemed to be out-dated and irrelevant, whereas other clergy were actively engaged in the practice.[27] However, it is a little known fact that every diocese in England has its own exorcist.

The remainder of the Protestant and Free Church family will have a mixture of approaches, from denial where theology and modernist culture dominate, to those that have some practical guidance, to others where it is an essential component of their theology (Pentecostal and some Charismatic). Space does not allow us to explore these fully, but we can note the variety of understandings and approaches that can be found. Few will have a liturgical framework, but many will still focus on the minister/pastor/elder as the primary provider for this type of ministry.

It is also worth noting that the Anabaptist tradition has made its own unique contribution through such authors as Hendrik Berkhof[28] and John Howard Yoder.[29] There has been a recent shift in both theological understanding and practice that brings many of these churches in line with a more Charismatic understanding of the powers and therefore of exorcism.[30]

Witch Hunts and European Dangers

One of the many historic memories of Christianity overtaken by powers rather than overcoming them is the various witch trials both in Europe and North America.[31] In both continents, the period of the Reformation followed by the Thirty Years War is the cultural and historical backcloth. The trials were conducted during the early modern period of history, roughly 1480–1750. It is estimated that somewhere between 40,000 and 100,000 executions took place. The last executions in Europe took place in the

26. See further, Green, *I Believe in Satan's Downfall*, 15.

27. The conclusion of their letter is a poignant illustration of how the theological framework along with the dominant culture has informed their thinking: "It is, we think, mistaken to suppose that loyalty to Christ requires the church to recreate, in late-twentieth-century Europe, the outlook and practices of first-century Palestine. Such an attempt invites ridicule, not to mention the harm that may be done. We urge all who hold high office in the church to ensure that the practice of exorcism receives no official encouragement and gains no official status in the church." *Christ Triumphant*, 13.

28. Berkhof, *Christ and the Powers*.

29. Yoder, *The Politics of Jesus*.

30. Burkholder, "The Theological Foundations of Deliverance Healing," 38–68

31. Levack, *The Witch Hunt in Early Modern Europe*; Cohn, *Europe's Inner Demons*..

eighteenth century. In North America, the most famous of the witch trials took place in 1692–93 in the village of Salem in Massachusetts.[32] Sadly, far too much of this was concerned with an abuse of power, some theological concerns about the millennium, and often little substantive evidence of any form of witchcraft.[33]

The Demythologization of Theology

One of the outcomes and legacies of classical liberal and modernist theological study has been the practice of removing the seemingly obscure parts of the Bible through the lens of the historical-critical method. While this Enlightenment paradigm offered great and important insights, it also led to a broadly dismissive approach to the miraculous,[34] including the demonic. This came to be seen as either a culturally-conditioned understanding that this was the worldview of less enlightened believers, now superseded, or was transposed to be understood primarily in terms of a purely psychological framework, equally dismissive of a biblical construct.[35] For some

32. An online project that documents the event can be found here: Salem Witch Trials: Documentary Archive and Transcription Project, 2002, http://etext.virginia.edu/ salem/witchcraft/ (accessed April 13, 2015).

33. Almond, *Demonic Possession and Exorcism in Early Modern England*, 16, notes some of the thinking during the sixteenth century on the matter: on occasion, the causal relation of witchcraft and possession was reinforced by the claim that the death or imprisonment of the witch cured possession. The cessation of possession demonstrated the truth of the verdict. The execution of the witches both acted as a judicial exorcism and demonstrated the authenticity of the possession.

34. Rudolf Bultmann is perhaps the best known New Testament scholar championing this cause. For three decades he influenced much of the theological horizon. He defined an understanding of a split between faith and history. Much of this is set out in his text *The New Testament and Mythology* and *Kerygma and Myth*. A good summary and understanding of Bultmann's position and contribution can be found in Dunn, "Demythologising—The Problem of Myth in the New Testament," 285–307. More popularly Bultmann's views could be seen in the writings of Bishop John Robinson, particularly his works *Honest to God* and *But That I Can't Believe*, both of which were highly influential during the 1960s.

35. While doing some basic training in psychology during the 1970s, the core textbooks I used all spoke of any biblical experiences of the demonic as primarily indications of psychological disturbances, thereby dismissing any involvement of exorcism. One psychiatrist who moved from this position to that of belief in demons and exorcism, and eventually belief in God, is Peck, *People of the Lie*.

Christian denominations, this methodological approach led to a similarly dismissive approach to exorcism.[36]

The Rise of Pentecostal Theology[37]

This is, of course, a huge jump forward in church history—much is being overlooked for the sake of brevity and practical engagement. The importance of this movement is the realization that ministry among the people of God, often referred to as the priesthood of believers, was not just a theological construct but was rather a practical expression of faith through people gifted by the Holy Spirit. Therefore the practice of this type of ministry was beginning to be moved from the clergy-dominated approach to a much broader potential for body ministry.[38] It does need to be stated, however, that even within the development of Pentecostal and latter Charismatic theology, the tendency to once again maintain the authoritative power of leadership within a few experts rather betrayed some of the pioneering work of the early protagonists.

Wimber's "Third Wave"

John Wimber's theology,[39] a development of the pragmatism of the American church growth movement and George Ladd's theology,[40] once again

36. Twelftree notes that, whereas the Anglicans were divided theologically and went to press with open letters (as noted above), the Methodists expressed their differences in a working document agreed at their conference in 1976. The Church of Scotland equally produced a working document in 1976 on parapsychology, which, while acknowledging a diversity of views, concluded that the rite of exorcism had no place in the Reformed Scottish tradition. Twelftree, *Christ Triumphant*, 14–15.

37. We do not have sufficient space to explore the understanding and contribution of Pentecostal theology. The reader is encouraged to explore this in such works as Anderson, *An Introduction to Pentecostalism*; Dempster, Klaus, and Petersen, ed., *The Globalisation of Pentecostalism*; Hollenweger, *Pentecostalism*.

38. Some of the earliest writings on exorcism and deliverance come from early Pentecostal leaders. See especially Penn-Lewis *The Warfare with Satan and the Way of Victory*, and Penn-Lewis and Roberts *War on the Saints*. This latter work comes from the experiences and practices of those ministered to during the Welsh revival.

39. In particular, John Wimber's power books set the pace for many within the developing Charismatic world and paved the way for the rise of the Vineyard churches and the teaching in the Alpha course.

40. Wimber's contribution is discussed more fully in section 2 above.

brought the issue of power to the fore.[41] Wimber introduced in a popular form the issue of the kingdom coming now, inevitably leading to a power encounter with the spirits of this age and the spirits of the age to come. This was practiced through healing and deliverance, which became known as the "Third Wave." Certainly David Pytches classic work *Come Holy Spirit* owes much to this approach, as does Clark Pinnock in his theology of the Holy Spirit. Pinnock goes on to say:

> Without falling into superstition, let us not make the mistake of minimizing the titanic struggle between God's kingdom and the powers of evil. God's sovereignty is not contested in this world, and his kingdom does not come without a fight. There are people who need to be delivered from Satan's power, and the church is responsible for ministering deliverance.[42]

Exorcism and the Developing World[43]

Outside of Western Europe where the modernist framework provides the plausibility structures of society, we find regular engagement in the practices of exorcism. Three regions in particular are noted here: Africa, India, and Japan. There are numerous studies that have been written up about these regions, which are worth consulting.[44]

Beyond the developing world exorcism continues today[45] while there have been many and various challenges to this by newspapers, TV documentaries, and theologians, there is no doubt that his ministry is still in

41. Wimber has not been without his critics. In particular see Hunt, "Deliverance: The Evolution of a Doctrine"; Percy, *Words, Wonders and Power*.

42. Pinnock, *Flame of Love*.

43. We do not have the space to investigate deliverance ministry within other faith communities such as Judaism, Islam, and New Age spiritualities. One recent publication based upon PhD research that compares Christian and Islamic experiences and practices is Philips, *Exorcist Tradition in Islam*.

44. Some recent studies in include: Ferdinando, "Biblical Concepts"; Meyer, *Translating the Devil*; Onyinah, "Akan Witchcraft." I am grateful to Graham Rusell Smith who is completing his PhD at the University of Birmingham for these references.

45. A very recent thorough study from a North American perspective on Catholic, Charismatic, and Evangelical theology is Cuneo, *American Exorcism*, who focuses primarily on the sociological and anthropological issues. In addition Hunt provides a good overview of practices and influences. See Hunt, "Deliverance." Also see Theron, "Critical Overview," 79–92.

demand.[46] Training courses and conferences, books, CDs and DVDs, and websites abound.[47] In this context there are a few things to note:

There have been a number of challenging issues over recent years that have caused the general public as well as church authorities to be concerned.[48] This will continue to be a challenge. What type of practices should we encourage or allow when this approach to ministry is taking place? What about the need for helpful training? I have witnessed far too many potential "abusive" situations where the person is treated as an object rather than a person, or where the focus on the deliverance is on the demons rather than on Jesus as the exorcist. Bad theology is as problematic as bad praxis, and often leads that way. In particular a dualistic worldview, where good vs. evil is on an equal par, is a departure from Christian theology. Good practices[49] are needed in order to gain a balance between the word as truth and word as confrontation, thus focusing less on demons and more on providing a place of holistic healing and support for those traumatized and needing to be set free. These practices will enable deliverance leading to a new life in a loving and healthy community.[50]

Postscript: Challenging Issues for Mission

The challenges of a coherent engagement with this type of ministry inevitably lead to thought-provoking issues that the contemporary Christian leader must face if he/she is to fully engage missionally in Western culture. Three initial considerations may provide food for further thought. First, we ask, can a Christian be possessed/demonized? With the rise in interest

---

46. Smith, "The Church Militant."

47. Some of the more important popular works include: Subritzky, *How to Cast Out Demons and Break Curses*; Prince, *Blessing or Curse*; MacNutt *Deliverance From Evil Spirits*; Koch, *Christian Counselling and Occultism*; Kraft, *Defeating Dark Angels*.

48. Hoskins, "Exorcism Mania Breeds Child Abuse," *The Sunday Times*, June 5th 2005.

49. There is much helpful advice in the Lausanne Movement Documents, "Deliver Us from Evil." It can be downloaded from the Lausanne website.

50. A recent publication seeks to work alongside churches to arrive at safer experiences. Cf. "Child Abuse Linked to a Belief in Sprit Possession," http://www.proceduresonline.com/coventry/scb/chapters/p_spirit_belief.html (accessed July 2014). Also see the important document "Working Together to Safeguard Children: Safeguarding Children From Abuse Linked to a Belief in Spirit Possession," http://www.education.gov.uk/consultations/downloadableDocs/Spirit%20possession%20pdf.pdf.

in alternative spiritualities, the issue of what effect any of this has on a Christian is something that has come once again to the fore. In particular, the issue of whether someone who is already a Christian believer can be somehow infected/affected by evil is both a pastoral and a missional issue.[51]

Secondly, "warfare" terminology, which uses power when confronting the powers, raises the questions: How does one engage in the use of power when confronting powers without becoming contaminated by the experience? Does the language of spiritual warfare itself help promote this issue? How does one's own cultural understanding play into this?

Finally, the aim of exorcism is inner peace and freedom but such terms as "casting out" utilize power language that on the surface might seem strange from the perspective of peace and wholeness. Jesus is portrayed as the prince of peace, but he also brings a sword. How might an engagement with justice and peace be understood as an expression of deliverance and exorcism? Perhaps we should let C. S. Lewis provide us with a final word:

> There are two equal and opposite errors into which our race can fall into about the devils. One is to disbelieve in their existence. The other is to believe, and to feel an excessive and unhealthy interest in them. They themselves are equally pleased by both errors and hail a materialist or a magician with the same delight.[52]

---

51. Cf. Arnold, *Crucial Questions*, for a thorough discussion on various ways of understanding this dilemma.

52. Lewis, *The Screwtape Letters*, 3.

7

The Semiotic and Hermeneutical Analysis of Power Language and Behavior

Andrew R. Hardy

Semiotics and Divine Self-Revelation

Homo-sapiens[1] has probably used language beginning emergently at a point near the appearance of so-called mitochondrial Eve.[2] The actual appearance of pictures on cave walls and worked rock surfaces probably goes back at least 30,000 years if not longer.[3] The use of pictographs, which evolved to become developed signs and symbols, can be particularly witnessed in Egyptian hieroglyphs[4] as well as in ancient languages such as those that arose in ancient China.[5] The verbal articulation of words that were represented in the more highly developed hieroglyphs of ancient Egypt, for example, bear testament to the behavior of verbal articulation of sounds in structured grammatical sentences as a primary means used by modern man to communicate reciprocally. The use of non-pictorial symbols in Indo-European languages developed out of earlier pictographic semiotic systems of representation. Semiotics has much to do with the study of signs

1. Bandelt et al., *Mitochondrial DNA*.
2. Ibid.
3. Sanz and Keenan, *World Heritage Papers*, 131.
4. Churchward, *Signs and Symbols*.
5. DeFrancis, *Chinese Language*, 54.

and symbols used in writing down what was originally articulated orally. There is power in the use of written signifiers (words, symbols, etc.), which communicate something about how any given person thinks and feels regarding subjects or objects, whether concrete or abstract, about which they wish to communicate.

In the Genesis account of the creation of humankind, Yahweh enables humanity to name created animals and things.[6] Thus, the Genesis creation account expresses the fundamental conviction of the redactor that God made humankind with the ability to think creatively and to construct meanings based on language. Both creation accounts picture a creation of the cosmos based on structure, reason, and purpose. God utters creative words that frame all things with purpose and meaning so that they can be understood by humanity who is made in God's semantic image.[7] Yahweh speaks and what he utters and formulates takes on structure, meaning, and life, which humankind can discover as part of the hidden semantics of a structured, ordered, and thought-through creation design, full of Yahweh's semantic footprints.[8] The psalmist puts it well: "*The heavens are telling the glory of God; and the firmament proclaims his handiwork. Day to day pours forth speech, and night to night declares knowledge.*"[9]

The constant theme of the biblical narrative resonates with the overarching claim that God has made a world that is to be understood. To look into its deep, intricate workings demonstrates a semantic understanding of order, design, and logic, which is intrinsic to created reality. As much as this Judeo-Christian book of sacred memories may have been challenged as an authentic communication of God's revelation to humankind by nineteenth- and twentieth-century liberal scholars, it is unmistakably clear that, in it, God wants to communicate with humankind.[10] The very notion of the Jewish and Christian communities as people of "the book" says something profound about the power of language as a key means of the Godhead's desire to reveal his purposes to his creation. This is especially true for humankind made in the image of God thus enabling them to "think God's thoughts after him," as Einstein once so aptly articulated it.[11] It is this two-

---

6. Gen 1:26, 27; 2:20.

7 Gen 1:3, 6, 9, 14, 20, 24, 26

8. Ps 19; Prov 8:22–36; John 1:1–18.

9. Ps 19:1, 2 (RSV).

10. John 1:1–18.

11. Dragash, *Made in the Image of God*, 91.

fold revelation of God through the natural revelation of creation and the special revelation of Scripture that work together to convey meaning to life.

The power of God's self-revelation, particularly in Scripture, is meant to help God's people construct the meaning of life in light of what is communicated about God's purposes for his people and his creation. It is this power of God's self-revelation, particularly through Jesus Christ and in the written accounts about his identity as the Son of God,[12] that has challenged believers and unbelievers alike to make choices about who Jesus is or was. One thing seems certain, the words of Scripture have power to form and transform human identities; even if for some it means they do not accept what is communicated as an authentic set of revelations from God.

In this chapter it will be important to explore the power of the signs, symbols, and signifiers of Christian Scripture. It is impossible to do this without some reference to, firstly, how symbols and signifiers take on different meanings in different cultures. Secondly, the question of hermeneutics will need to be considered and how interpretation is the product of agreed meanings that various groups gather around. And thirdly, the question of authority must be considered in a postmodern age where semiotic and hermeneutical theory challenges the notion that understanding of commonly-shared meanings, intended by the original writers of Scripture, can be recovered by present day people.

The Power of Semiotics in Culture

The term semiotics derives its original meaning from the Greek word *semeion*, which at a basic level means a sign by which something is known or understood. Thiselton identifies two main categories of semiotic communication, the first concerns "the nature and status of codes through which texts communicate meanings."[13] This first form of semiotic semantics has been referred to (above) as present in Christian Scriptures as well as, at a deeper level, in the chemical languages found in the genetic codes that structure biological lifeforms in the natural world, which may be thought of as a way of touching base with natural revelation about God or godlanguage (at supra- or super-natural levels, depending on our worldviews). The second basic category of semiotic theory focuses on "forms of non-verbal social behaviour which, through the presupposition of a code, become

12. Mark 1:1.

13. Thiselton, *Horizons in Hermeneutics,* 80.

signifiers."[14] In this second case body language, and the tone or volume of a voice can convey semiotic meanings. Moreover, gestures of gifts given to a loved one can signify love and friendship, with the token gift saying in effect "I love you or like you." It is in this second form of semiotics that culture-specific codes come to light that encode meanings based on any number of gestures that may be made to convey meaning. Thiselton comments on an example of coded language in Scripture that is preeminently hard for modern people to relate to meaningfully:

> The culture-specific nature of codes is underlined when we examine the second feature to which we referred in semiotics, namely the role of non-verbal behaviour. The conventions of apocalyptic can be no more strange to the modern western world than the code which forms the basis for the operation of traffic lights might seem to the ancient world. The existence of such a code (based on arbitrary colour-contrasts) gives rise to extended and metaphorical applications.[15]

In fact, in the Apocalypse of John power-laden semiotic metaphors exist that were full of rich symbolism to the Christians of the mid to late first century AD. The beast that comes out of the sea in Revelation 13 is empowered by Satan essentially to persecute the Messiah's people.[16] The power represented by this beast can soon be deciphered in the context of the revelation to refer to pagan Rome.[17] The battle that is fought has to do with who is worthy to be worshiped: Is it God or the devil?[18] In chapter 13 the power symbolism of the beast, replete with the fierce qualities of the beasts of Daniel chapter 7, is combined into the one creature thus demonstrating the exercise of authority and power based on physical force and manipulation to make people do its biddings.[19] The lamb-like beast at the end of chapter 13 actually speaks like a dragon and also engages in force and aggression to win its presupposed right to be worshiped by all, including Christians. The lamb and his followers pictured in Revelation 14 symbolize Christ and are contrasted with the force used by the anti-lamb of chapter 13 in order to challenge people to action. The messianic lamb has followers

14. Ibid.
15. Ibid.
16. Rev 13:1, 2.
17. Rev 17:9—Rome was built on seven hills.
18. Rev 4–5.
19. Compare Rev 13 with Dan 7.

who want to follow him because he has proved himself worthy through sacrifice, as depicted earlier in Revelation chapter 5. The manner in which "the lamb who was slain"[20] exercises authority is based on sacrifice because of the love of God for his creation.[21] The power of forced compulsion over against the persuasion of the lamb that sacrifices himself for his creation is the basis of the power of God's sacrificial love to win convinced followers who want to follow the one they trust. This latter conclusion is at the very least strongly implied in terms of the chiastic semiotic structures evident in apocalyptic literature.

The heavily-coded language of the apocalypse seems foreign to modern Christians, but it was a language with a rich heritage of meanings known to early Christians.[22] Recovering this deeper meaning of the apocalypse, regarding the worthiness of the lamb to receive worship, is often lost to those who do not understand the rich cultural semiotics of ancient Near Eastern apocalyptic. Language like the term "the global web" is the closest that modern people might come to understanding encoded symbolic meaning that has similar power to symbols like "the lamb." It is not hard to imagine how this modern symbolic language could easily become a mystery to a future generation, if in a thousand years' time they were to see it used in a modern Christian devotional text. Suppose such a text used coded language like the term the "global web" to describe how the Holy Spirit is omnipresent in God's creation; it would prove hard to grasp such language if all memory of the internet was lost. The semiotic power of language operates if it is understood without the need to have to go into long explanations of what it meant in a past, different cultural setting. The more work people have to put into understanding something the more they will give up trying to understand it. This is a lesson for the missional church; if it uses an outmoded language when it seeks to communicate with postmodern people, it will lack the power to grab their interest.

These examples go some way toward demonstrating the necessity for missional leaders to acquire the skills to communicate the words of Scripture to postmodern people in semiotic forms that are encoded within culturally relevant language. Only thus will they help people understand what the contemporary relevance of Christian faith is for their lives. In order for Christian language to have the power to transform non-Christian

20. Rev 5:12.

21. Rev 1:5.

22. Humphries, *Christian Origins*, 3.

worldviews it must be easy for the receiver group to understand it.[23] Put in other terms, the point of view of the coded language of Scripture needs to be conveyed in a way that can give it the power to be embodied in the semiotic code language of another cultural group's context-rich semiotic language systems.[24] Kraft classically stated this when he discussed the translation of the Bible into another language: "God's desire to convey his message to humans within the human cultural and linguistic frame of reference necessitates the translation of God's casebook [the Bible]. God's Spirit has therefore been very active through the years in leading people to translate the Bible."[25]

Kraft's pneumacentric theology, linked as it was to the revelation of the written word of God, directly correlated the messages of God found in Scripture with the work of the Holy Spirit, which he believed motivated missionaries to take the living word of God to a new people in their own semiotic rich language. He further discussed the challenges of sharing the gospel within a cultural context such as the church arguably now has to do on its own doorstep in the postmodern secular world of the West:

> But the question must be asked concerning just how adequately these translations are conveying the message of God to those for whom they are intended. For, even beyond the tremendous handicap of intelligibility . . . it must be observed that many of these translations are not giving the impression that God has really mastered the language into which his Word has been translated. The readers of such translations, therefore, often assume that God is a foreigner or out of date or, perhaps, that he has a speech defect. [26]

Translations of Scripture are obviously Kraft's focus in this context. What it is important to note is that too often the missional church can be significantly out of step with the "in-language" of the next generation in its own local context. One important way of empowering the language the church uses to communicate with the next generation will be the need for it to take time to learn and understand the deeper meanings of the signs, symbols, and metaphors the emerging generation is using. One of the lessons the present writer learned when engaged with youth and family ministry with postmodern teenagers, in the UK, was that words like "cool"

23. Thiselton, *Horizons in Hermeneutics*, 80.
24. Kraft, *Christianity in Culture*, 262.
25. Ibid.
26. Ibid., 263.

were certainly "un-cool" to use when speaking to them. "Chill out" was acceptable. At base level I learned once again that the gatekeepers of the un-churched youth community I was knocking on the door of, first of all needed to assess my acceptability as a person who could understand their language. In other words the use of "in-language" in groups such as this particular tribe was the first power hurdle to negotiate in order to get a hearing. I had to start by communicating something about myself that they would accept, let alone the message of Scripture somewhere down the road.

In missional terms it is vital to understand the semiotic power of language as well as the non-verbal signifiers that are used to communicate with others. It is all very well to talk about the power of the Word of God to speak meaning into people's lives, but it must not be forgotten that the language used in a translation, even one like the New International Version of the Bible, will be a foreign language to any number of postmodern tribes that currently exist as part of Generation Y. One important reason for the church's loss of ability to communicate with youth tribes and young adults age 18–30 years, could be because it has not understood the lack of power of the words of Scripture, written or preached, as an accepted medium of communication by younger people. Something far more engaging than words alone is needed. In order to communicate powerfully with postmodern people we need to consider the whole person, including their experiences, in order to assess whether the spoken word has actually made any difference to them at all. This is where the broader concerns of semiotics beyond simple words and sentences can help in assessing how to communicate effectively with the newer generation.

The researcher Albert Mehrabian classically formulated the thesis that 7 percent of a message is verbal, 38 percent of a message is vocal (which includes the tone of voice used in communication, inflections and sounds), and 55 percent of a message was non-verbal (i.e., what is communicated by body language, such as expressions on the face and postures of the body).[27] Pease and Pease have more recently revisited this research and have reinforced his findings.[28] Beattie has also furthered research into body language following the work of Argyle,[29] which has done much to overturn many assumptions in modern psychology about verbal and non-verbal transactions. Modern psychologists have tended to assume that higher psychologi-

27. Mehrabian, *Social Influence;* Mehrabian, *Silent Messages.*
28. Pease and Pease, *Body Language.*
29. Argyle, *Bodily Communication.*

cal language functions are superior to body language. According to Beattie, there is clear evidence that even complex ideas are communicated as much by non-verbal cues, such as are expressed by body language and vocal cues, as by words themselves. Beattie comments on Argyle's findings:

> These results led Michael Argyle to the conclusion that nonverbal communication is twelve and a half times more powerful than language in the communication of interpersonal attitudes, specifically on the friendliness-hostility dimension, and over ten times more powerful in the communication of a different interpersonal attitude, namely superiority-inferiority.[30]

Argyle and Beattie argue that non-verbal communication is much more effective for communication in face to face interactions between people than spoken words are alone. In semiotic terms this is not unexpected as body language, tone of voice, and so on, are powerful communication forces. These findings challenge the word-based ministries of the traditional evangelical and Protestant word-focused ministry. Such an approach to ministry does not take into account the incarnational experiential power of the Word of God pneumatically brought into life in the experience of the living person and through other non-verbal cues that convey passion for what is communicated.

Boison and Gerkin classically spoke of the power of the living "human document," which they understood in terms of the involvement of the whole person in communication so that not simply spoken or written words are used to achieve meaningful exchange of ideas.[31] The Spirit-filled Christian brings the words of Scripture alive as they are completely expressed through every fiber of their beings. The effect of written or spoken words taken from Scripture only have 7 percent communication impact on those who hear those words for the first time. Hence the power of the Word of God needs to take on 93 percent of its communication impact through believers who convey it through their body language and vocalisations, that is, the whole person. For the words of Scripture to have full impact on generation Y, found as they are in various young adult and youth tribes, missional disciple-makers need to incarnate the living word as living human documents, whose whole beings and behaviors convey the meaning of God's love for the world through their whole approach to life in general. Beattie agreed with Mehrabian's findings that verbal language will normally

30. Beattie, *Visible Thought*, 29.
31. Gerkin, *Human Document*, 1–10.

be dismissed if interpersonal relationships are poor and if body language and vocal articulation communicate attitudes that conflict with a message being communicated.[32] In order to meaningfully communicate the message of salvation and influence a person to explore Christian faith it is necessary to utilize the power of the other 93 percent of the communication process.

Communication of the gospel must be a holistic process if the word of God is to be communicated with power. It is important for the missional disciple-maker to live and breathe the semantics of the message of God's grace through every fiber of one's being. In this way Christ speaks power-fully through his missional kingdom people when they become holistically incarnate on a semiotic level with those with whom they wish to share their faith.

The Power of Culture-Specific Exegesis and Hermeneutics

The late anthropologist Paul Hiebert focused on an important aspect of the exegesis and, therefore, of the hermeneutics and semiotics of sharing the gospel message between two different people groups, where the sender group acts as the conveyor of the message of the gospel to the receiver group. Most of his academic missiological thinking was orientated toward classically defined missionaries going into another nation and culture different to their own in order to make new disciples. However, in the multicultural, pluralistic, and postmodern context in Western society it is no longer safe to assume that there is one national culture in the cosmopolitan melting pots of most of our cities. Hence, Hiebert's insights concerning the communication of the gospel by, let us say, cultural group A to cultural group B is useful in this new context. He stated in terms of classical missions, "We must communicate that gospel to humans who live their every-day lives in worlds far different from our own."[33] Owing to contemporary pluralism and multiculturalism some peoples in our own milieu have come from "worlds far different from our own" to live among us it is important to consider the insights taken from the mission fields outside the West. In addition, the emerging generation Y youth and young adult tribes in our own society also come from "worlds" somewhat "different from our own" if we are from the boomer generation or generation X. They have moved

32. Ibid., 29.

33. Hiebert, *Gospel in Human Contexts*, 12.

beyond the cultural world that shaped the boomer generation and to a large extent that of generation X as well.[34]

Hiebert's thought challenges the missional church to conceive ways and means to enhance its power to communicate the gospel, by first of all learning not only to exegete Scripture so that it can be interpreted by Christians today but also to engage in cross-cultural exegesis of subcultures surrounding our churches. Only thus will the church be able to interpret and understand their worldviews to alternative groups so that the message of the gospel can be meaningfully shared with them too. He commented: "Unfortunately we receive little training in the exegesis of human beings and their contexts. At best we may have taken a course on how to learn a new language. Consequently, the gospel we preach goes off into space and does not reach the people we serve."[35]

He later adds: "It is increasingly clear that we must master the skill of human exegesis as well as biblical exegesis to meaningfully communicate the gospel in human contexts."[36] We cannot go into a detailed examination of how to go about cultural exegesis, but it is important to note that the "meaningful" communication of "the gospel in human contexts" requires missional disciple-makers to understand the semiotic language of the group to which they seek to convey the message of the gospel. The receiver group needs to be addressed in a semiotic system that they can grasp. Hiebert taught that it is essential "to study the social, cultural, psychological, and ecological systems in which humans live in order to communicate the gospel in ways the people we serve understand and believe."[37] The vital point Hiebert raised was the authority of Scripture, which is based on the ultimate power and authority of God to transform societies. This means that the authority inherent in the message of Scripture could be held captive to new cultural contexts. However, this possibility must be avoided if we want to allow the word of God to speak without losing its power.[38] Hiebert commented further:

> The gospel is not simply information to be added to current cultural understandings. It is a transforming power that changes individuals and societies into signs and witnesses of the kingdom

34. Possamai, *Generations X and Y*, 20–29.

35. *Gospel in Human Contexts*, 12.

36. Ibid.

37. Ibid.

38. Ibid., 13.

of God. Moreover we must learn to exegete our own contexts because these shape the way we understand and communicate the gospel. We often speak of this encounter between gospel and human contexts as indigenization or contextualization.[39]

Hiebert thought of these facets of cultural exegesis and hermeneutics as missional theology.[40] Missional theology has to do with the power of the meaning of signifiers (words, body language, symbols, etc.) that can convey the message of Scripture in a way that a receiver group will understand, in terms as close as possible to their whole semiotic communication system. Consequently the earlier example of how I sought to work with a new youth community consisting of generation Y youth demonstrated the need to engage in cultural exegesis of their symbolic world, so that they would accept not only me but also possibly, in the end, what the whole of my life as a Christian might mean for their lives. There is genuine power in taking time to exegete a receiver group's semiotic worldview and what it means to them so that it can become possible for the power of God's word to be conveyed, not in words alone but also through the whole living "human document" of the missional disciple-maker.

This more holistic level of communication needs to go beyond individuals in a community with whom a missional leader may seek to share the gospel—it also needs to focus on the broader community in which individuals exist. If the semantics of the gospel is to make a meaningful impact on the public debate on the role of faith in Western society then it needs to transform the communities found in that society as well. This means that for lasting change to happen secular culture itself needs to be changed by the Christian story. Thiselton, following Gadamer and Ricoeur, seeks to convey the need for community involvement in the process of people coming to understand anything, including the gospel message. He comments: "Gadamer sees the role of the community as being of key importance for processes of understanding, just as Ricoeur sees interaction with 'the other' as important for the ethical discussion of avoiding 'narcissism.'"[41] He adds a little later: "Contrary to the rationalism of the secular Enlightenment, which elevates the autonomous individual above inherited traditions and values, Gadamer calls for 'the rehabilitation of authority and tradition.'"[42]

39. Ibid.

40. Ibid.

41. Thiselton, *Hermeneutics,* 19.

42. Ibid.

Gadamer's thesis, as well as Ricoeur's, obviously requires "interaction with the other" in order for the sender of the message not to be isolated from interaction with the receiver. This would inevitably lead to the deluded belief that a message can only really be confirmed or disconfirmed if it is understood and accepted by the receivers. In terms of the need for community cultural traditions to validate a message it is vital, as Hiebert articulated, for the message to become part of a community and for it to transform that community as a living representation of the power of the gospel. Thus, the meaning of the Christian story needs to inhabit deeper unconscious cultural strata not just shallow culture. The challenge facing the Christian faith in the West today is for secular and postmodern semiotic cultural systems to take on a suitably contextualized gospel tradition that can transform them from the inside out. The power of Gadamer's thesis that the community itself needs "rehabilitation of authority and tradition" to take place, will require a new exegesis of non-Christian aspects of societal semiotics within the public square. A new incarnational semiotic language needs to be found in order to start the transformation of post-Christian cultures. To enable the missional church to take the gospel into the public square it is important to help postmodern people re-engage with the message of Scripture and the gospel in new ways. One way this could be done is by learning from postmodern literary theories such as reader-response criticism and narrative criticism. This chapter will be confined to briefly focusing on one of these approaches.

Reader-Response

The development of reader-response theories that took place in the 1970s and 1980s came about as a reaction to new criticism and its theories, which claimed that the text of Scripture should be treated as autonomous, in a manner that simply left the texts of the Bible isolated from their authors, their subject matter, and its readers. If all that could be known about a text was in isolation from the original context it emerged within and from, then readers who might want to learn from it could not do so because it was impossible to recover its intended meaning. Moreover, "It appeared to lose any anchorage in the public world, or reality."[43] So serious were the implications of this thesis that a new movement emerged

---

43. Ibid., 19.

that in effect tended to supersede the New Criticism. This movement promoted the view that the key determinant for the produc-
tion of meaning was the reader or readers. Meaning was less a
product of the author or the text as such, or even of the relation
between the text and its author, than a product of the relation
between the text and its readers. How readers responded to the
text came to be regarded as the main source and determinant of
meaning.[44]

Reader-response theory is useful in that it takes seriously the power of
a text, or passage, to actually shape the person's own life story and worldview. It takes an interaction between the text, and the reader's response to it,
which will inevitably transform the outlook of the reader in some manner
in response to what is perceived to be the meaning of a text. Left to itself,
the theory is weakened, but allowing for the added work of the Holy Spirit
on the reader offers a useful tool to help people engage with the living word
of God that can help them to reinterpret their life stories in the light of the
Christian story.

In terms of making sure that a biblical passage is conveyed in a suitable
translation, even if it is amplified like *The Message Bible*,[45] it is important for
the language to be expressed in such a way that its message provides the
best possible chance to understand the text in language forms with which
they are familiar. The closer this interface between the recipient's cultural
language and the written word, the better the chance that the read text
will be paid attention to by the recipient. This will lead them to respond
by having their outlook on God and the world transformed negatively or
positively.

All that we have written so far demonstrates that it is very important
to consider the correspondence between what is communicated and what
is heard and understood by a receiver group, if what is communicated is to
have power to affect their understanding of the Christian gospel message.
The power of the Holy Spirit to transform the semantics of the human soul
must not be underestimated by a missional church seeking to discern the
missio Dei.

44. Ibid.

45. Peterson, *The Message Bible*.

Newbigin on the Question of Authority

The question of the usage of language suited to communicate the gospel effectively to differing cultures calls attention to more than missional theology *per se*. It also calls attention to contextual theology that seeks to make the Christian gospel understandable to any given receiver group. Contextual theologians are inevitably interested in maintaining the impact of the gospel message in terms adapted to the milieu of a given people group or subculture. There are at least six different models of contextual theology, each of which has its own merits; Bevans includes: the translation model, the anthropological model, the praxis model, the synthetic model, the transcendental model, and the countercultural model.[46] Out of these models Lesslie Newbigin formulated his own countercultural model, built on certain prerequisites that started with the authority of the gospel of Christ and the Lord's authority to call every human cultural expression to purify itself with reference to Christ. Bevans captures the countercultural model well:

> It recognizes that human beings and all theological expressions only exist in historically and culturally conditioned situations. On the other hand, however, it warns that context always needs to be treated with a good deal of suspicion. If the gospel is to truly take root within a people's context, it needs to challenge and purify that context: "if it is truly the communication of the gospel," writes Lesslie Newbigin, "it will call radically into question that way of understanding embodied in the language it uses. If it is truly revelation, it will involve contradiction, and call for conversion, for a radical metanoia, a U-turn of the mind."[47]

The countercultural model seems best suited to the radical claims to authority that Jesus Christ made for himself including God's mission to renew creation by the establishment of his eternal kingdom.[48] Newbigin wagered his whole life on the service of *missio Dei*, based on his conviction of the authority of Jesus. Classically he asked the question in *The Open Secret* "By what authority?" He founded his theology of mission on the basis of a theology of the authority of the economic Trinity.[49] He responded to the question in three ways:

46. Bevans, *Contextual Theology*, 3–21.

47. Ibid., 117.

48. Matt 28:19.

49. Newbigin, *Open Secret*, 15, 54.

1. "My answer to this question is a personal commitment. I am in Pascal's famous phrase—wagering my life on the faith that Jesus is my ultimate authority."[50]

2. "The confession I am making is that Jesus is the supreme authority or, using the language of the New Testament, that "Jesus is Lord." This confession implies a claim regarding the entire public life of mankind and the whole created world."[51]

3. "I make this confession only because I have been laid hold of by Another and commissioned to do so. It is not primarily or essentially my decision. By ways that are mysterious to me, that I can only faintly trace, I have been laid hold of by one greater than I and led into a place where I must make this confession and where I find no way of making sense of my own life or of the life of the world except through being an obedient disciple of Jesus."[52]

Each of these three ways essentially formed a confessional missional spirituality that helped Newbigin map his whole theology of mission. It would seem fair enough to suggest that a similar set of confessions of this type is open to everyone who wishes to engage in semiotic power encounter. The power of the living Father, Son, and Holy Spirit are at the foundation of Newbigin's contextual theology. Building on the basis of their authority, the semiotic laden message of the power of the gospel of the living Christ was and is to be taken to all cultural contexts to be found in the world today.

Newbigin's Trinitarian *missio Dei* theology has been further developed in the work of a number of contextual and practical theologians, who use Trinitarian theology as a lens through which to engage with people of today. One such thinker is Peter Holmes, who has mapped out a psycho-spiritual concept of discipleship in the context of what he calls therapeutic faith communities.[53] Among other facets of his theology that are useful is his emphasis on making disciples who can do more than just simply read the Bible, but who can also hear God's inner voice as well. This kind of pneumacentric theology has the potential to vivify the Christian community as well as secular communities that are the focus of such community-centered missiology. His concept of salugenic discipleship formation is built around

50. Ibid., 15.
51. Ibid., 16.
52. Ibid.
53. Holmes, *Becoming More Human*, 13–23.

a phenomenological spirituality. In his view, a therapeutic faith community is one where people are shaped by reference to the primary foundation of a social Trinity engaged in an inter-trinitiarian perichoresis with them as a community, thus making each person of the faith community a participant in the Trinity's community.[54] He comments:

> Scirghi helpfully summarizes this view, following Himes and Himes and Boff, that the three persons of the Godhead are a model for human community, through both kenosis and inclusion. Following Eastern Orthodoxy, Scirghi sees perichoresis as an interpenetration of all persons who are a perfect harmony through their relation with one another.[55]

In this sense, the healing faith community is one where people are enabled to become whole, and to be enabled to live in harmony and good relations with one another, because they model their community's identity on that of the perichoresis of the economic and imminent Trinity (as far as that is possible). Central to Holmes view of the power that transforms people, as well as healing them, is the work of the Holy Spirit. He frames his theology on the concept that people are equipped to hear the Spirit of Christ's voice on a deeper spiritual level, which is experienced phenomenologically as a communication with one who is in them, but at the same time separate from them.[56] Holmes suggests:

> listening to God's voice forms the basis of a journey of therapeutic discipleship. The Rapha promise makes it clear that God expects us to listen to Him and respond. Contemporary spirituality likewise places strong emphasis on wholeness change. So, it seems, does Yahweh (e.g. Ex. 33:5, Ps. 32:8–9; 55:19, Acts 11:5ff.). When Christians refuse to change in response to God's voice, they are refusing to harmonise their lives with Christ, with imago Dei wholeness.[57]

The question is how does this relate to semiotics and the power of the Word of God? In Holmes's view it has everything to do with it. Scripture itself attests to its own claim to enshrine something of God's voice as well as calling readers or conveyors of the word to hear that voice for themselves

54. Ibid., 59.

55. Ibid., 196.

56. Ibid., 127.

57. Ibid.

on an inner spirated level. It is through this inner power of the living and active Spirit of Christ within believers—as well as going ahead of the church in the world, preparing hearts and minds to receive the gospel of the living Jesus—that the missional semiotic power of the word, contextualized for receiver communities, will cause a response conveyed by the written and spoken word alike. However, entering communities with the living contextualized word also calls for Christian communities to model the deeper perichoretically formed life that will, in turn, demonstrate what it means to function as perichoretic communities, living by the power of the Spirit. In this way, in their corporate life they will become examples of what it means to be healed by the God who loves to restore and heal communities.

No chapter on semiotic power in the Christian missional context can ignore the work of the lifegiving power of the Spirit. It will fundamentally be the work of the Spirit to guide God's people to exegete the communities among which they are called to engage in *missio Dei*. Unchurched people will best respond to the voice of God as it is lived out through his people within their own communities and among those of seeking peoples. This will happen as the people of God and their Christian communities take their place as living human documents based on the semiotic power of shared lives, grounded on love and grace lived out with each other and those with whom they share the gospel. It is the Spirit that gives life and power to the semiotics of such missional communities.

8

The Psychology of Power Encounter and Counseling the Overpowered

Andrew R. Hardy

Social psychology has particularly provided rigorous analytical insights that enable pastoral psychologists and counsellors to understand the phenomenology of the psychology of power encounter. Any mature discussion of the theology of power encounter must take the insights of psychology seriously as it offers critical models which enable the missional church to be more aware of the abuse or misuse of power. This chapter will not consider the actual abuse of power in the church as this will be undertaken in chapter 9. The focus of this chapter will be based on seeking an understanding of the social psychology of power as well as a guideline discussion of key principles for counselling the overpowered.

Obviously a chapter focused on the psychology of power encounter and counselling the overpowered will be limited. An important part of framing this discussion starts with an appraisal of social influence theory as it is particularly understood by social psychologists. What will follow will be a psychosocial exploration of the exercise of theological beliefs and practices on existing believers, as well as on seekers who want to explore the Christian faith. This chapter will pick up on general observations about the application of theological power to the practice of the Christian faith and end with a short discussion focused on counseling the overpowered.

Social Influence and Power Encounter

The social psychologists Hogg and Vaughan discuss the relationship of social influence compared to the critical discipline of social psychology:

> Social psychology has been identified as "an attempt to understand and explain how the thoughts, feelings, and behaviours of individuals are influenced by the actual, imagined, or implied presence of others." This widely accepted and often quoted definition of social psychology identifies a potential problem for the study of social influence—how does the study of social influence differ from the study of social psychology as a whole? There is no straightforward answer.[1]

It is impossible to observe brain behaviors in a detailed fashion to offer an account of how the brain's neural community interacts to motivate and cause people's reactions.[2] It is only possible to study deeper psychological motivations by inference or reports of inner mental processes, making it harder to affirm whether deeper psychological drivers have been properly uncovered, to help in uncovering psychological influences affecting interactions between persons on a social level. Indeed, sociologists focus attention on the social construction of reality and the possibility of the existence of an independent social reality,[3] thus challenging the notion that it is easy to observe social behaviors that make simple explanations of social influences obvious to infer. The social constructivists Berger and Luckman classically deconstructed the idea that social reality existed as a separate category to be investigated apart from how people within their cultures actually construct reality.[4] For example, what might be common-sense knowledge for a person from *Culture A* may not be common sense knowledge for another person from *Culture B* since there is not, as such, a stable social reality that transcends cultures. The sociologist Giddens offers an incisive observation about this fundamental deconstruction of social reality, which adds much to the study of power encounter due to social influences in civil and spiritual societies such as the church:

> Social constructivists believe that what individuals and society perceive and understand as reality is itself a construction, a

1. Hogg.and Vaughan, *Social Psychology,* 236.
2. Newberg, *Principles,* 214.
3. Giddens, *Sociology,* 273–75.
4. Berger and Luckmann, *Social Construction of Reality,* 24–44.

creation of the social interaction of individuals and groups. Trying to "explain" social reality is to overlook and to reify (regard as a given truth) the processes through which such reality is constructed. Therefore, social constructivists argue that sociologists need to document and analyse these processes and not simply be concerned with the concept of social reality they give rise to.[5]

Constructivists challenge the idea that there is a stable construct, or constructs, of social reality to be discovered as independent realities outside of individual, persons, structures, and cultures that fashion a specific social system under consideration. Hence, the study of social influences acting as conscious or unconscious forces that motivate power encounters implies they are constructed at a far deeper psychological and social level and act as drivers by which individuals seek to exercise influence and power over others. In this sense it is possible to place the study of social influences upon a psychological footing because basic human psychological drivers may be thought of as the source of energy making individuals seek to get others to do what they want them to do compared to what they do not want them to do. Social psychology is useful in that it seeks explanations for sociological behaviors and the psychological motivations behind those behaviors. Hogg and Vaugham comment:

> Social psychologists are interested not only in behaviour, but also in feelings, thoughts, beliefs, attitudes, intentions and goals. These are not directly observable but can, with varying degrees of confidence, be inferred from behaviour; and to a varying degree may influence or even determine behaviour.'[6]

What is important to note is that human social interactions are driven by deeper psychological motivations. It is possible to formulate a simple analysis of how a social interaction between two people could be analyzed. For instance what about a person who has a ministry in deliverance from demonic forces—how might a power encounter between such a person and a potential recipient of a deliverance ministry be analyzed? *Person 1* (the deliverance minister) may feel driven to help *Person 2* (the recipient of the deliverance ministry) to accept that he has some form of, let us say, demonic oppression, which he needs *Person 1* to help him to be delivered from. The first question that could be asked is what is *Person 1's* drive to help *Person 2*? Should it not be open to interpretation as motives are important in terms

5. Giddens, *Sociology*, 273.
6. Hogg and Vaughan, *Social Psychology*, 4.

of the reflective practical theology of most Christian traditions? Why does *Person 1* really want to help *Person 2* to receive a particular type of intervention, in order to release *Person 2* from *Person 1's* interpretative-driver, which assumes that *Person 2* has demonic oppression? What does *Person 1* get out of having his diagnosis of *Person 2* as demon oppressed if *Person 2* accepts *Person 1's* diagnosis? Both of these questions are important as they speak to norms of behavior that *Person 1* and *Person 2* assume can be inferred by how each person responds to the other's interactions, as well as to the expectations and values that form the opinions of both persons that will lead to *Person 1* being granted power to act by *Person 2,* or not. Obviously in this case it will be vital for any evaluation of motives for the exercise of power over another to take place with reference to some key Christian values within the Christian community where *Persons 1* and *2* fellowship together. What these values are and how they are perceived and understood by *Persons 1* and *2* will be important to measure, in some fashion, in order to judge what is potentially healthy or unhealthy about them. Given that some of those who may be thought of as demon-oppressed may be extremely open to manipulation due to an underlying vulnerability coming from a mental illness, it is very important to consider whether power is being used in a harmful way. This requires some reflection on how social psychology understands the way social influence and power works.

Analysis of Social Psychological Power in Churches and Missional Work

To begin the analysis of social psychology's contribution to power encounter it is important to distinguish between behaviors of compliance and conformity. Social psychologists consider that conformity is a product that is largely socialized into individuals from a young age. It is largely a sociocultural by-product that helps define what acceptable behaviors are based on, as they are defined by norms and values of a given culture and society as they are acculturated into the young. A large variety of norms could be mentioned—among them we may identify high power and low power distance cultures.[7] In high power distance cultures it is normative for there to be respected elders or leaders who have rights to exercise power over people lower in the social system[8] without those lower in the system feeling

7. Cardwell et al., *Psychology,* 325.
8. Livermore, *Cultural Intelligence,* 103.

it is wrong for those with higher status to have more rights to the exercise of power being given to them.[9] Many such leaders do not formally get awarded power but a family's reputation can refer power and prestige to a person without reference to a formal process of putting them in a place of authority with attendant higher social recognition potential as a matter of class.[10] To be part of a family that has a royal or noble bloodline also affords and refers prestige to people in a family, as well as to how people consider them to be more powerful than themselves because of higher claims to social recognition and status. It has struck the writer that some African men in church leadership positions trace their heritage back to high status family names, such as to a chief or king of a given tribe or people in their homelands. It is noticeable that members in their churches pay special respect to them. High power distance cultures that work on such a normative-values set are based on an expectation that people should know their place in society, and accept it, and also know the place of those higher up in society and show special deference and respect to them.[11] Those higher up in the system are considered to be more worthy of deference than those lower in the system. Those lower in social ranking are expected not to challenge their superiors. Non-western societies are often high power distance cultures which tend to have less democratic forms of government, although there are rapid changes going on in the world which are introducing differing versions of democratic systems to societies.

Conversely, low-power distance cultures are most often democratic in nature and leaders do not expect that they have the privilege to go unquestioned or even uncriticized for their leadership decisions.[12] In low-power distance cultures each individual is held to account for their actions,[13] and often those in the most responsible areas of government are held up for greater scrutiny than members of the general public are. In both high- and low-power distance cultures the assumptions of how power is recognized, perceived, and exercised are part of the norms that are socialized into citizens as they grow up and take on roles and statuses in adult life. Conformity to the norms for how leaders are treated and related to are encoded into the way people relate in everyday life. What the discussion of high-power

9. Barnard and Spencer, *Encyclopedia*, 23, 27, 65, 89, 93, 333.

10. Ibid., 89.

11. Hiebert and Hiebert Menses, *Incarnational Ministry*, 106.

12. Cardwell et al., *Psychology*, 325.

13. Livermore, *Cultural Intelligence*, 98–102.

and low-power distance cultures does to help in the discussion of power encounter is especially important to grasp in a multicultural or multiethnic church setting. If, for example, a multiethnic church has members who come from an African high-power distance culture, and white European people who come from a low-power distance culture, then a potential conformity-based power encounter may occur. African participants may expect leaders to act with more authority and to have the natural right to exercise it without question, whereas Westernized members may expect their leaders to be their equals and to act in a democratic rather than an autocratic fashion. Without a whole case study to illustrate the challenges this may raise in such a multiethnic church, it is probably self-evident enough to predict that conflict could arise simply because of two different culturally socialized norms, making each group expect different things of their leaders. One can also imagine that, if a black leader of such a church expected to be treated with special deference, with conformity happening automatically to conform to his leadership expectations, that Westernized members would not conform so readily without questioning his motives for wanting to exercise a more autocratic leadership style. In other words, the power encounter in this case would arise not out of a desire to use power abusively, but rather out of a different assumed cultural norm for how power is expected to be exercised by those with a higher status.

This is an important example of the difficulty for multicultural and multiethnic churches to be planted in the West unless these issues can be addressed and resolved as a crosscultural change management process where people can start to understand how expectations for conformity are conditioned within different cultural groups as socially accepted norms. What the missional church has to recognize in this case is that not every form of assumed abuse of power is actually intentional abuse, given that different cultures have different normalized expectations for how power should be exercised. It will be important not to assume spiritual abuse where actually a perceived abuse of power is only viewed to be abusive by a different cultural group which does not share the same norms-and-values set compared to another group, which understands them and accepts them as a healthy form of leadership. It also needs to be added that feminist theology has raised the whole question of male abuse of power over women in the context of leadership in the church.[14] The conformity of women to a particular theological paradigm (or hermeneutic) over the role

14. Fulkerson and Briggs, eds., *Feminist Theology*, 1, 2.

of women in church in these cases has to do with accepting a subcultural norm (hermeneutical code or tradition), which they must accept in order to be fully integrated into that community. The writer observed a case example of a woman openly vocalizing her agreement with the subordinate role of women in the church at a Reformed church leader's conference he was invited to attend. The lady concerned spoke from the rostrum to about 600 delegates. She was engaged in leading a women's ministry and had been asked to say something about it at this conference. She spent two thirds of her presentation making supporting statements for the subordinate role of women in the church and the rest of her time was spent on talking about her work. This is a good example of compliance to a male-dominated power structure. The male dominance in Christian leadership of this particular Reformed hermeneutical code led to a conformity behavior in order for this woman to be accepted by her membership group.

Having highlighted some of the slippery issues of social-psychological analysis of the power of accepted norms, which condition conformity behaviors, it is next important to move on to behaviors of compliance and the dynamics identified for their operation. Compliance is most often achieved when people change their behaviors only while they are under surveillance. When they are not being observed they no longer comply by behaving in accepted ways by those who expect these behaviors. In the Western context the issue of compliance in migrant monocultural churches has raised some interesting questions. For example, in a group of African churches known to the writer there has been a growing conflict between male leaders and feminist groups within these churches. The authority of male leaders has been challenged to such an extent by some powerful women in these congregations that the leaders have had to comply with some of the demands made by the influential women. In social-psychological terms this is an interesting phenomenon to observe as it demonstrates that these women are perceived to have real power to influence congregations, with which the male leaders feel they must comply. This feminist power is based on the influence of these women on other women in their congregations, who having moved to the West are now expecting to be treated like Western women in terms of how women in low-power distance cultures expect more equal statuses with male counterparts. One very positive outcome in this case is that some of these women are now leaders in their own right in their congregations alongside male pastors. It is also important to note that these women exercise some degree of coercive power over male leaders, because they have a strong following among other female members who are not willing to remain silent on issues about which they disagree with their male leaders.

It is also vital to take note that it is not just ethnic diaspora groups, now living in the West, who may exercise coercive power; this can also be witnessed in more Reformed evangelical traditions as well as in white charismatic free churches. A near classic example can be taken from the 1980s in terms of the heavy shepherding movement.[15] Leaders in emerging charismatic congregations claimed apostolic and prophetic powers, which made their leadership decisions as good as the very words of God. The type of coercive compliance in these cases did not just achieve compliance to the leaders' wishes while members were under surveillance, but also when they were not under surveillance. In other words, the theological power exercised by these leaders led members to privately accept ideas, beliefs, and the practices that members were told they needed to adopt because they purported to come from the authority of God's new apostles and prophets.[16]

It is worth taking stock at this point of how social psychology works in terms of helping Christian leaders to analyze power encounters in their work. Firstly, we discussed conformity and how this is defined to be the product of less conscious forms of power encounter. The power encounters that lead people to conform are based on accepted norms that have been socialized into members of a society from the earliest age. It is hard for leaders who are embedded in one culture and who have not lived in another culture for some years to be aware of the power of socialized norms that cause members in their own monocultures to conform to socially accepted norms and values. However, many ministers who have led churches made up of other cultural groups living in the West, often develop an awareness of how different cultural norms lead members to conform in different ways compared to the minister's own cultural norms. It proves useful for culturally intelligent church leaders to take stock of their congregations, asking what their accepted norms are and how these cause people to conform to a variety of social conventions, norms, values, and expectations. It is also important to recognize that different church traditions, which people have chosen to become members of, have their own subcultures, and that these subcultures are also based on accepted norms the broader culture these

15. More, *The Shepherding Movement*.

16. *Shepherding*, 14:39. Cult Information Services of Northeast Ohio, cisneoinc.org (accessed March 21, 2014).

members come from does not adopt. Hence there are ecclesiastical structures that create plausible norms and values to which members in a given tradition are expected to conform. These ecclesiastical subcultures exercise theological power through beliefs and practices that members agree to keep in order to belong to a particular group. Social psychologists call these "membership groups." Membership groups set objective criteria for people to become members based on the social consensus of the group concerned that being a member, and remaining a member, calls people to conform and comply with the socially agreed values and norms.

It is interesting to note that church membership groups founded on ecclesiastical traditions are not attractive to many postmodern people. The reasons for this are complex, but John Drane has suggested that among them is the perceived failure of the mainline denominations, beginning in the 1960s, to be able to address the questions postmodern people are asking.[17] Another issue has to do with the failure of the traditional churches to form meaningful friendships with these emerging postmodern people by socially identifying with segments of society they live among, in order to help them explore their spiritual journeys in their own contexts.[18] Moreover, beginning in the 1960s, the boomer generation started asking spiritual, theological, and philosophical questions *en masse*, which the mainline denominations did not understand and feared as examples of anti-Christian propaganda. The net result was that the church began to lose its power to influence people in society, as it called for people to join its membership groups on the church's own terms rather than by meeting on some newer middle ground. The traditional churches did not meet the need for more flexible structures that would missionally welcome the new questions of generations X and Y.[19]

This is an interesting point to reflect on in terms of what is missionally new in the ways Christian groups are now trying to encounter the postmodern secular powers. Kelly discusses the relationship between membership groups and reference groups.[20] Reference groups are significant psychologically to people as they feel that these groups act as referents to their own attitudes and behaviors. Postmodern people relate especially well to these kinds of groups. Reference groups do not require membership as such but

---

17. Drane, *Do Christians Know How to Be Spiritual?*, 1–40.
18. Ibid.
19. Brierley, *Reaching and Keeping*, 16, 151, 173.
20. Kelly, "Reference Groups," 410–14.

provide a positive sense of norms that people can accept and live by. For example, celebrities have websites that set out a "celeb" look-a-like popular cultural agenda as an example of a kind of reference group.[21] Alternatively, reference groups can also be negative and those who relate to these groups agree with their ideas in opposition to broadly accepted norms. In the case of positive reference groups members will align themselves with group ideas and will support what is acceptable to them within that arena. An example of this would be the action of households that recycle products to save much needed earth resources. In the case of negative reference groups an example would be public marches that take place in cities to protest about green issues, animal rights, or other social issues.

In terms of the emerging church situation Hirsch and Frost recognize the many creative alternatives that Christians use to relate to postmodern people.[22] For example, in a small town near Oxford in England there is a Costa coffee shop that opens outside of normal evening hours to allow access to a missional group appealing to young people who hang around in the shopping mall. Here, in a familiar environment, they come and talk about their life questions. Emerging churches are much more like reference groups than membership groups. They do not seek to get members to accept, conform, and comply with their norms, but rather they seek to meet people incarnationally where they are situated, and to help these secular people think through what the Christian faith might look like in their own secular segments of society.[23]

Missional theologians and anthropologists have much to say about the power of the gospel to transform a society from within. Gill suggests that Weber's thesis that transposition of Christian religious virtues has largely shaped the present Western virtues of industriousness and having morals that guide decisions and policy making.[24] To this extent, postmodern society is still founded on the power of the high Christian values that helped shape modern Western culture. This kind of power to transform a society is also part of the work of the Holy Spirit who is the power of God transforming all who will listen to his voice. Rahner suggested that

21. Cf. Cheryl Cole's website, http://cherylofficial.com (March 21, 2014, which demonstrates the popular iconic followings that celebrities achieve.

22. Frost and Hirsch, *The Shaping of Things to Come.*

23. Gibbs and Bolger, *Christian Community,* 51 -53.

24. Gill, *Shaped by Theology,* 56, 57.

the Spirit universally reveals himself to every human person.[25] The great strength of this type of power theology is that it puts potency into the hands of seeking people, to converse with believers and to be influenced by the Spirit of Christ and to shape their lives in ways suited to their own contexts. This is not too unlike what the early church did when it took the gospel into cities and market places in order to engage people where they lived on their own terms and with reference to their own needs, norms, and values. The crucial lesson to learn from the Pauline Epistles is that many groups that then formed into small ecclesial communities were helped to reshape themselves into contextually relevant groups offering an alternative way of living to the predominant Greco-Roman culture.[26]

In this section the aim has been to provide examples and relevant discussion of how social-psychological analysis of various kinds of power encounters can be better understood by applying some simple analytical tools so that it is possible to deconstruct positive and negative forms of power encounter with reference to mission. In order to help churches or missional ventures to engage better with conflicting power systems, whatever they may be, it is important to be able to deconstruct what is potentially going on in any given encounter that challenges the healthy interactions of peoples in communities. Another aspect of the deconstruction of group dynamics has to do with individual and group needs for counseling by leaders and their team members who feel overpowered. The writer, as a constructivist, holds that no social-psychological power system can be understood unless there is a positive deconstruction of the various systems that influence power relations in a group or society. In terms of counseling the overpowered, social psychology offers a simple grid of differing types of power systems that can be said to help in the positive diagnosis of the powers that are abusing or positively influencing a person or group.

Counseling the Overpowered

The other side of a study of the psychology of power encounter is the counseling of those who have been overpowered by their experience with those who exercise power. The church is not immune to the use and misuse of power by leaders or members. It is possible to view what goes on in any human social interaction as a power encounter. The psychologists French

25. Kärkkäinen, *Pneumatology*, 112.

26. Moynagh and Harrold, *Church for Every Context*, 379–404.

and Raven in the late 1950s identified five bases of social power.[27] Some six years later French expanded the five to six bases consisting of: reward power, coercive power, informational power, expert power, legitimate power, and referent power.[28] These six bases to the exercise of social power have proved to be useful designations to help social psychologists understand how different types of power come to influence people in society. In terms of pastoral psychology and counseling of the overpowered these six designations can prove to be very useful in helping victims of power abuse to understand what sort of power has overcome them. All six types of power are exercised to different degrees in churches to be found across the Christian traditions. At this stage it is not possible to engage in an in-depth analysis of which traditions use which of these different categories of social power. Rather, this section will focus more generally on using insights from these categories to help pastoral counselors and their clients to understand the types of social power they have succumbed to. The simplest approach to adopt is to consider each of the categories and to offer comments on how power works in each of them, and how identifying the power exercised in each case can lead counselors and clients to a new frame of reference capable of liberating victims from power abuse.

Firstly, consideration will be given to reward power. Leaders or individuals who use reward power exercise their ability to give rewards or to promise rewards for compliance to their wishes or demands. In business settings reward power can work in very positive ways when employees are promised bonuses for good work outcomes. These promised rewards act as good motivators to achieve conformity among employees to meet company or corporate goals. Within the church, reward power can be exercised in a number of important ways. For instance, giving tithes to the church is often associated with a theology of reward for the giver. The reward elements are often based on three important criteria, firstly, that it is good to engage in sacrificial giving as this will help to maintain the church and its professional ministers so that the gospel can be preached in local contexts. Secondly, there is a practical theology that the one who pays their tithes to the church will receive special financial rewards and other benefits from God to make up for sacrificial giving. Thirdly, in some congregations tithing is made a requirement for full membership, as it is claimed that paying at least 10 percent of one's income to the church is a sign of real conversion

27. French and Raven, "Social Power," 118–49.
28. Raven, "Social Influence," 371–82.

and commitment to God, and the reward in this case is for a person to be admitted as a full member of the Christian group with full rights to take part in all of its provisions to members, often including the right to vote at members meetings on issues facing the community.

None of these practices and beliefs may be called abusive in themselves, but they can be open to misuse by leaders if the underlying theology of blessing, for instance, was used to make members believe that not having paid tithe is the cause of some financial disaster like losing a job. More worryingly in some very fundamentalist Pentecostal and Charismatic churches a theology of reward can develop around healing, health, wealth, and the believer's faith level.[29] In the context of prosperity gospel theology a person who is not blessed with healing, health or wealth is often considered not to have the right faith level in order to be rewarded with these blessings.[30] From a pastoral-psychological perspective this is open to special abuse, because there is a skewed theology of reward that does not take biblical theology into account in a balanced way. There is a loss of a theology of suffering spoken of by Jesus, Paul, Peter, and the Revelator within the biblical theology of the prosperity gospel movement.[31] This breeds disregard for the possibility of persecution or illnesses. More could obviously be mentioned here, but the sign of the abuse of power in this case is that the lack of reward for one who is suffering in some way is taken to be a sign of weakness and a lack of faith. In turn, members who constantly do not get the level of required prosperity come to feel undervalued, and can be viewed as part of an underclass, who can suffer from constant anxiety and depression as a result of feeling like a second-class Christian. It may be hard to unpick all the reasons why people can come to feel this way, except it seems obvious enough that there is an unhealthy theological use of the power of reward, in this instance, given its skewed biblical theology.

Secondly, coercive power is by far the most obvious type of power encounter. Its use in the church is more subtle for the most part compared to other forms of social-control mechanisms. Coercive power is the ability of a group, social system, or individual to give or threaten punishment for non-compliance with expected behaviors. The time when churches use coercive power is most obvious when it comes to dis-fellowshiping or excommunicating a member, who has broken expected norms of behavior, or who

29. Coleman, *Globalisation*, 27.

30. Ibid., 27.

31. Luke 9:23; Phil 1:29; 1 Pet 1:6; Rev 6:9, etc.

is living in what is thought to be open sin without being willing to change those behaviors. Coercive power can also arise through preaching beliefs such as punishment in hell for those who do not respond to the gospel message. This type of preaching is less often used in Westernized churches today, but there are still fundamentalist Reformed evangelical churches that utilize this kind of manipulative tool to win compliance from new converts who they wish to join them.

Coercive power can also be witnessed in some churches where a leader has the strong support of the majority of members. Those members who are not liked by a leader or church in a minority group may be punished by removing them from holding an office in the church. There is not so much a real offence against established membership criteria, but rather a personality clash that leads to those in power exercising power to remove responsibilities from people they do not like in order to get their own way. This is simply a power play to disallow them from positions of influence. In counseling those who have been overpowered by the use of coercive power it will be important to explore exactly how the application of this type of power works and their part in allowing it to be used against them. Part of successful counselling might be to empower the counselee with insights into coping with the grief and anger produced by being at the receiving end of coercive power.

Thirdly, information power has to do with the target's belief that the influencer has more information than they have. It is interesting that throughout church history information power has often been mainly available in a more cultured form within the church.[32] Indeed it was often priests and monks who served in the courts of kings in the medieval period who brought learning to the realm and government.[33] In the time of Galileo and Copernicus the new learning about the solar system became an informational power issue, with the church claiming its own ancient cosmology as the legitimate version compared to the new heliocentric view. The birth of liberal historical criticism starting in the late eighteenth century up until the present period challenged the historical credibility and authenticity of biblical information. Indeed, the early twentieth century witnessed a strong reaction to liberal theology with the birth of fundamentalist evangelical churches.[34] This represented an attempt to return to the Bible as a straight-

32. Riley, *Christian Education,* chapter 7.

33. Peterson, *Warrior Kings,* 152.

34. Olsen, *Evangelical Theology,* 77.

forward reliable historical document accompanied by a radical denial of liberalism and its radical deconstruction of the historical Jesus.

All of these examples demonstrate the use of informational power by the church and responses to it. In the West, the power of Christendom, based on acceptance of its interpretation of biblical information, has shifted to the current context where the church as a whole feels broadly disempowered from having a strong voice in a secular society. One of the largest areas of loss in terms of church attendance is among young people aged eighteen to thirty years who are no longer reared in the church. This emergent postmodern generation no longer trusts that any one informational power system can claim absolute truth, or have authority over their lives. Those in this age range who remain in the faith, or who are coming to it, are looking for an experience of God that is real around which they can construct their identities. This generation can feel overpowered by competing information systems in the secular Western environment, hence finding the living Spirit of Christ will often convince them that there is an information-system/narrative they can live their lives by, which provides a plausibility structure to guide them on life's journey.

Fourthly, expert power is based on the target's belief that the influencer has generally greater expertise and knowledge than themselves. This is an interesting area to consider given that most mainstream denominations and traditional churches in the West put great emphasis on higher education for their clergy and in some cases for other key roles in the church. This has to do with the need to equip church leaders with an equivalent kind of expert power, compared to their often middle-class members who hold professional jobs of significant responsibility. The argument is that this higher level of ability is required so that ministers can properly serve their congregations, as well as be respected by them since they understand the rigors of achieving expertise or a recognized professional status. In this fashion church leaders can feel overpowered by the demands of the expert power of their congregations. How can a church pastor who has limited experience of just managing a church compete with captains of industry who understand how to direct large organisations? In the megachurch context the corporate model of church leadership is derived from the corporate world. Of course some members in churches feel that expert clergy with high level MA and PhD qualifications know about faith matters far better than they. Sometimes this leads smaller congregations to feel disempowered to share their faith; instead they leave the job of teaching and evangelism to the expert minister. In the free church sector quite a number of leaders who have planted churches without going through any formal ministry preparation course, have later gone on to find training for themselves, or have put together their own training courses based on their experience—covering years or decades in church leadership. The type of expertise these kinds of leaders have is based on their success in planting and growing larger congregations. This type of expert power is that of professional experience based on the credibility achieved with others in the formation and establishment of congregations that attract large audiences.

Fifthly, legitimate power is founded on the target's belief that the influencer is authorized by a recognized power structure, or group, to command and make decisions they must obey. In churches like the Anglican and Catholic denominations priests hold legitimate power that is either supported by recognition as a state church, such as the Anglican Church in the UK, or because of ancient traditions that support the hierarchy of popes, cardinals, bishops, and priests. The legitimization of power by such hierarchies makes it hard for lay members to be empowered to take active roles within churches beyond a certain point.

It is interesting to see how power is legitimized in congregational churches by comparison. The concept of the body of full members having the right to vote and shape the life of the church means that power is legitimized based on consensus. The minister is hired by the church, new members are accepted by the vote of members gathered in members' meetings. Legitimate power is often exercised in established congregational churches of up to about 130 members, by accepted norms and "how we do things around here." Many a congregational member, or minister, understands how this sort of legitimated power is based on those who hold position in congregations. Those who do not recognize the power of established members who have come to be the king makers, or power brokers, within a congregation will be disempowered. Disempowerment for ministers in these churches results if they fail to agree with the established dynasty, which is often made up of a coalition of long-term family members.[35] The minister only has legitimate power as long as the dynasty gives it to him or her.

Finally, referent power has to do with identification with, attraction to, or respect for the source of influence who holds power due to charisma, friendships, or relationships with those who like a person or a group that hold the kinds of values "we like." House churches may be a

35. Croft, *Transforming Communities*, 50.

good description of this type of power. Much the same could be said for churches of forty members or less. People refer the right to be influenced and led by significant others in these groups, because they want to be part of something that meets their need to be wanted and liked by such a person or persons. The power exercised by charismatic small-group leaders can be very influential, and if leaders in these groups do not like those who want to join them, or who they have come to dislike as they have got to know them in a group, they can disempower them by seeking to undermine their reputations or characters. In smaller groups that have charismatic leaders of this type, another potential charismatic personality who wants to join can be perceived as a threat. Sometimes the existing charismatic leader can be forced by popular opinion to allow a new charismatic likeable person to join them. The net result can be a fracture in the group, with some staying with the initial leader and others joining the new leader, or with the disempowerment of one compared to the other, leading to expulsion from the group because sides are taken by those who refer power to one leader compared to the exclusion of the other for the sake of group harmony and happiness. Of course, larger churches can be based on referent power of this type as well. This is also the case for varieties of emerging churches that have people more loosely associating in pub churches, coffee shop churches, and other informal structures.

Conclusions

Social psychology helps leaders in churches to analyze how social influence and power operates within their congregations and networks. Enough has been achieved in general terms to understand some of the basic concepts that can help in the understanding of the psycho-dynamics of power encounters based on psychological reactions to human behaviors, or reactions to power structures that exist in society at large and within the church. Clearly it is important to understand how power encounters work in this context. When evaluating whether power is being used for good or bad purposes, the concept of a theology of grace that seeks to liberate people from domination systems and unhealthy relationships needs to be held center-ground. The church is not immune from the abuse and misuse of power that leads to injury of people. Hence it is important to seek to address non-Christian ways of exercising power that can harm rather than heal people. Pastoral counselors need to help clients to identify what kind of power has led to harm or personal disempowerment. The steps that follow on from this will have to do with helping the counselees to be liberated from systems that disempower them in their Christian journeys and as they seek healthy growth into the likeness of Christ. After all, it is he who exercises the power of grace and forgiveness for the healing and healthy psychological functioning of his people.

9

The Religion of Power:
Engaging the Abuse of Power in the Church

Dan Yarnell

"On the side of the oppressor is power"

ECCLESIASTES 4:1.

"Power tends to corrupt, and absolute power corrupts absolutely. Great men are almost always bad men."

LORD ACTON, 1887

Introduction

Of all the many and various challenges that face contemporary missional leadership, the right use of power clearly stands out as central to our experiences. Whether in the fields of politics, commerce, industry, sport, entertainment, or faith communities, the effects of the misuse of power can easily be demonstrated. This is often related to ethical and moral failures that have informed and exacerbated the situation to produce a world where leadership is not only ineffectual but highly damaging and abusive.

Beasley-Murray provides one of the more recent and well-researched explorations of this issue of power and Christian leadership. Based upon findings conducted within the membership of the Richard Baxter Institute for Ministry, he notes:

> Christian people suffer from a considerable degree of naivety, if not self-inflected blindness. We know that power games are a reality in the world of politics and in the world of business, but we do not want to accept that they are also a reality in the church.

He goes on to remind us:

> It is scarcely an exaggeration to say that within every strand of the New Testament we can find evidence of power struggles affecting the life of God's people. Yet time and again we seem to close our eyes to this underlying reality, and many of us apparently prefer to live with an "ideal" picture of the church.[1]

Parsons further explores this issue within the framework of fundamentalist/Charismatic forms of Christianity within Britain. His work focuses on family values, counseling, occult fears, and other Bible issues that have become a fulcrum for power issues.[2] While not as academic and nuanced as Beasley-Murray, his exploration, primarily through a type of case study, is another reminder that these issues are still very much part of the contemporary church scene. In this chapter, we want to explore this growing challenge of leadership to enable us to identify, inform, understand, and develop approaches that will help us to find better ways of using and thereby not abusing power in our leadership.

Leaders Who Abuse

The Christian church has countless stories of wonderful leaders emulating their master Jesus through humility, generosity, and vulnerability. Sadly this same history equally contains a plethora of personnel who exhibit the style of leadership that creates fear, frustration, and demoralization of those under their care.

The prophet Ezekiel, in the Hebrew Bible, indicates that leadership is to be modeled upon the compassion and care of YHWH, the real shepherd of Israel (34:1–10). This points the way for Peter to express leadership in

1. Beasley-Murray, *Power For God's Sake*, 1–2.
2. Parsons, *Ungodly Fear*, 43–49.

his epistle in terms of an under-shepherd, following the model of Jesus the chief shepherd (1 Peter 5:1–11).

Abusive leadership comes in a variety of forms. Some of the more contemporary practices are often related to expressions of authority.[3] This can be both recognized and unrecognized. Where it is known, the absolute importance of healthy and robust accountability is crucial, and even then this style of leadership can often go unreported or ignored. More often, it is unknown or perhaps unstated until such time that great damage occurs, mostly to very vulnerable people who have sought safety, care, and a loving parental figure or a loving family to engage with.[4]

A significant case study in the UK context in recent years, which hit the national headlines, was the rise and fall of the Nine O'Clock Service in Sheffield (NOS) under the leadership of Chris Brain.[5] This was a radical, emerging, and culturally engaging youth service, which focused on the arts and club scene in the late 1990s. It experienced hundreds of youth regularly queuing up for services at each event. It ultimately and sadly led to the rapid dislocation of these same youth from the church through the ongoing sexual, psychological, social, and theological abuse evidenced within the leadership and its structures.

In recent years, many of the denominations in Britain have undergone the shocking discovery that some of their more trusted leaders have been abusers,[6] more often than not amongst young children.[7] It is often this kind

3. Hahn, *Growing in Authority*, helpfully seeks to explore the issue of authority in a more empowering way.

4. Parsons, *Ungodly Fear*, 282–86. Following a Jungian reading, he identifies the importance of knowing the shadow sides of leadership and urges greater training in theological colleges and universities as well as ongoing input from denominations and networks.

5. Howard, *The Rise and Fall of the Nine O'Clock Service*. A YouTube video additionally explores the rise and fall of this innovative expression of church in youth culture and the effects it has had on various victims. https://www.youtube.com/watch?v=ANRZ_ELqLcE&feature=relmfu (accessed April 16, 2015).

6. Chevous, "Breaking the Silence," 22–25. She notes that in the USA, 20 percent of clergy and priests have been involved in sexual abuse of their parishioners. She also notes in a recent UK study amongst 141 Christian leaders, 21 percent indicated they had been involved in inappropriate sexual behavior. This does not take into account the growing rise of internet pornography amongst Christian leaders.

7. A few of the numerous examples that have come to light in recent years: "Pope begs forgiveness for church sexual abuse," *Telegraph*, 9th July 2014; "Boys Brigade pervert jailed more than 50 years after abusing youngster in Leeds," *Yorkshire Evening Post*, 24th June 2014. It is worth noting that this kind of institutional child sex abuse is not limited

of story that hits the tabloids and adds to the growing mistrust of all those in authority. While inquiries have been undertaken within denominational structures, pressure and support groups have provided the challenge to make this more robust.[8]

What is often less known, or identified, are abusive leadership practices that are often tolerated for years by church members who feel it inappropriate to challenge, question, or raise any concerns. This approach to leadership is usually more subtle,[9] as often the leader is considered to be a great person of faith, or is well versed in the Bible and theology, or has years of experience that causes those on the receiving end to feel inadequate or undermined in raising any challenges to their authority. In a few cases this can be seen to be tantamount to questioning God himself, since the perpetrator is one of God's anointed leaders.[10]

Forbes[11] posits the necessity of understanding the important distinction between power and authority. Power focuses on the leader getting their own way and using others. It is assumed, and often destructive. Authority, on the other hand, is positive and is a right that has been conferred within appropriate boundaries. She notes,

> The exercise of power always implies coercion and violence because the purpose of power is to reproduce itself. Whatever tries to prevent this reproduction must be disposed of. An exercise of authority, however, should have nothing to do with coercion, violence or manipulation. Yet in our zeal for God's work we decide that if someone won't recognise our authority, we will force him with our power.[12]

A good illustration comes from the recent retelling of Tolkien's *Lord of the Rings* trilogy. In director Peter Jackson's film version, the desire for power is seen to be ultimate and creates a drivenness by all who are affected by the influence of the one ring of power. All apparently fall under its spell,

to those in church leadership—it affects all kinds of public positions. Recent media coverage of famous children entertainers is a case in point.

8. One positive response has been key church leaders calling on the government to provide a full public enquiry. Victims and concerned individuals have set up the web site: http://stopchurchchildabuse.co.uk. See also www.oneinfour.org.uk.

9. Forbes, *The Religion of Power*, 81–88. She identifies this as "power through piety."

10. Parsons, *Ungodly Fear*, notes this issue throughout.

11. Ibid., 84.

12. Ibid., 85.

except one lone hobbit, Bilbo Baggins, and his fellowship of friends, who aid him to destroy it. The journey is costly, and not all complete it, but the outcome is the power to choose, to love, to serve, and to overcome through the subversive action of friendship and accountability. Bilbo uses the authority bestowed upon him by the council to eventually fulfill the task, even though he nearly succumbs to the powerful influence of the ring.

While there are clear systems of accountability within many denominations and networks, these are often quite limited. Helping leaders who are affected by these issues is as important as protecting the vulnerable who are often their prey. This is a massive challenge to which all those who work with leaders need to be attentive and seek to provide greater resourcing, support, and discipline as required.

In addition to this, the culture of celebrity is a continuing challenge and feeds the issue of abusive power. The desire for "fifteen minutes of fame"[13] is continually fed through the successful ministries that are paraded on Christian TV, in our conferences (where the largest and best are always given attention), and even the author of the latest books. Jesus, of course, faced this issue head on in the synoptic gospel accounts of his wilderness temptations as well as the ongoing challenges to his leadership. His way of dealing with it was regularly to withdraw and find his identity and acceptance from his father in heaven, rather than from the powers in culture, the crowds, or even his own disciples or family. Jesus regularly practiced self-emptying (the Philippian hymn suggests this clearly in chapter 2:1–11).

Preece, following the contribution of Herrick, draws our attention to this importance of self-emptying as a spiritual discipline.

> Vanessa Herrick, in her Grove booklet, Limits of Vulnerability, explains the importance of self-emptying, particularly in relation to pastoral ministry. This voluntary letting go of power through personal choice liberates the one ministering and the one receiving ministry. It means coming into connection with another human being without a prescriptive agenda. It requires a deep listening and humility that allows the entry into another person's world before we dare suggest direction of movement.[14]

Learning to hold onto all forms of leadership lightly can be a helpful corrective to the sway of identity and ownership. Hengel, reflecting on the

---

13. The frequently alluded to phrase of Andy Warhol. The actual quote is: "In the future everyone will be world famous for fifteen minutes."

14. Preece, *Understanding and Using Power*, 17.

life of Jesus amidst the political and religious power structures of his time, notes that, for Jesus, "true freedom is freedom from the compulsion to assert oneself at all costs . . . The overwhelming disarming power of Jesus' message—then as well as now—lies not least in this fundamental renunciation of external means of exerting power."[15]

A final type of leadership abuse can often occur when those with leadership powers within church structures limit or prohibit others from being recognized or developing their own leadership. While there is greater improvement in opportunities for women within Christian leadership, there are still continuing issues around younger leaders and those from differing cultures or ethnicities than the power brokers of the denomination or network.[16]

These kinds of tensions more often than not develop mistrust, angst for younger, emerging leaders, and provide a display of power that undermines the kind of godly leadership we are ultimately wishing to express. Developing ways of giving permission within helpful boundaries of relationship and authority are more appropriate expressions that in the end foster the growth of trust and multiply leadership for the work of God.

Nouwen, reflecting on the importance of identity in being chosen as "the beloved of God," formulates this approach to enabling others:

> When we claim and constantly reclaim the truth of being the chosen ones, we soon discover within ourselves a deep desire to reveal to others their own chosenness. Instead of making us feel that we are better, more precious or valuable than others, our awareness of being chosen opens our eyes to the chosenness of others. That is the great joy of being chosen: the discovery that others are chosen as well. In the house of God there are many mansions. There is a place for everyone—a unique, special place. Once we deeply trust that we ourselves are precious in God's eyes, we are able to recognize the preciousness of others and their unique places in God's heart.[17]

---

15. Hengel, *Christ and Power,* 18–19.

16. A helpful and important contribution can be found in Lingenfelter, *Leading Cross-Culturally.*

17. Nouwen, *Life of the Beloved,* 52–53.

Abusive Churches

There are occasions where the abuse of power comes not from within the leader *per se*, but rather from toxic church structures with a long history of control and marginalization. There are entire Christian communities that utilize abusive forms of governance and formation. This seems to be more frequent in Free Church denominations that are congregationally organized, but it is equally present in other expressions of the body of Christ. This can, at times, be hard to separate from leadership practices since they are often closely connected.

A colleague informed me that in his native Australia there was a church that was notorious in the local community and its denomination for a very long history of bad incidents in the treatment of its members. Church leaders were equally taken advantage of, and sadly no one seemed to enjoy sharing in its life. The pinnacle was finally reached and the church was closed for a year in order to be restarted with a new set of values, practices, and leadership. One may wonder why this was allowed to continue for so long. Often, ecclesiological structures give authority exclusively to the local church without any strong reference to any other influences. Typically there can be a family or a strong lay leader who is the one that is really in charge, regardless of any other recognized leadership. This creates a hiatus as to how authority is recognized and adhered to within the life and health of the local church. This is such a growing tendency that there are now various online websites providing advice. Moreover, a growing literature demonstrates the worrying proliferation of several forms of dysfunctionality in local churches.[18]

Abusive Theology

Absolute Unquestioning Control

This is perhaps the most common example of abusive theology popular amongst certain expressions of Charismatic and Pentecostal theology, and some minority ethnic forms of leadership. However, it is not unknown amongst Reformed and other highly structured forms of ecclesiology. Often, such unquestioned authority is related to a more fundamentalist

---

18. Redeger, *Clergy Killers*; Greenfield, *The Wounded Minister*; Davis, *Healing a Wounded Leader*.

theology and, ultimately, it becomes so unquestioned and absolute as to amounting to playing God.[19]

The real danger in this expression of leadership is the assumed and implied authority found within the leader themselves, or in their interpretation of the Bible. It was this kind of abuse (as well as the fear of it) to which some of the Reformers took exception and against which they set up the sole authority of the Bible as protection. They did not consider that, as more and more Bibles became available through the introduction of the printing press, a vacuum of interpretation, now solely based on the individual reader, would be created. With the rise of the plethora of new denominations, the potential scale of abuse also increased so that any power-driven person could set up their own authoritative framework and thereby achieve more power to abuse others with whom they disagreed. This is especially true for the Anabaptists who found themselves at the receiving end of abuse from both Rome and Geneva. There are some expressions of this theology that assume that asking questions is tantamount to unbelief. This, of course, presents a significant challenge in a Western context, where critical thinking and questioning are part and parcel of the culture of most people. Ethnic minority churches in a European context are soon confronted by a different mindset to their accustomed understanding of authority thereby create a polarizing framework of a "do as I say/teach or depart" model of leadership.

Power and the Demonic

This second form of abusive theology has become prevalent within wider British and European culture. Social workers in the UK are now trained to understand this phenomenon and to provide a context in engaging with faith communities who regularly practice this type of ministry, especially with underaged children.[20] Of course, this is not purely a minority ethnic issue. Once again, mainly within Pentecostal and Charismatic Christian communities (and Jewish and Muslim as well), there are clear examples

---

19. Haon, "Identifying Leadership Power Abuse and its Prevention in the Local Church," 107–8.

20. HM Government, "Safeguarding Children from Abuse Linked to a Belief in Spirit Possession," http://webarchive.nationalarchives.gov.uk/20130401151715/http://www.education.gov.uk/publications/eOrderingDownload/DFES-00465-2007.pdf (accessed 1 June 2015).

of power abuse. The recent conduct of the American TV faith healer Todd Bentley demonstrates that this approach and understanding is still widely evident amongst certain persuasions of the faith-based community and is a significant expression of their theology.

The challenge here is to note that this expression of ministry can and does have a valid expression as a form of gospel engagement. All the authors have had some experience in this type of ministry. What needs to be noted is where the undergirding theological framework creates and perhaps distils an unhealthy focus on methodology that produces potential and real dangers. In some circles, the author has noted that the focus on the demonic seems to be the central issue, rather than a more holistic expression that includes this explanatory framework among others.

Degradation of Gender, Ethnicity, and Class

Another significant area of potentially abusive theology is where those who are "other" than us are demeaned through the leader's use of language, education, position, or influence, based upon certain theological understandings. This has historically been particularly experienced within the context of class, ethnicity, and human sexuality and is especially noteworthy in relationship to the ways in which expressions of communication are related to through expressions of fellowship within the Christian community. Drawing on the challenges raised by Foucault around power and communication, Kearsley notes,

> This means that its circulation of communication reflects its power relations and their associated power patterns. Hence the widely varying influence on channels of communication often mirrors forms of inequality in a group, such as class, upbringing, gender, ethnicity, knowledge, age, confidence or wealth etc. Even a fairly monochrome social group contains this economic and cultural diversity, revealing varying backgrounds and fortunes with their consequent 'asymmetries' or imbalances. As a result of those disparities, experiences of communication most likely would vary.[21]

There is a long history of the marginalization of women in forms of leadership and mission, and yet within some areas of Christian mission it is the women who are the ones that have been the real pioneers. This has not

21. Kearsley, *Church, Community and Power*, 93.

been a key issue in some denominations,[22] but most Western expressions have found that the contribution of women, while important, has been at the least limited on the grounds of gender. While the issue of women and leadership can be a debatable issue from history, exegesis, and tradition, it is important to note that dismissive expressions of power simply due to one's biological makeup is a limiting theology, and thereby an expression of one form of power abuse.

The history of apartheid in South Africa was at least partially based upon the theological tenets of a type of Calvinistic reading of Scripture that disempowered native Africans from even being considered eligible for salvation and church membership, let alone leadership, thereby creating a divide between white and black, not only culturally but spiritually. This approach can be seen in various other cultures as well. With the rise of reverse mission, whereby receiving nations of Western Christian mission are now bringing mission back to the West, this same approach can be witnessed. The challenge of creating multicultural churches and leadership is huge, but within the new Europe that is beginning to emerge it is necessary one.[23]

A final consideration is related to the issue of class, and one's place in society. While some might suggest this is no longer a genuine concern it is noteworthy, in Britain at least, that few churches are intentionally pioneered amongst the white working classes, which by and large are still mostly unaffected by the gospel.[24] It is perhaps even more noteworthy in places like India where caste and class divisions are more clearly understood to be part of the social structure.

Often, leaders bring their class distinctions into poorer working class areas, creating difficulties around the exercise of power and a consequent lack of empowerment. Historically these were perhaps more clearly defined, but they can continue to be expressed in more subtle ways. For some denominations, middle-class values are assumed and generated in choosing recognized leaders as evidenced in education, dress, styles, and approaches to leadership practices. This may lead to power issues where others are seeking leadership recognition without forms or structures that support other inherent sets of values. This kind of subtlety can prevent new leadership emerging since it is not the recognized norm.

---

22. Most notably many Pentecostal denominations.

23. Hardy and Yarnell, *Forming Multicultural Partnerships*, chapter 1.

24. Gamble, *The Irrelevant Church.*, is one key text that seeks to address this head on.

Deconstructing and Enabling the
Subversive Element of Power

In seeking to provide some signposts to enable healthy expressions of leadership and right use of power, some potential forms of protection and safety need to be considered. The factors noted below suggest ways one might create and explore a system of responsible working practices that would encourage good and trusted leadership in the right use of power and authority.

Honest Accountability

Real use of power should always be invested authority. In some denominations this is more clearly expressed than in those that are more independent. Self-awareness and self-discipline are vitally important, but the likelihood of self-deception is always present. Having an intentional mentor, a close friend or ministry colleague, one's spouse as well as a healthy support structure will be some of the tools that will enable a safer environment to explore the expression of leadership.

Far too often, it is the very expression of contemporary Christian leadership that can create the seedbed of moral failure. By this I mean the fact that far too much leadership can be expressed in isolation, thereby unknowingly nurturing an environment of loneliness. Many of the moral failures have this as a part of their root cause. Devenish observes,

> One of the sad factors of church life, however, is that many pastors are lonely. Although some pride themselves on their independence, many long for accountable relationships. In particular, their heart cry is for a fathering style of relationship, where they can be cared for pastorally as well as mentored in the development of spiritual gifts and practical skills for their ministry. This is accountability, not within a formal structure but within the context of loving friendship.[25]

Even with all of this, I have known leaders who have still failed morally, ethically, and spiritually by abusing others. We cannot underestimate the kind of temptations that affect those in spiritual leadership. That being said, leadership and power is also a position of trust, once that trust

---

25. Devenish, *Fathering Leaders*, 11.

is broken, as in the example of the Nine O'Clock Service in Sheffield, the effects on countless human lives can be devastating.

Clear Protocols

One helpful framework emerging in recent years has been the safeguarding agencies and policies around child protection. These have ensured that, at the very least, there are some reasoned and recognized strategies seeking to provide a safe environment for vulnerable children within the care of the Christian community. There is equally much work to be done with vulnerable adults and other marginalized people under church ministry and leadership. New initiatives are being explored, which, as with children, will provide a potentially safer environment and good working practices.[26]

In the same way, leaders need to identify and seek to follow clear personal and professional protocols that are appropriate for their own communities and spheres of influence. This means not only a sensitivity to their cultural environment, but also setting in place some frameworks that indicate how they will operate in varying situations.

It is also good practice to clearly state these in advance and make them publically known so that relationships are kept intact. It will then become clear if the protocols are breached, thereby limiting any collateral damage. Often this may mean working with a gender mixed team and not on one's own. This provides a model of support and compassion while at the same time keeping each other in check.

Good Use of Authority

It was noted above that one form of power is spiritual elitism that arises when senior leaders have more experience, especially in interpreting the Bible, which creates its own form of power that can lead to abuse. This relates to the use of authority and finding good and helpful expressions in its use.

With reference to faith documents, such as the Bible or other kinds of denominational creeds or statements, clear teaching and information is needed for all leaders and members. Too often people can be hoodwinked

---

26. One important initiative in the UK is the enabling church movement sponsored by churches for all (www.churchesforall.org.uk).

because they are misinformed or even at times deliberately kept in the dark about key issues or are denied formative teaching. Encouraging other voices than just the lone pastor/priest also brings some helpful corrective. There is a need for robust and intentional discipleship whereby we teach and empower others to take on responsibility for their own learning.

Further danger of misuse of authority may also result from the authority of office or positional leadership. The named leader and the title that goes with it (apostle, bishop, vicar, priest, pastor, leader, teacher, youth worker, etc.) can bring an assumed authoritative form of leadership. While common in some traditions and cultures, this approach can carry with it elements of non-accountability, misuse of power, and rationalizations of expressions that would not be tolerated in other work environments. This does not mean that titles are worthless, but that they need to reflect the nature of the work more than the position of the person who is invested with the title.

In his day, the apostle Paul presented us with some sound warnings against his adversaries as he pointed to the responsibilities accompanying his own position of leadership. In 2 Corinthians 11:22–33 he intentionally notes a long list of challenges that he personally faced in fulfilling the role of leadership. These include imprisonments, beatings, and floggings, stoning, being shipwrecked, sleepless nights, and dangers from within the religious communities and dangers without, as well as his daily concerns for the churches. Those who seek to invest in positional leadership would do well to reflect on this list and see how they relate to these experiences of authentic leadership.

Robust Forms of Correction

Because of its nature, the regular use of power will inevitably cause struggles for those who wield it and sadly there will be failings. Often leaders can be trapped into the coercive use of power and need correctives to challenge, rebuke, and restore them to right practices. Within some structures there will be leaders in more senior positions who will hold some form of accountability responsibility that will address the failings as they occur. Others will need to find alternative ways of seeking to stay alert and find assistance if the proper use of authority is violated. The challenge is for leaders as individuals to allow others to provide the needed corrective input into their lives. Often when leaders fail, such precautions have been missing or have only been observed in the breach.

It is worth noting that some of the necessary correction is not just about personal misuse of power. Inadequate and unhelpful theologies, as noted above and throughout this book, generate a context that creates unhealthy dependence on a leader, or produce an environment where toxic forms of abuse can flourish. While we need to remember that we are all flawed creatures whom God is renewing, our thinking and subsequent actions reflect our core theological beliefs, especially in reference to power and the powers.

Dawn, writing in reference to the demythologizing approach of Bultmann to the language of the powers, and the noted limitations of Wink's contributions, observes,

> My concern in these chapters is for Christians to estimate rightly the capacities of the powers so that they do not lead us and our churches astray. It is also essential that we recognise that each church—as one of the created powers—constantly wrestles with its own fallenness and often fails to live by the power of the Holy Spirit in genuine fulfilment of its true vocation.[27]

Not just believing everything we hear or read or are told is a healthy approach to our thinking and development of theology and practices. Seeking to continue to learn through key forms of input will also keep us abreast of crucial issues as well as providing another form of development and engagement with power that may work as a corrective.

Note the Danger Signs

Power rarely becomes dangerous without first exhibiting some signs of development. Most failures did not begin from intentional harm, but gradually grew and morphed into something devious and destructive. Here are some potential warning signs that power is beginning to be misused.

Demanding Leadership

Any form of the use of power in leadership will require some form of demands. When the leader's identity or role in using power is harnessed to

27. Dawn, *Power, Weakness and the Tabernacling of God*, 22–23.

create a culture that demands to be obeyed or followed this often ultimately leads to abuse. This is especially difficult where leadership is attained through the exercise of charismatic personality since the open and exuberant nature of this person will carry others along.

Self-Deception

Those who regularly exercise leadership over others must be aware of the dangers of the personality cult. Soon we are noted, respected, and followed because of who people think we are or what we can do for them. Ego demands can soon cause us to begin to believe we are more important and more needed than we really are. This can easily lead to self-deception and the adoption of a Messiah-complex leading us to believe we are brought in to save the situation. The temptations are subtle and can be frightening; this is often where a good leader suddenly goes wrong.

Dysfunctionality

Since no leader is fully mature and whole, there will often be elements of unmet needs where acceptance and approval are being sought. This creates a challenging dilemma in discerning the right use of power. Abuses can often be traced back to forms of personal dysfunctionality that create a tendency to abusive leadership. Psychological, physical, social, and even spiritual dysfunctions all add to complexity in the use of power. This is not only relevant to leadership, since many Christian faith communities can also, as we have already noted, embody forms of dysfunction that may lead to corporate abuse.

Recognizing the Shadow Side of Leadership

One corrective that can be employed is in understanding the Jungian approach to our shadow sides. This relates to our personalities, our preferences, and our actions. Some of the personality indicators, such as Myers-Briggs, that are often used by business, education, and increasingly in faith communities provide one kind of engagement with an understanding of this corollary. Many training colleges are making more use of these kind of tools to enable developing leadership to understand more about their preferences and how these can be both an aid and a potential obstacle in leadership and the exercise of power.

Parsons makes the plea that more could and needs to be done in early stages of training new ordinands in leadership. He suggests,

> For a start, power issues could be far more openly acknowledged in the training colleges for clergy and ministers. In Jungian terms, ordinands need to be taught to enter their own personal wilderness, meet their personal shadow and befriend it. Like Jesus, they have to own up to their temptation to exercise power wrongly before it can be transcended and avoided. Ordinands and trainee ministers need to realise that it is not surprising to have within the psyche such a mixed-up motivation, but training should help them to identify it and not allow it to be acted out.[28]

Of course, not all power is bad. Foster notes that, while real destructive forces may be unleashed by power, destroying relationships, communities, and cultures, it can also have the effect of being a great, creative, healing force for good. In the context of reflecting on its use by William Wilberforce and his tireless campaign to end slavery, he states,

> The power that creates gives life and joy and peace. It is freedom and not bondage, life and not death, transformation and not coercion. The power that creates restores relationship and gives the gift of wholeness to all. The power that creates is a spiritual power, the power that proceeds from God.[29]

In the life of Jesus, we see a healthy corrective as he deals with all kinds of issues that surround power as he seeks to transmit some of the values of the kingdom and its approach to power and leadership to his disciples. As he is confronted with issues of infighting, pettiness, position, and potential abuse, he says this:

> When the ten heard it, they were angry with the two brothers. But Jesus called them to him and said, "You know that the rulers of the Gentiles lord it over them, and their great ones are tyrants over them. It will not be so among you; but whoever wishes to be great among you must be your servant, and whoever wishes to be first among you must be your slave; just as the Son of Man came not to be served but to serve, and to give his life a ransom for many." (Matt 20:25)

28. Parsons, *Ungodly Fear*, 285.
29. Foster, *The Challenge of the Disciplined Life*, 196.

Van Gelder reminds us, "They [Christians leaders] are called to a lifestyle of suffering service that is willing to let the power of powerlessness unmask the principalities and powers that have already been defeated through Christ's death and resurrection (Col 2:15)."[30]

Here is perhaps the best approach to the use of power. To deconstruct it along the lines of a kingdom ethic that denotes the upside-down values of the followers of Jesus. We all will make use of power in our lives and leadership. The question that remains is how will we therefore live with it? Will it enslave and ensnare us in fulfilling our leadership thus letting it destroy us, or will we allow this great gift of God to be a creative tool for the coming kingdom? The jury is out, but we are the entrusted bearers and change agents of the kingdom for our generation.[31]

30. Van Gelder, "Defining the Issues Related to Power and Authority in Religious Leadership," 13–14.

31. A recent and helpful book on good use of power as a leader is Walker, *The Undefended Leader*.

10

Incarnational Missional Community: Transforming the Use of Power in Society

Richard Whitehouse

Incarnational Community: The Church for Itself?

The church currently finds itself in a different situation from any that it has experienced over the past five-hundred years. We stand at the cusp of a new paradigm of church and mission brought on by seismic changes in society as a whole and in the church's relationship with the rest of society. In his book *Missional Map-making* Alan Roxburgh charts some of these changes and compares them with changes in information technology and the way it has both grown exponentially and at the same time altered patterns of decision making while spearheading the direction of change in society.[1] The problem in terms of the church's mission is that, in the face of social change, we have continued to do things the way we always have on the mistaken assumption that working harder on the same agenda will deliver better results while ignoring the aphorism that digging harder in the same hole only produces a deeper hole. As Roxburgh observes, the church in general has responded to social change by seeking to improve its programs and training both of which are aimed at serving the church in an effort to make it more effective in meeting the needs of its members while, apart

1. Roxburgh, *Missional Map-making*, 3–10.

from occasionally sallying forth in evangelistic outreaches or short term mission, largely ignoring what is happening in the wider world.

Michael Frost, along with a host of other commentators, concurs with Roxburgh in pointing out that the church's focus has largely been upon finding ways to increase and maintain membership and, in doing so, has become "a market-shaped church."[2] The focus is on producing religious goods and services designed to recruit and retain members, yet at the same time the church is losing traction with the rest of the world and so, even from a marketing point of view, its appeal is shrinking. As Frost comments, "If the institutional church is the only doorway to experiencing the reign of God, we are in an increasingly tenuous position as institutional religion loses its grip on society."[3] In an earlier work Roxburgh speaks of the church transitioning from a creative and innovative "emergent zone" and giving way to a "performative zone" where it hones skills and capacities developed in the emergent era. The problem is that in this performative zone:

> The organizational culture focuses on performing well what has been learned and proven to work. The primary values are not in-novation but skilled performance of a regular pattern of habits and actions. A performative zone congregation grows not through connecting with the people in its context but through people switching from other congregations. A good performative culture is creative; it thrives but increasingly lives off capital that was built in the emergent zone. Performative congregations and leaders have been the dominant form of organizational culture for North American churches throughout the twentieth century.[4]

This has also been true for the few growing churches in Europe where the social milieu is different, but, nevertheless, the church's response there has been much the same. One response to the changing social context of the church has been to reexamine its nature and purpose. Thus debate about both Christology and ecclesiology has been high on the theological agenda in recent years. Among these responses was Hauerwas and Willimon's *Resident Aliens*, which posits that the church is called to be a countercultural remedy to the stance of the world providing an alternative perspective by which the world may be judged and held to account.[5] In

2. Frost, *The Road to Missional*, 63.

3. Ibid., 67.

4. Roxburgh and Romanuk, *The Missional Leader*, 45.

5. Hauwerwas and Willimon, *Resident Aliens*. Cf. also Hauwerwas and Willimon,

their view, rather than trying to reform society or to offer political solu-
tions the church is meant to focus on developing Christian life and community so as to offer an alternative set of ethics. Since Hauwerwas was then
a Methodist theologian-ethicist teaching in a Catholic University theology
department it is not too surprising that he would characterize himself as
"a high church Mennonite"! This stance seems to fit into Niebuhr's "Christ
against culture" categorization, although the approach of *Resident Aliens* is
somewhat more nuanced than this would suggest. However, in terms of a
missional approach to engagement with the world the classification of the
church as resident aliens is inadequate. The fact that the church is resident
suggests continuity and even longevity while labelling it as "alien" flags up
the church's role in questioning the world's values and even as a prophetic
pointer to an alternative future, but it falls short of engagement that offers
a listening ear and the possibility of transformation. The one great gain in
their approach lies in the fact that it rejects the psychological nurturing
role of the church, which panders to individualistic emotional and spiritual
needs in favor of a vision of the church as a colony, a holy nation a family
"standing for sharply focused values in a devalued world." This has the benefit of drawing attention to the corporate nature of salvation and spiritual
nurture away from a post-Enlightenment individualism.

Nevertheless, something more is required and an increasingly popular
alternative model of the church that is frequently proposed is that of incarnational ministry. Darrell Guder has been leading the charge on this for
several decades. In his short book *The Incarnation and the Church's Witness*
he states that mission is the church's primary calling and that in order to
fulfill this it needs to incarnate Christ's presence in the world:

> If Christ's calling defines the church's purpose, and if the called
> community is to incarnate the good news, then, to put it bluntly,
> neither the institution's existence nor its maintenance is to be its
> priority. . . . The problem is not *that* the church is institutional,
> but *how* it is institutional. . . . Is our communal institutional life
> an embodiment of the good news? Does the way we live, decide,
> spend money and make decisions as organizations reveal both the
> character and purposes of God for humanity?[6]

Roxburgh and Romanuk state that, in spite of the fact that congregational life is written off by many as hopelessly compromised by the spirit

---

Where Resident Aliens Live.

6. Guder, *The Incarnation and the Church's Witness*, 24–25.

of the world in which we live, "[t]hrough the Incarnation, we discover that God's future is at work not where we tend to look but among the people we write off as dead or powerless to make things different."[7]

This notion of the church as an incarnational community is based on the idea that just as God revealed himself concretely in history through the birth and life of Christ so his people can also embody the gospel through flesh and blood presence in the world that makes Christ real to outside observers. In some versions of this vision it is felt that incarnational presence is first and foremost for the benefit of God's people as an incarnational community. This is the line taken by Peter Holmes who seeks to form therapeutic communities of Christ's presence. Holmes grounds this incarnational approach to community wholeness in the relational character of the Trinity as a whole commenting that this runs counter to the way the church was formed in the Christendom era. He says that, "in looking at Augustine of Hippo we are near the beginning of the era when the Church was being conceived as an Institution, mediating grace to the individual, rather than as a community formed on the analogy of the Trinity's *interpersonal* relationships."[8] Beginning from the notion of the church as a relational community modeled on the social Trinity, which brings renewal to the wider community through the presence of God, Holmes seeks to visualize:

> a divine community and a redeemed people, living within a renewed community, enjoying the presence of their God. Such a community is the life of Christ on earth, having a *Theocentric heart*, where God speaks to each personally, while actively and manifestly dwelling among them corporately.[9]

This raises the question, How is the church as an incarnational community to effectively mediate the presence of Christ in the world?

The Church in the World

Todd Billings contests the whole notion of incarnational ministry seeing it as a false path. Billings concedes that key points in his own life as a missionary were shaped by this new approach to ministry and he admits:

---

7. Roxburgh and Romanuk, *Missional Leadership*, 9.

8. Holmes, *Becoming More Human*, 41.

9. Ibid., 191.

The incarnational ministry model challenged me to take my own
identification with the culture very seriously—including how I
lived, the language I spoke, and the relationships I formed. There
is something extremely appealing about this relatively new way of
conceiving ministry—as imitating the act of incarnation, in which
God came close to us in Christ.[10]

Nevertheless, as a missionary-turned-academic he identifies practical
theological problems in applying this notion and he rejects it as impossible to harness in practice. The missionary, or individual Christian in the
world "can find it impossible, practically speaking to become 'one' with the
people they are ministering to. Indeed, the goal itself can easily seem to be
an illusion."[11] Further, Billings alleges that, since no Christian can become
Christ, they cannot truly identify either with Christ or with the people with
whom they are seeking to relate. He questions whether identification with
the culture should become an end in itself as if Christian presence rather
than the presence of Christ can become redemptive. He comments: "This
kind of thinking can easily slip into individualistic attempts to 'make Christ
incarnate' in the world as opposed to participating in a worshipping community that is empowered for ministry."[12] Billings's critique may point to a
misunderstanding of what is intended by most advocates of incarnational
ministry—and one that is to be avoided—but it remains true that the idea
of embodying Christian truth as lived out experience is a vital means of
making Christ real to a watching world.

In an earlier work Frost and Hirsch borrowed the term "liminality"
from field anthropology,[13] a term which has been picked up by Roxburgh
and others. It describes a state of transition from a known, tried, and tested
context to one of uncertainty where many of the markers are removed and
previously assumed realities are called into question. In such contexts previous guidelines for conduct and successful existence are no longer com-
pelling. Liminality best characterizes the situation of post-Christendom
church in a postmodern context and gives rise to the search for new ways
of moving forward in relation to its mission to the rest of the world. In a
later work Frost and Hirsch point out that "mission is one of the elements

10. Billings, *Union With Christ*, 125.

11. Ibid.

12. Ibid., 126.

13. Frost and Hirsch, *The Shaping of Things to Come*, 125; Billings, *Union With Christ*,
125.

of liminality" and that "mission, by its very nature creates the conditions of liminality."[14] They go on to point out that both church and mission always take place in a liminal context since God's kingdom, of which both are a part, is inaugurated but yet to be fulfilled, and they conclude, "By its very nature, then, mission (especially evangelistic mission) is a liminal activity. It sits between what is and what is to come."[15] For them mission is a risky venture calling the church to love and serve others as a demonstration of God's reign.

What all of this suggests is that the church is meant to become an incarnational community not for its own sake, but for the sake of the world. Greene and Robinson call the church to create a missional narrative. They say that the ecumenical movement missed the point in the 60s through to the 80s when it saw mission purely as God at work in the world that people should join. Although charismatic renewal, on the other hand, seemed to promise the possibility of a retelling of the Christian story, a reconnection with the power of primitive Christianity it, too, missed the way since:

> What was required was neither a renewalist theology that sought only to renew the institution of the church, nor a secular theology that called the church into the world. What was required was a public theology of radical cultural engagement that called the church to be constituted not for itself, nor even for the world in an abstract sense, but towards the remaking of human communities as deeply incarnational expressions of the church in mission.[16]

This means that in order to become truly incarnational and to engage with the world it is necessary for the church to reinvent itself and to reexamine its practices and its language, not least its formative stories and their relevance to, and transforming possibilities for, society as a whole. As Greene and Robinson comment:

> The distinctiveness of the church lies not in its life as an institution but in its founding story that calls the church to repentance just as it simultaneously calls the word to a new vision of its future. To truly engage the host culture the church has to learn how both to indwell that narrative and to reconfigure it around the key issues that the culture must see and hear for its own salvation.[17]

14. Frost and Hirsch *The Shaping of Things to Come*, 39.

15. Frost and Hirsch, *The Faith of Leap*, 39

16. Greene and Robinson, *Metavista*, 188.

17. Ibid., 189.

In order to be effective in its mission the church needs to learn to listen to the people it seeks to serve. For too long we have been saying "Jesus is the answer—what is your question?" instead of seriously engaging with the concerns of society at large. In order to meet needs we first have to discern what those needs are and consider how they can best be met. It is vital to exegete the community before we even begin to attempt a relevant exegesis of Scripture. Cultural exegesis comes before textual exegesis if, as Newbigin urged long ago, the church is to become the hermeneutic of the gospel.[18] In the process, we need to arrive at contextual local theologies rather than generic catch-all explanations as we attempt to forge links between God and human need. We have already examined Robert Schreiter's advocacy of local theologies in chapter 5 pointing to the fact that the complexities of postmodern culture create new questions to be addressed and demand new approaches to meeting them. This is a process which will not be easily or quickly solved but we have suggested that one attempt to address these issues is found in the New Monasticism and is echoed in many forms of emerging church, which seek to live out a disciplined life in small units within the community in order both to relate to it more easily and to demonstrate an alternative way of living. This way of living may be as necessary for the church as for the wider community that it seeks to address. A research paper for California State University points to the influence of Robert Bellah's book *Habits of the Heart*[19] that refers to the cancerous toxicity of American individualism, which employs utilitarian measures such as self-actualization, self-satisfaction, and self-expression to evaluate marriages, family life, careers, education, public institutions, and churches. The report concludes that Bellah's analysis has influenced New Monasticism, provoking a counter-movement that rejects individualism and privatized faith.

> Unlike the majority of evangelical churches who cater to the individualistic sensibilities of its parishioners, New Monasticism is marked by a pronounced religious communalism. The emphasis is decidedly on the impact that religious involvement has on the group and society at large.[20]

In his survey of the literature that has grown up around the New Monastic movement Erik Carter mentions the influence of The Confessional

18. Newbigin, *The Gospel in a Pluralist Society*, especially chapter 18.

19. Bellah et al., *Habits of the Heart*.

20. Lowitzki and Kim, "New Monasticism."

Church's reaction to Nazi incorporation of the church and Bonhoeffer's response in *Life Together*[21] and goes on to note the connection between it and the emergent church movement. Luther Smith surveys sixty-eight intentional communities of both types seeing them as catalysts for change in the world but, as Carter observes, "intentional Christian communities are, in essence, modest proposals for the few prepared to commit." Nevertheless, they may have a ripple effect, since "[t]hose not poised to join are more likely to be persuaded by those whose faith is accompanied by action, and whose life is oriented around one's neighbour and characterized by a passion for God not just by a social justice issue."[22] Smith avers, "Radical discipleship occurs through the invitation to see the word made flesh."[23]

Of course, as other commentators have observed, the New Monasticism is not monastic in the strict sense at all but, like the original monastic movement of the third century onwards, is a protest against an effete church that has, to a large extent, capitulated to the values of the dominant society. In doing so, it also contributes toward a thrust to mission that does not focus merely upon congregational expansion but, rather, on the ideals of the kingdom of God. In the process, it concentrates not so much on programs or even structures as on a way of living that forms disciples whose focal point is outwards toward engagement with the world. As such it has affinities with other mission-minded movements throughout church history. In his survey of New Monasticism Tim Muldoon observes:

> The common feature is that new monasticism seeks to share with these other movements a radical discipleship, in the sense of eschewing participation in the structural/social sins endemic in contemporary American life: not only racism, but also individualism, economic disparity, and participation in war-making.[24]

Convergence on the issue of discipleship is shared by monastic and emergent movements as well as by Dallas Willard and Richard Foster's Renovare initiative. Willard's classic work *The Divine Conspiracy*[25] called attention to the gospel as a call to discipleship. In it, he trenchantly insisted that salvation is a way of life in opposition to what he characterizes as the "gospel of sin management" (repent once as a guarantee of heaven when

21. Carter, "The New Monasticism: A Literary Introduction," 271.

22. Ibid., 279.

23. Smith, *Intimacy and Mission*, quoted by ibid.

24. Muldoon, Review of *The New Monasticism*, 124.

25. Willard, *The Divine Conspiracy*.

you die) that is the staple presentation of fundamentalist evangelicalism. His contribution, along with the thought of Newbigin, has been a catalyst for current attitudes to discipleship as a way of life, not as a diploma lecture course or "how to" manual but as an alternative way of living that acts as a sign and foretaste of the kingdom of God.

How then in the light of such a deconstructed approach to church, is mission to be realized relationally in the world? Swart and colleagues argue for a view of mission as participation both in God and the world. They argue that "participation is characteristic of the overall biblical narrative"[26] and, furthermore, suggest that participation is essentially an expression of the Trinitarian nature of the godhead. Following Moltmann they affirm that "God is self-communicating love. Love requires self-giving reciprocity both within the life of God and in salvation history"[27] and with Ziziuoulas, from an Orthodox point of view, that "the real gap between God and the world is bridged in and through the Incarnation."[28] In developing a Trinitarian and eschatological account of the doctrine of creation Swart and his colleagues suggest that God maintains communion with his creation through a reciprocal relationship with the world and he calls the church to participate in this process:

> In *ongoing* creative work in the world, God calls forth in Christ and through the Spirit a new humanity, the church, whose participation in the life of the triune God and the world is the social embodiment of *missio Dei*. This view of mission as participation is characterized by the tensions of history and eschatology, life in creation and life in Christ, openness to God and openness to the world. Because the church in *missio Dei* is constituted by participation with the triune God and the world, the missional church cannot see the world or culture as extrinsic to its own life. The missional church comprehends its embeddedness in the world and culture and receives its identity in God's work of new creation begun in the Incarnation, culminating in the cross and resurrection, and continued in the transforming work of the Spirit.[29]

This rather long quotation carries profound significance for our understanding of the church's conduct of mission, placing it within a

26. Swart et al., "Toward a Missional Theology of Participation," 78.

27. Ibid., 80

28. Ibid., 85

29. Ibid.

thoroughly biblical and theological framework. The authors go on to speak of God's hospitality in terms of his indwelling of believers through the work of Christ as a model for our involvement in the world as we offer hospitality to it. They say, "As the church receives the hospitality of the triune God, the church socially embodies God's hospitality in its proclamation, worship, fellowship, service and willingness to suffer."[30] All of this calls for discernment as we respond to the word of God and trace God's activity as he moves ahead of us; discernment as participation in the world requires an evangelical conversation: "Such an open ended image of communal discernment," they say, "leads naturally to the understanding of mission as 'prophetic-dialogue.'"[31] This entails listening to the world in order to be able to answer its questions.

It would take a long time to flesh this out in practice—indeed, this could take the form of a further volume—but, for now, we will move on to consider the implications such an analysis entails for reciprocal relationships as we seek to conduct mission in the world. The liminal context in which we currently find ourselves demands a new vocabulary that will enable a fresh approach to mission in the world and the way in which, from an incarnational standpoint, the church confronts the powers that dominate the world as a whole and the individual societies in which we move and to which we are asked to relate. Alan Roxburgh notes that this is not the first time that the church has been asked to make such a cultural shift in order to make the gospel relevant to shifting ground. He believes that the key to missional church lies at local neighborhood level and he asks, "How will we indwell both the gospel and the people in neighbourhoods where we live and work so that we hear God speak to us in and through them?"[32] Note the change of emphasis from speaking to listening—a theme to which we will return later. In the meantime, Roxburgh observes that the first-century church entered just such a crisis when its eschatological expectations were not immediately met. He maintains that Luke launched his two-volume work of Luke-Acts in order to change the discourse. Roxburgh utilizes the concept of "language-houses"—by which he means universes of discourse encompassing vocabulary and the stories we tell—in order to explain Luke's strategy. He suggests that Luke changed the "language-house" for Mediterranean Christian communities who faced a crisis of identity by telling a

---

30. Ibid.

31. Ibid., 86.

32. Roxburgh, *Missional: Joining God in the Neighborhood*, 48

different story. He says, "They were asking fundamental questions about who they were and what it meant to be Christians in the midst of this empire." The crisis they were confronting "was characterized by a fundamental questioning of the nature of God's mission in the world, the meaning of what had been taken for granted as the self-evident nature of the gospel, and unfulfilled eschatological hope."[33] The questions they were asking were:

1) What's gone wrong?

2) What is God up to in the world?

3) What then does it mean to be the church in this new space?

Roxburgh proposes that "these are precisely the questions that lie just under the surface for a North American [and European] church still lost in a monologue about its own health, effectiveness, style, growth, and future."[34] With their eschatological expectations dashed the early church needed to regroup and Luke helped the process by retheologizing their vocabulary by telling a different story. As Roxburgh puts it:

> Luke turns his attention to these questions because he understands that until these small communities can discover a different narrative, a different way of understanding what God was about in Jesus, they would be stuck in these other narratives and, therefore, unable to enter the new space of Christian life that had emerged by the end of the first century.[35]

Roxburgh suggests that Luke's retheologizing provides an example for the church in the West today, which is asking the same questions. He asks:

> What if the life-giving Spirit is saying to us that nothing has gone wrong but that he is breaking apart the five-hundred-year-old boxes in which we have so conveniently placed the movement of God since the European Protestant reformations? What if the period we are in is another of those times when the boundary-breaking Spirit is pushing apart the settled, managed, and controlled ecclesiologies that came out of a specific period of European history with its nation-states and the emergence of its hegemony over all of the world? What if the great shifts of global populations,

33. Ibid., 93.

34. Ibid., 101.

35. Ibid.

which have changed the face of continents, are all elements of this boundary-breaking work of the Spirit?[36]

Finally he closes this argument by issuing a challenge to the church in the West:

> If you want to discover what God is up to in the world just now, stop trying to answer this question from within the walls of your churches. Like strangers in need of hospitality who have left their baggage behind, enter the neighbourhoods and communities where you live. Sit at the table of the other, and there you may begin to hear what God is doing.[37]

It is to this issue of addressing the reciprocal nature of power and decision making within and beyond the church that we must turn if we are to understand the balance of power in the public square and ways in which the church can become a partner engaging in the dialogue that takes place there. Central to this process are the arts of hospitality and of listening; before we can advise or even venture an opinion it is crucial for the church to become part of the debate. The dominant powers on the public square can only be confronted through engagement rather than sniping from the sidelines, offering critiques and remedies that are not even couched in language that is understood there.

Shift of Power: How to Engage in the Debate

In a practical paper on community-based ministry written from an Adventist perspective Gaspar Colon suggests the ministry of Jesus as a model for bringing the influence of the kingdom of heaven to bear on the communities that we try to reach. He asks,

> Is the church, as the body of Christ, content to live on the sidelines as passive victims of the entropy of humanism and its resulting post-Christianity? Does the church even perceive itself as an incarnational entity through which Christ showers his blessings to a world filled with self-centeredness, suffering, and pain? Does the church strive to earn social capital and trust by reflecting the ministry of Jesus?[38]

36. Ibid., 114.

37. Ibid.

38. Colon, "Incarnational Community: A Leadership Model for Community

In asking these questions Colon implies that incarnational ministry is not a matter of seeking to *be* Christ so much as to imitate his approach to touching the lives of people and his reference to social capital suggests that the Christian community has something to offer to society as a whole. The concept of social capital is drawn from *Bowling Alone*, Robert Putman's classic study of contemporary American life that highlights the increasingly privatized nature of personal experience. Robin Gill points out that a gradual shift from public worship to privatized spirituality and a corresponding shift away from religious and civil forms of marriage as well as from political membership are indicators of a diminution of social capital.[39] But what is meant by "social capital"? Putman defines it in this way

> By analogy with notions of physical capital and human capital— tools and training that enhance individual productivity- the core idea of social capital theory is that social networks have value. Just as the screwdriver (physical capital) or a college education (human capital) can increase productivity (both individual and collective), so too social contacts affect the productivity of individuals and groups. Whereas physical capital refers to physical objects and human capital refers to the properties of individuals, social capital refers to connections among individuals—social networks and the norms or reciprocity that arise from them. In that sense "social capital" is closely related to what some have called "civic virtue."[40]

Thus, social capital in terms of networks of relationships among people has an ethical and civic dimension since it is evidenced in "civic virtue." Putman's work shows that engagement with such social virtues as charity, volunteerism, and philanthropy is measurably greater among church attenders than the rest of the population. He finds that, in the case of America,

> religion is today, as it has traditionally been, a central fount of American community life and health. Faith-based organizations serve civic life both directly, by providing social support to their members and social services to the wider community, and indirectly by nurturing civic skills, inculcating moral values,

---

Transformation," 10.

39. Gill, *Society Shaped by Theology*, 126.

40. Putnam, *Bowling Alone*, 18–19.

encouraging altruism, and fostering civic recruitment among church people.[41]

The church's social capital is increasingly recognized by government and its agencies in the UK, too, as they have increasingly come to rely on the unpaid manpower that it provides to help fund social services of various kinds. A high proportion of volunteers in service based programs ranging from youth work and caring for the elderly and the vulnerable, such as street people, through to reaching out to refugees, come from the churches. Faith-based programs supplement the shortfall in government provision in many areas of civic life and this is a significant feature of what the church has to bring to the table when it comes to the debate about policy in the public square. The ability to deliver these services comes from two sources: compassion, which is part of Christian response to the gospel, and the ability to listen both to God and the needs of the wider community. A case in point is the way in which the provision of food pantries to supplement the straightened income of the out-of-work during the recent economic crisis has been dominated by church and parachurch organizations. As Greene and Robertson point out, "Politicians recognize the capacity of faith groups in general to motivate and mobilize large numbers of people."[42] As they comment, the ability to do so arises from the capacity for Christians to build community and from the persuasion that the gospel story offers hope in every situation and is good news that needs both to be lived out and proclaimed. What the church needs in the context of liminality is to move from being a compliant majority to becoming a subversive and yet servant minority that is a catalyst for change, challenging negative secularizing powers.

This flags up consideration of ways in which the nature of power has changed and is being redistributed both in the church and society at large. It is no longer acceptable or efficient to engage in mission from a position of power; in order to make headway in touching the lives of the unchurched it is necessary to listen to them and share with them in such a way that they have a part in making decisions about their own futures. Within the church, hierarchical decision making from the center no longer works; increasingly decisions have to be made nearer to the point of delivery if they are to be either relevant or fruitful. One of the reasons for this is that it is the people nearest to the point of need or delivery who are best positioned

41. Ibid., 79.
42. Greene and Robinson, *Metavista*, 220.

to read the situation and discern the needs. As Roxburgh observes, we are moving from the luxury of reading pre-prepared maps in favour of becoming map makers who read the terrain. Thus, he comments, "It will be among the ordinary people of God that the ability to discern what needs to take place in their neighborhoods and communities must emerge. The new maps come from among the people."[43] What is taking place in churches is a mirror of what is already happening in the world in general. We live in an age of interconnectivity, which is characterized by bottom-up local interactions. Part of the background to this is the changing importance and shape of cities as human environments aided and abetted by the proliferation of cyber connectivity. This means that cities no longer work as centrally commanded structures, they are increasingly broken down into smaller discrete but interconnected units, often ethnically differentiated, and it is at these levels that decisions are normally made. Often these decisions have more wide-ranging impact than is possible with centrally commanded policy making. Basing his observations on the work of Jeb Brugman,[44] Roxburgh notes:

> In the emerging global city, small districts, remote provincial towns and entirely new cities are playing major roles in world affairs and changing the concrete order of the world. More and more, it is the unmanageable, unthinkable, and unpredictable events at local levels in the cities that shape the future of life on this planet rather than national governments or multinational organizations.[45]

In such contexts it is imperative that a missional church learns to confront the powers through a biblical, Christ-centerd power encounter, one that utilizes Christ's own strategy of overcoming power through weakness—reigning through servanthood. This will best be done by learning map-making skills in this new space; Roxburgh identifies three steps to map making in such new spaces. First, he advocates assessing how the environment has changed in the local context; it is no good offering the same attractional model of church in an environment that is not attracted by it! Second, he recommends focusing on developing a new core identity; this does not mean totally abandoning past experience; rather it entails paying attention to the founding stories of the group that give clues to the real reason for its existence in the first place. From this base it is necessary to

43. Roxburgh, *Missional Map-making*, 137.

44. Brugman, *Welcome to the Urban Revolution*.

45. Roxburgh, *Missional Map-making*, 210.

cultivate the habit of listening to God and one another while observing the neighborhood contextually. Roxburgh comments: "To cultivate a people in our local churches who are asking questions about what the Spirit is up to in their neighbourhoods requires a church environment where people feel safe enough to listen to God and one another as a basic habit of their lives."[46] Roxburgh's third step is to create a parallel culture. By this he intends resocializing Christians into habits and practices of the Christian life thereby creating parallel communities of Christian life that offer alternative models for social living, thus contributing to civic virtue and inviting outsiders to join them on the journey. In the process, these new communities of faith will form new centers of power that challenge the coercive powers that dominate popular and public cultures, thus demonstrating the power of Christ's incarnational presence in the world.

These moves do not mean, in spite of Billing's assertion, that Christians are seeking to incarnate Christ, but rather that through the indwelling power of the Spirit they are seeking to demonstrate the dynamic of his incarnate presence through his people. Latin American missional theologian Orlando Costas contends that theology in general, and missional theology in particular, is always a contextual reflection on the actions of God. Thus, theology consists of historically-based reflection on God's revelation. He says, "Precisely because of this fact, we must interpret and communicate Jesus Christ in the light of contemporary history. Reflection on God in the light of the incarnation is not simply meditation on a past factual reality, but also on the contemporary meaning of the incarnate God."[47]

For Costas, this means Christ is to be seen, served and experienced among the poor and disenfranchised, but he asks, "[I]n our world where Jesus has been distorted (we might add, 'beyond recognition') by oppressive powers and principalities. How then can we be sure that the Christ we experience in the context of the poor and dis-enfranchised is not a distortion of his true identity?"[48]

His answer is to go back to the New Testament text to encounter Christ's true identity as bringing liberation to the poor. This foundational text is important because it establishes the theological relevance of the church's mission. For Costas (and this applies to any situation, not only to

46. Ibid., 137.

47. Costas, "Contextualization and Incarnation," 26.

48. Ibid., 28.

that of the poor) our experience of Christ must be verified by the transformation of the contexts into which we minister. As he comments:

> This proceeds from the very character of Jesus Christ as Lord and Saviour of the world. He did not come into the world to leave things as they were. He came to bring a new order of *life*. He both proclaimed and embodied the kingdom of God, the new order of love, justice and peace which aims at the total transformation of history and demands a radical conversion as condition for participation in it. To incarnate Christ in our world is to manifest the transforming presence of God's kingdom among the victims of sin and evil. It is to make possible a process of transformation from personal sin and corporate evil to personal and collective freedom, justice and wellbeing.[49]

This stirring summary alerts us to the fact that it takes an incarnational missional community: to begin to transform the use of power in society, thereby challenging malign alternative powers that seek to usurp the reign of God in Christ. It may seem unlikely that such an end can be achieved through such a modest proposal, but that is the glory of incarnation—the testimony that strength comes through weakness.

49. Ibid., 29.

Bibliography

Almond, Philip. *Demonic Possession and Exorcism in Early Modern England*. Cambridge: Cambridge University Press, 2004.

"An Introduction to Wicca and Wican Beliefs." Witchway, 1999–2008. http://www.witchway.net/wicca/what.html.

Anderson, Allan. *An Introduction to Pentecostalism: Global Charismatic Christianity*. Cambridge: Cambridge University Press, 2004.

Argyle, M. *Bodily Communication*. London: Routledge, 1996.

Arnold, Clinton E. *3 Crucial Questions About Spiritual Warfare*. Grand Rapids: Baker, 1997.

———. *The Colossian Syncretism: The Interface Between Christianity and Folk Belief at Colossae*. Tübingen: Mohr, 1995.

———. *Power and Magic: The Concept of Power in Ephesians*. Cambridge: Cambridge University Press, 2001.

Aulen, Gustav. *Christus Victor: An Historical Study of the Three Main Types of the Idea of Atonement*. New ed. New York: Macmillan, 1969.

Balz, Horst, and Gerhard Sneider, eds. *Exegetical Dictionary of the New Testament*. 3 vols. Edinburgh: T. & T. Clark, 1990–2003.

Bandelt, H., et al., eds. *Human Mitochondrial DNA and the Evolution of Homo Sapiens*. Berlin: Springer, 2010.

Barker, C. *Cultural Studies*. 3rd ed. London: Sage, 2008.

Barnard, A., and J. Spencer. *Encyclopedia of Social and Cultural Anthropology*. London: Routledge, 1997.

Barrett, C. K. *The New Testament Background: Selected Documents*. Rev. ed. London: SPCK, 1987.

Bartholomew, Craig, and Thorsten Moritz, eds. *Christ and Consumerism*. Carlisle, UK: Paternoster, 2001.

Beasley-Murray, Paul. *Power For God's Sake*. Carlisle, UK: Paternoster, 1998.

Beattie, G. *Visible Thought: the New Psychology of Body Language*. Hove, UK: Routledge, 2004.

Bell, R. *Love Wins*. London: Collins, 2011.

Bellinger, Charles. "Yoder's Christ and Girard's Culture: With Reference to Kierkegaard's Transformation of the Self." Paper delivered at Brite Divinity School, University of Notre Dame, March 8, 2002, pp. 1–13.

Bellah, Robert N., et al. *Habits of the Heart: Individualism and Commitment in American Life*. Berkeley: University of California Press, 1996.

Berger, P., and T. Luckmann. *The Social Construction of Reality: A Treatise in the Sociology of Knowledge*. New York: Doubleday, 1966.

Berkhof, Hendrik. *Christ and the Powers*. 2nd ed. Scottsdale: PA, 1977.

Bevans, S. B. *Models of Contextual Theology*. Maryknoll, NY: Orbis, 2012.

Bietenhard, H. "Demon." In *New International Dictionary of the New Testament*, edited by Colin Brown et al., 1:450–53. Grand Rapids: Zondervan, 1975.

Billings, Todd J. *Union With Christ: Reframing Theology and Ministry*. Grand Rapids: Baker, 2011.

Blood, Linda Osborne. "Shepherding/Discipleship." Cult Information Services of Northeast Ohio, 2004–2009. http://www.cisneoinc.org/articles/shepherding.htm.

Böcher, O. "δαμων, ονος, ὁ δεμον." In *Exegetical Dictionary of the New Testament*, edited by Horst Balz and Gerhard Schneider, 1:271–74. Edinburgh: T. & T. Clark, 1990.

Bosch, David J. *Transforming Mission: Paradigm Shifts in Theology of Mission*. Maryknoll: New York, 1995.

Boyd, Gregory. A. *God at War: The Bible and Spiritual Conflict*. Downers Grove, IL: IVP, 1997.

Brierley, P. *Reaching and Keeping Tweenagers: Analysis of the 2001 RAKES Survey*. Beckenham, UK: Cox and Wyman, 2002.

Brown, Peter. "Sorcery, Demons and the Rise of Christianity: From Late Antiquity into the Middle Ages." In *Religion and Society in the Age of St. Augustine*, 119–46. London: Faber and Faber, 1972.

Brown, C. *Philosophy & the Christian Faith*. Downers Grove, IL: IVP, 1968.

Brown, Colin, ed. *New International Dictionary of the New Testament*. Vol. 1. Grand Rapids: Zondervan, 1975.

Brugman, Jeb. *Welcome to the Urban Revolution*. Toronto: Viking, 2009.

Bryman, Alan. *Social Research Methods*, 3rd ed. Oxford: Oxford University Press, 2008.

Burkholder, Lawrence. "Let My People Go: A Mennonite Theology of Exorcism." MA thesis, Conrad Grebel College, 1999.

———. "The Theological Foundations of Deliverance Healing." *Conrad Grebel Review* 19, no. 1 (2001) 38–68.

Bultmann, R. *Theology of the New Testament*. Translated by Kendrick Grobel. London: SCM, 1968.

Burnett, David. *Dawning of the Pagan Moon*. London: Pickering, 1992.

Cardwell, M., et al. *Psychology*. London: Collins, 2004.

Carter, Erik. "The New Monasticism: A Literary Introduction." *Journal of Spiritual Formation and Soul Care* 5, no 2. (2012) 268–84.

Catholic Doors Ministry Website. http://www. catholicdoors.com/prayers/english/p01975b.htm.

Chevous, Jane. "Dark Secrets: Breaking the Silence." *Third Way* 26, no. 1 (2003) 22–25.

Churchward, A. *Signs and Symbols of Primordial Man*. New York: Cosimo, 2007.

Cohn, Norman. *Europe's Inner Demons: The Demonization of Christians in Medieval Christendom*. Rev. ed. Chicago: University of Chicago Press, 1993.

Cole, Cheryl. http://www.cherylcole.com/.

Coleman, S. *The Globalisation of Charismatic Christianity: Spreading the Gospel of Prosperity*. Cambridge: Cambridge University Press, 2000.

Collins-Mayo, S., and P. Dandelion, eds. *Religion and Youth*. Farnham, UK: Ashgate, 2010.

Colón, Gaspar F. "Incarnational Community-Based Ministry: A Leadership Model for Community Transformation." *Journal of Applied Christian Leadership* 6, no. 2 (2012) 10–17.

Coventry Safeguarding Children Board Procedures Manual. "Child Abuse Linked to a Belief in Sprit Possession (including Witchcraft)," 2013, amended June 2014. http://coventryscb.proceduresonline.com/chapters/p_spirit_belief.html.

Croft, S. *Transforming Communities: Re-imagining the Church for the 21st Century.* London: Dartman Longman and Todd, 2007.

Cuneo, Michael W. *American Exorcism: Expelling Demons in the Land of Plenty.* New York: Doubleday, 2001.

Davies, B. *Philosophy of Religion: a Guide and Anthology.* Oxford: Oxford University Press, 2000.

Davis, Wendell J., Sr. *Healing a Wounded Leader.* Xlibris Corporation, 2013.

Dawkins, Richard. *The God Delusion.* London: Black Swan, 2007.

Dawn, Marva. *Power, Weakness and the Tabernacling of God.* Grand Rapids: Eerdmans, 2001.

DeFrancis, J. *The Chinese Language: Fact and Fantasy.* Honolulu: University of Hawaii Press, 1986.

Dempster, M. A., et al, eds. *The Globalisation of Pentecostalism.* Oxford: Regnum, 1999.

Devenish, David. *Demolishing Strongholds.* Milton Keynes, UK: Authentic Media, 2005.

———. *Fathering Leaders, Motivating Mission.* Milton Keynes, UK: Authentic Media, 2011.

Dragash, F. *How Then Should We Reason: Made in the Image of God a Christian View of the Philosophy of Life and Family.* Bloomington, IN: Authorhouse, 2007.

Drane, John. *Do Christians Know How to be Spiritual?: The Rise of New Spirituality and the Mission of the Church.* London: Darton, Longman and Todd, 2005.

———. *What is the New Age Still Saying to the Church?* Grand Rapids: Zondervan, 1999.

Dunn, James D. G. "Demythologising—The Problem of Myth in the New Testament." In *New Testament Interpretation: Essays on Principles and Methods*, edited by I. Howard Marshall, 285–307. Carlisle, UK: Paternoster, 1979.

Ellul, Jacques. *The Subversion of Christianity.* Grand Rapids: Eerdmans, 1986.

Engelsviken, Tormod. "Missio Dei: the Understanding and Misunderstanding of Theological Concept in European Churches and Missiology." *International Review of Mission* 92, no. 367 (2003) 481–97.

Enroth, Ronald, M. *Churches That Abuse.* Grand Rapids: Zondervan, 1992.

Evans, Craig. *Mark 8:27—16:20.* Word Biblical Commentary 34b. Nashville: Nelson, 2001.

Fee, Gordon D. *God's Empowering Presence: The Holy Spirit in the Letters of Paul.* Peabody, MA: Hendrickson, 1994.

———. *Paul, the Spirit and the People of God.* Grand Rapids: Baker Academic, 1996.

Ferdinando, Keith. "Biblical Concepts of Redemption and African Perspectives of the Demonic." PhD diss., London Bible College/CNAA, 1992.

Fisher, David. "British Film and Video Censorship and Classification." Terra Media, October 7, 2006. http://www.terramedia.co.uk/reference/law/british_film_censorship.htm.

Forbes, Cheryl. *The Religion of Power.* Bromley: Marc Europe, 1986.

Forster, Roger, & Paul Marston. *Reason Science & Faith.* Crowborough: Monarch Books, 1999.

Foster, Richard J. *The Challenge of the Disciplined Life: Christian Reflections on Money, Sex and Power*. New York: HarperOne, 1989.

France, R. T. *Gospel of Mark: New International Commentary on the Greek Testament*. Grand Rapids: Eerdmans, 2002.

French, J. R. P., and B. H. Raven. "The Bases of Social Power." In *Social Power*. Edited by D. Cartwright, 260–64. Ann Arbor, MI: Institute of Social Research, 1959.

Friedl, J. *Cultural Anthropology*. New York: Harper's College Press, 1976.

Frost, Michael. *The Road to Missional: Journey to the Center of Church*. Grand Rapids: Baker, 2011.

Frost, M., and A. Hirsch. *The Faith of Leap: Embracing a Theology of Adventure, Risk and Courage*. Grand Rapids: Baker, 2011.

———. *The Shaping of Things to Come: Innovation and Mission for the 21st-century Church*. Peabody, MA: Hendrickson, 2003.

Fulkerson, M. M., and S. Briggs, eds. *The Oxford Handbook of Feminist Theology*. Oxford: Oxford University Press, 2013.

Gamble, David, et al. *Time For Action: Sexual Abuse, the Churches and a New Dawn For Survivors*. London: Churches Together in Britain and Ireland, 2002.

Gamble, Robin. *The Irrelevant Church*. Monarch, UK: Tunbridge Wells, 1991.

Gibbs, E., and R. K. Bolger. *Emerging Churches: Creating Christian Community in Postmodern Cultures*. London: SPCK, 2006.

Giddens, A. *Sociology*. 6th ed. Cambridge: Polity, 2012.

Gill, R. *Society Shaped by Theology*: Sociological Theology 3. Farnham, UK: Ashgate, 2013.

———. *Theology Shaped by Society*: Sociological Theology 2. Farnham, UK: Ashgate, 2012.

Girard, Rene. *Things Hidden Since the Foundation of the World*. Stanford, CA: Stanford University Press, 1978.

Greene, C., and M. Robinson. *Metavista: Bible, Church and Mission in an Age of Imagination*. Milton Keynes, UK: Authentic Media, 2008.

Greenwood, Chris. "Boy, 15, Tortured to Death with Hammer and Chisels on Christmas Day Because Relative Thought he was a Witch." Daily Mail online, Sunday, Jan. 8th, 2012. http://www.dailymail.co.uk/news/article-2082618/Kristy-Bamu-15-tortured-death-witch-claim-Christmas-Day-Newham.html.

Gerkin, C. C. *The Living Human Document: Re-visioning Pastoral Counselling in a Hermeneutical Mode*. Nashville: Abingdon, 1989.

Green, Michael. *I Believe in Satan's Downfall*. London: Hodder & Stoughton, 1981.

Greenfield, Guy. *The Wounded Minister*. Grand Rapids: Baker, 2001.

Guder, Darrell. L. *The Incarnation and the Church's Witness*. Eugene, OR: Wipf and Stock, 2005.

Guelich, Robert E. *Mark 1–8*. Word Biblical Commentary 34a. Dallas: Word, 1989.

Guthrie, D. *New Testament Introduction*. London: IVP, 1985.

Hahn, Celia Allison. *Growing in Authority, Relinquishing Control*. Washington, DC: Alban Institute, 1994.

Haon, Abel. "Identifying Leadership Power Abuse and its Prevention in the Local Church." *Melanesian Journal of Theology* 29, no. 1 (2013) 104–21.

Haralambos, Michael, and Martin Holborn. *Sociology: Themes and Perspectives*. 7th ed. London: Collins, 2008.

Hardy, Andrew, and Dan Yarnell. *Forming Multicultural Partnerships: Church Planting in a Divided Society*. Watford, UK: Instant Apostle, 2014.

Hauwerwas, Stanley, and William Willimon. *Resident Aliens: Life in the Christian Colony.* Nashville: Abingdon, 1989.

Hauweras, Stanley. *Where Resident Aliens Live.* Nashville: Abingdon, 1996.

Hearne, Kevin. "The Demonization of Pan." Student Paper, Online Mesa Community College, 2008. http://www.mesacc.edu/~thoqh49081/StudentPapers/pan.html.

Heiser, Michael S. "Divine Council." In *Dictionary of the Old Testament: Wisdom, Poetry, and Writings,* edited by Tremper Longman and Peter Enns, 112–16. Downers Grove, IL: IVP, 2008.

Hengel, Martin. *Christ and Power.* Translated by Everett R. Kalin. Philadelphia: Fortress, 1974.

Hesselgrave, David G. *Communicating Christ Cross-Culturally: An Introduction to Missionary Communication.* 2nd ed. Grand Rapids: Zondervan, 1991.

Hick, J. *God Has Many Names.* Westminster: Knox, 1982.

Hiebert, Paul G. "Conversion and Worldview Transformation." *International Journal of Frontier Missions* 14, no. 2 (1997) 83–86.

———. "Culture and Cross-cultural Differences." In *Perspectives on the World Christian Movement,* edited by Ralph D. Winter, and Steven C. Hawthorne, 367–79. Pasadena: William Carey Library, 1992.

———. *The Gospel in Human Contexts: Anthropological Explorations for Contemporary Missions.* Grand Rapids: Baker Academic, 2009.

———. "Spiritual Warfare and Worldviews." *Direction: A Mennonite Brethren Forum* 29, no. 2 (2000) 114–24.

Hiebert, Paul, and E. Hiebert Menses. *Incarnational Ministry: Planting Churches in Band, Tribal, Peasant, and Urban Societies.* Grand Rapids: Baker, 1995.

HM Government. "Safeguarding Children From Abuse Linked to a Belief in Spirit Possession." 2007. http://webarchive.nationalarchives.gov.uk/20130401151715/ http://www.education.gov.uk/publications/eOrderingDownload/DFES-00465-2007.pdf.

Hogg, M. A., and G. M. Vaughan. *Social Psychology.* 6th ed. Harlow, UK: Pearson Education, 2011.

Holder, A., ed. *The Blackwell Companion to Christian Spirituality.* Chichester, UK: Wiley-Blackwell, 2011.

Hollenweger, Walter J. *Pentecostalism: Origins and Developments Worldwide.* Peabody, MA: Hendrickson, 1997.

Holmes, Peter R. *Becoming More Human: Exploring the Interface of Spirituality, Discipleship and Therapeutic Faith Community.* Milton Keynes, UK: Paternoster, 2005.

Holy Trinity Brompton. http://www.htb.org.uk.

Hooker, Morna D. *Gospel according to St Mark.* Black's Commentaries. Hendrickson, MA: Peabody, 1991.

Howard, Roland. *The Rise and Fall of the Nine O'Clock Service: A Cult within the Church?* London: Mowbray, 1996.

Houreld, Katharine. "African Children Denounced as 'Witches' by Christian Pastors." Huffington Post World, December 4th, 2012. http://www.huffingtonpost.com/2009/10/18/african-children-denounce_n_324943.html.

Humphries, M. L. *Christian Origins and the Language of the Kingdom of God.* Carbondale, IL: Southern Illinois University, 1999.

Hunsberger, G. R., and C. Van Gelder, eds. *The Church between Gospel & Culture.* Grand Rapids: Eerdmans, 1996.

Hunt, Stephen. "The Anglican Wimberites." *Pneuma: The Journal of the Society for Pentecostal Studies* 17, no. 1 (1995) 105–15.

———. "Deliverance: The Evolution of a Doctrine." *Themelios* 21, no. 1 (1995) 10–16.

Johnson, Richard. "Archive: Exorcism." BBC Four-Part Documentary on Exorcism. http://www.bbc.co.uk/worldservice/specials/1512_exorcism/index.shtml.

Julian of Norwich. "The Westminster Cathedral/Abbey Manuscript of Julian of Norwich's *Showing of Love*." Translated by Julia Bolton Holloway. http://www.umilta.net/westmins.html.

Kärkkäinen, V. M. *An Introduction to Ecclesiology*. Downers Grove: IVP Academic, 2002.

———. *Pneumatology: The Holy Spirit in Ecumenical, International, and Contextual Perspective*. Grand Rapids: Baker Academic, 2002.

Kearsley, Roy. *Church, Community and Power*. Farnham, UK: Ashgate, 2008.

Kelly, H. H. "Two Functions of Reference Groups." In *Readings in Social Psychology*. Edited by G. E. Swanson et al., 410–14. New York: Holt, Reinhart and Winston, 1952.

Kim, K. *Joining in with the Spirit*. London: Epworth, 2009.

Kimball, D. *The Emerging Church*. Grand Rapids: Zondervan, 2003.

Koch, Kurt. *Between Christ and Satan*. Grand Rapids: Kregel, 1961.

———. *Christian Counselling and Occultism*. Grand Rapids: Kregel, 1965.

Kraft, Charles H. *Christianity in Culture: A Study in Dynamic Biblical Theologizing in Cross-Cultural Perspective*. Maryknoll, NY: Orbis, 1979.

———. *Christianity with Power*. Ventura, CA: Gospel Light, 1989.

———. *Defeating Dark Angels: Breaking Demonic Oppressions in the Believer's Life*. Ann Arbor, MI: Servant, 1992.

———. "What Kind of Encounters Do We Need in Our Christian Witness?" *Evangelical Missions Quarterly* 27, no. 3 (1991) 258–65.

Küng, Hans. *Christianity and the World Religions: Paths of Dialogue with Islam, Hinduism, and Buddhism*. New York: Doubleday, 1986.

Lane, William. *The Gospel of Mark*. New International Commentary on the New Testament. Grand Rapids: Eerdmans, 1974.

Leeper, Elizabeth. "The Role of Exorcism in Early Christianity." *Studia Patristica* 26 (1993) 59–62.

Lewis, C. S. *The Screwtape Letters*. London: Bles, 1942.

Levack, Brian. P. *The Witch Hunt in Early Modern Europe*. 3rd ed. London: Longman, 2006.

Lingenfelter, Sherwood. G. *Leading Cross-Culturally: Covenant Relationships for Effective Christian Leadership*. Grand Rapids: Baker Academic, 2008.

Livermore, D. *Leading with Cultural Intelligence: the New Secret to Success*. New York: AMACOM, 2010.

Longman III, Tremper, and D. Reid. *God Is A Warrior*. Grand Rapids: Zondervan, 1995.

Lowitzki, David, and Sharon Kim. "New Monasticism: The Emergence of Incarnational Communities." Unpublished Research Paper, Department of Sociology, California State University, 2000, pp. 1–20.

Lyons, John. "The Fourth Wave and the Approaching Millennium: Some Problems with Charismatic Hermeneutics." *Anvil* 15, no. 3 (1998) 169–80.

McAlpine, Thomas H. *Facing the Powers: What are the Options?* Monrovia, CA: MARC, 1991.

McKim, D. K., ed. *Dictionary of Major Biblical Interpreters*. Downers Grove, IL: IVP Academic, 2007.

McLaren, Brian D. *A New Kind of Christianity.* London: Hodder & Stoughton, 2010.

McGrath, Alister E. *Christian Theology: An Introduction.* Chichester, UK: Wiley-Blackwell, 2011.

McManners, J. *The Oxford Illustrated History of Christianity.* Oxford: Oxford University Press, 2001.

MacNutt, Francis. *Deliverance From Evil Spirits.* Grand Rapids: Chosen, 2009.

Malia, Linda. "A Fresh Look at a Remarkable Document: Exorcism: The Report of a Commission Convened by the Bishop of Exeter." *Anglican Theological Review* 83, no. 1 (2001) 660–81.

Mehrabian, A. *Tactics in Social Influence.* Englewood Cliffs, NJ: Prentice-Hall, 1969.

Meilander, Gilbert, and William Werpehowski, eds. *The Oxford Handbook of Theological Ethics.* Oxford: Oxford University Press, 2010.

"Meme." Dictionary.com, 2015. *Collins English Dictionary—Complete & Unabridged 10th Edition.* New York: HarperCollins. http://dictionary.reference.com/browse/meme.

Merton, Thomas. *Contemplation in a World of Action.* Colorado Springs: Image, 1973.

Meyer, Birgit. *Translating the Devil: Religion and Modernity Among the Ewe in Ghana.* International African Library. Edinburgh: Edinburgh University Press, 1999.

Meyer, K. *Four Old Irish Songs of Summer and Winter.* London: Hutt, 1903.

Michael, S. Heiser, "Divine Council." In *Dictionary of the Old Testament: Wisdom, Poetry, & Writings,* edited by Longman Tremper III and Peter Enns, 110–17. Downers Grove, IL: IVP, 2008.

Miller, Patrick D, et al. "The Divine Council and the Prophetic Call to War." *Vetus Testamentum* 18 (1968) 100–124.

Monaghan, John, and Peter Just. *Social and Cultural Anthropology.* Oxford: Oxford University Press, 2000.

More, D. *The Shepherding Movement.* New York: Continuum, 2004.

Moulton, H. K. *The Analytical Greek Lexicon Revised.* Grand Rapids: Zondervan, 1981.

Moynagh, M., and P. Harrold. *Church for Every Context: an Introduction to Theology and Practice.* London: SCM, 2012.

Muldoon, Tim. Review of *New Monasticism: What it Has to Say to Today's Church* by Jonathan Wilson-Hartgrove. *Spiritus* 10, no 1 (2010) 123–26.

Mullen, E. Theodore. *The Divine Council in Canaanite & Early Hebrew Literature: The Assembly of the Gods.* Missoula, MT: Scholars, 1980.

Murray, Stuart. *Post-Christendom Church: Mission in a Strange New World.* Milton Keynes; Paternoster, 2004.

The Nag Hammadi Library. http://gnosis.org/naghamm/nhl.html.

Newbigin, Lesslie. *The Gospel in a Pluralist Society.* London: SPCK, 1998.

———. *The Open Secret: Introduction to the Theology of Mission.* London: SPCK, 1995.

Newberg, A. B. *Principles of Neurotheology.* Farnham, UK: Ashgate, 2010.

Nouwen, Henri. *Life of the Beloved.* London: Hodder and Stoughton, 1992.

O'Brien, Peter. "Principalities and Powers: Opponents of the Church." In *Biblical Interpretation and the Church,* edited by D. A. Carson, 110–50. Exeter, UK: Paternoster, 1984.

O'Donnell, K. *Inside the World Religions.* Oxford: Lion, 2006.

Olsen, R. E. *The Westminster Handbook of Evangelical Theology.* Louisville: Westminster John Knox, 2004.

Onyinah, Opuku. "Akan Witchcraft and the Concept of Exorcism in the Church of Pentecost." PhD diss., University of Birmingham, 2002.

Pannenberg, W. *Systematic Theology*. Vol. 1. Translated by Geoffrey W. Bromiley. Edinburgh: T. & T. Clark, 1991.

Parsons, Stephen. *Ungodly Fear: Fundamentalist Christianity and the Abuse of Power*. Oxford: Lion, 2000.

Papademetriou, George C. "Exorcism in the Orthodox Church." www.goarch. org/ourfaith/ourfaith7079.htm.

Pease, B., and A. Pease. *The Definitive Book of Body Language*. New York: Random House, 2008.

Peck, Scott M. *People of the Lie*. New York: Simon & Schuster, 1983.

Penn-Lewis, Jessie, and Evans Roberts. *War on the Saints*. Rev. ed. Poole, UK: Overcomer Literature Trust, 1977.

————. *The Warfare with Satan and the Way of Victory*. 6th ed. Bournemouth, UK: Overcomer Book Room, 1951.

Petitpierre, Dom R., ed. *Exorcism: The Findings of a Commission Convened by the Bishop of Exeter*. London: SPCK, 1972.

Percy, Martyn. *Words, Wonders and Power: Understanding Contemporary Christian Fundamentalism and Revivalism*. London: SPCK, 1996.

Peterson, E. H. *The Message Bible*. Colorado Springs: Alive Communications, 1996.

Peterson, G. D. *Warrior Kings of Sweden*. Jefferson, NC: McFarland, 2007.

Philips, Abu Ameenah Bilal. *The Exorcist Tradition in Islam*. Birmingham: Al Hidaayah, 2007.

Philostratus. *The Life of Apollonius of Tyana*. 2 vols. Translated by F. C. Coneybeare. Loeb Classical Library. London: Heinemann, 1912.

Pinnock, Clark. *Flame of Love: A Theology of the Holy Spirit*. Downers Grove, IL: IVP Academic, 1996.

Possamai, A. *Sociology of Religion for Generations X and Y*. London: Equinox, 2009.

Preece, Roger. *Understanding and Using Power*. Cambridge: Grove Booklets, 2011.

Prince, Derek. *Blessing or Curse: You Can Choose*. Milton Keynes, UK: Word, 1990.

Putnam, Robert. D. *Bowling Alone: The Collapse and Revival of American Community*. New York: Simon and Schuster, 2000.

Pytches, David. *Come Holy Spirit*. London: Hodder & Stoughton, 1985.

Rainie, Lee, and Barry Wellman. *Networked: The New Social Operating System*. Cambridge, MA: MIT Press, 2012.

Redeger, G. Lloyd. *Clergy Killers: Guidance for Pastors and Congregations under Attack*. Louisville: Knox, 1997.

Riley, J. C. E. *The Heritage of Christian Education*. Joplin, MO: College, 2003.

Robinson, Martin. *Winning Hearts, Changing Minds*. London: Monarch, 2001.

Robinson, Martin, and Dwight Smith. *Invading Secular Space*. London: Monarch, 2003.

Roxburgh, Alan J. *Missional: Joining God in the Neighborhood*. Allelon Missionary. Grand Rapids: Baker, 2011.

————. *Missional Map-Making: Skills for Leading in Times of Transition*. San Francisco: Wiley, 2010.

————. *The Sky is Falling*. Eagle: ACI, 2005.

Roxburgh, Alan J., and Fred Romanuk. *The Missional Leader: Equipping Your Church to Reach a Changing World*. San Francisco: Jossey-Bass, 2006.

Ryall, J. "Kim Jong-un: 10 Ways North Korea's 'Dear Leader' is Different." *The Telegraph* 21st March, 2014.

Sanz, N., and P. Keenan, eds. *Heads, Human Evolution: Adaptations, Dispersals and Social Developments.* World Heritage Papers 29. Paris: UNESCO World Heritage Centre, 2011.

Samuel, Henry. "How to Become an Exorcist." *The Telegraph.* 30th March 2011.

Schreiter, Robert J. *Constructing Local Theologies.* Maryknoll, NY: Orbis, 1985.

Seinfeld, Katharine, ed. *The New Interpreter's Dictionary of the Bible.* Vol. 2. Nashville: Abingdon, 2007.

Sider, John W. *Interpreting the Parables.* Grand Rapids: Zondervan, 1995.

Silf, Margaret. *Soul Space: Making a Retreat in the Christian Tradition.* London: SPCK, 2002.

Skarsuane, Oscar. "Possession and Exorcism in the Literature of the Early Church." Lausanne Movement Documents, *"Deliver Us From Evil."* Nairobi, 2000. http://www.lausanne.org/content/historical-overview-1.

Smith, Graham R. "The Church Militant: A Study of "Spiritual Warfare" in the Anglican Charismatic Renewal." PhD diss., University of Birmingham, 2011.

Smith, Luther E., Jr. *Intimacy and Mission: Intentional Community as Crucible for Radical Discipleship.* Eugene, OR: Wipf and Stock, 1994.

Stobart, Elanor. "Child Abuse Linked to Accusations of 'Possession' and 'Witchcraft.'" Research Report no. 750, UK Government Department for Education and Skills, 2006. http://dera.ioe.ac.uk/6416/1/RR750.pdf.

Subritzky, Bill. *How to Cast Out Demons and Break Curses.* Auckland: Dove Ministries, 1991.

Swart, Jannie, et al. "Toward a Missional Theology of Participation." *Missiology: An International Review* 37, no. 1 (2009) 75–87.

Theron, Jacques. "A Critical Overview of the Church's Ministry of Deliverance from Evil Spirits." *PNEUMA: The Journal for the Society for Pentecostal Studies* 18, no. 1 (1996) 79–92.

Thiselton, A. C. *Hermeneutics: An Introduction.* Grand Rapids: Eerdmans, 2009.

———. *New Horizons in Hermeneutics: The Theory and Practice of Transforming Biblical Reading.* London: HarperCollins, 1992.

Tiénou, Tite, and Paul G. Hiebert. "Missional Theology." *Global Missiology* 3, no. 2 (2005) 1–14.

Townley, Jaramy. "Mimesis and Violence: Perspectives in Cultural Criticism." *Berkshire Review* 14 (1979) 9–19.

Trigg, J. W. *Origen.* London: Routledge, 2002.

Twelftree, Graham. *Christ Triumphant: Exorcism Then and Now.* London: Hodder & Stoughton, 1985.

———. *In the Name of Jesus: Exorcism Among Early Christians.* Grand Rapids: Baker Academic, 2007.

———. *Jesus the Exorcist: A Contribution to the Study of the Historical Jesus.* Tübingen: Mohr, 1993.

Van Gelder, Craig. "Rethinking Denominations and Denominationalism in Light of a Missional Ecclesiology." *Word and World* 25, no. 1 (2005) 23–33.

———. "Defining the Issues Related to Power and Authority in Religious Leadership." *Journal of Religious Leadership* 6, no. 2 (2007) 1–14.

Von Rad, G. *Holy War in Ancient Israel.* 1958. Reprint, Grand Rapids: Eerdmans, 1991.

Wagner, C. Peter. "Third Wave." In *Dictionary of Pentecostal and Charismatic Movements*, edited by Stanley M. Burgess and Gary B. McGee, 1141. Grand Rapids: Zondervan, 1988.

———. *The Third Wave of the Holy Spirit: Encountering the Power of Signs and Wonders Today*. Ann Arbor, MI: Servant, 1988.

———. "A Third Wave?" *Pastoral Renewal* July-August (1983) 1–5.

Walker, Simon P. *The Undefended Leader*. Carlisle, UK: Piquant, 2010.

White, T. B. *The Believer's Guide to Spiritual Warfare*. Ventura, CA: Regal, 2004.

Willard, Dallas. *The Divine Conspiracy: Rediscovering Our Hidden Life in God*. San Francisco: HarperCollins, 1998.

Wimber, John, and Kevin Springer. *Power Evangelism*. London: Hodder & Stoughton, 1985.

Wimber, John. *Power Healing*. London: Hodder & Stoughton, 1987.

Wink, Walter. *Engaging the Powers: Discernment and Resistance in an Age of Domination*. Minneapolis: Fortress, 1992.

———. *Naming the Powers: The Language of Power in the New Testament*. Philadelphia: Fortress, 1984.

———. *The Powers That Be: Theology for a New Millennium*. New York: Galilee Doubleday, 2010.

Wright, N. T. *Jesus and the Victory of God*. London: SPCK, 1996.

———. *The New Testament and the People of God: Christian Origins and the Question of God*. London, SPCK, 1992.

Yamauchi, Edwin M. "Magic in the Biblical World." *Tyndale Bulletin 34* (1983) 169–200.

Yoder, Howard. *The Politics of Jesus*. Grand Rapids: Eerdmans, 1972.

Yronwode, Catherine. "Paschal Beverly Randolph and the Anseiratic Mysteries." Sacred Sex, 1995–2003. http://www.luckymojo.com/tkpbrandolph.html.